The Fourth Evangelist and His Gospel

An examination of contemporary scholarship

Robert Kysar

Augsburg Publishing House
Minneapolis, Minnesota

Preface

A book which attempts to examine contemporary scholarship on the fourth gospel must, among other things, be useful. It is my hope that you will find this volume a useful tool in your study. No bibliography is included, because complete bibliographical data is available in the footnotes. There might have been an index of subjects, but I trust that the detailed table of contents will serve more effectively to guide you to the specific topics in which you are interested.

It is unthinkable to allow the following pages to appear publicly under my name without first acknowledging my profound debt to a number of persons and institutions. Of course, they cannot in any way be held responsible for whatever weaknesses this volume has. Still, without their contributions this work would have remained unrealized. First, I am grateful to Hamline University for its support of my sabbatical leave in 1973-74 during which the bulk of the research and writing was completed. Hamline was also kind enough to furnish resources for the typing of the final draft. Mrs. Judy Hamilton typed the final draft with a care which is most appreciated.

Yale University generously appointed me a Post-doctoral Research Fellow during my sabbatical leave which allowed me access to its rich library facilities. Among the numerous persons who aided my project is Professor Wayne Meeks of Yale. It was he who first encouraged the pursuit of a survey of contemporary fourth gospel criticism. He also continually supported the task with advice and eventually read Part One and offered helpful criticisms.

Most important, I am grateful to my wife, Myrna. Among her specific contributions are the long hours of typing the first draft during a hot, humid summer month in Washington, D.C. Moreover, her careful reading of the manuscript and her ruthless critique of her husband's style has produced a much more readable book. But above all, it was her undaunted optimism which kept me at the task until its completion. It is with profound gratitude and love that I dedicate this book to Myrna.

Robert Kysar

Contents

Introduction

"Someone has described the remarkable character of this gospel
by saying that it is a book in which a child can wade and an
elephant can swim."[1] The accuracy of this anonymous observation
is attested to by the assorted appreciations of the fourth gospel.
The beginning student may well find the thought of the gospel
rather obvious and understand its symbolism in a straightforward
manner. On the other hand, the lifetime scholar of the writing
will still be wrestling with the nuances of the gospel in the
fading years of his or her career. The gospel presents itself in
a manner not unlike that of the mysterious cave that entices the
mountain explorer. The entrance seems clear enough, but the deeper
one moves into the opening the less illumination there seems to be
and the more intense the darkness becomes. But, like the newly
discovered mountain-side cave, the fourth evangelist and his gospel
are irresistibly attractive to the historical explorer; the
enigmas and mysteries of the gospel cry out for explication and
beckon the student to undertake the probings of its inner recesses.
     This book is written for the student who would like to move
more deeply into the darkness of the fourth gospel in search of
light. It offers an introductory survey of the contemporary
critical efforts to solve some of the problems of the fourth
gospel. To shift the analogy away from our mountain cave, this
book endeavors to provide a road map through the terrain of recent
johannine scholarship, for much of that terrain is uncharted. The
survey is intended for the person who has had an introduction to
the fourth gospel and wants to inform him or herself more fully
with regard to the critical opinions currently held about it. The
book is not an introduction to the gospel, because the introductory
matters usually handled in the beginning pages of a commentary, for
instance, are taken for granted. So, while some critical orientation to the gospel is required, the survey does not presuppose

---

[1]Quoted in Siegfried Schulz, *Die Stunde der Botschaft:Einführung
in der Theologie der vier Evangelisten* (Hamburg: Furche, 1967), 297.

advanced knowledge of the gospel and its problems. It is hoped, therefore, that a wide range of persons curious about the state of current critical studies of the gospel will find the following pages helpful. What I have attempted to do is to summarize the major studies on the most significant questions in johannine scholarship and then try to bring those major studies into relationship with one another. It is intended that, in addition to summarization, the survey accomplish some degree of dialogue among the various positions. The task is to reveal the consensus and disagreements, the shades of differences, the variety of methods, etc., found in recent critical work on the fourth gospel.

Some further remarks concerning the nature of our project are called for: The survey is limited to critical work since 1963 for a number of reasons. This period of time represents, in my opinion, a significant period of johannine scholarship--one in which important contributions to the quest for understanding the fourth gospel have been made. There has been a near explosion of johannine studies in the 1960s and 70s. Yet, in spite of the abundance of scholarly work on the fourth gospel, no survey of that work has been done in the English-speaking world since C.K. Barrett's revision of W.F. Howard's *The Fourth Gospel in Recent Criticism and Interpretation* twenty years ago.[2] What follows is a modest effort to fill a part of that gap out of the conviction that recent scholarly literature merits investigation in and for itself.

I have tried to exercise a high degree of objectivity in the discussion of the range of studies covered. Fair and accurate summaries and representations of relationships among critics is the highest priority exercised in the work. Still, it must be confessed that that objectivity is undoubtedly qualified at a number of points. It was necessary, of course, to make decisions regarding the studies which would be given primary attention; the critical efforts which have been included are representative of what I believe to be the most important work done on the fourth gospel. The survey could not be entirely exhaustive, at least if the volume were to be kept within a reasonable length. For example, the survey does not give heed to the studies done on the literary structure of the gospel as a whole or selected passages within the gospel, except where those studies bear immediately upon other questions. This decision was made because those studies

---

[2]Wilbert Francis Howard, *The Fourth Gospel in Recent Criticism and Interpretation*, revised by C.K. Barrett (London: Epworth, 1955).

of structural analysis do not seem as creative and helpful as other
types of work. Similarly the question of the literary relationship
of the prologue to the remainder of the gospel has been relegated
to a comment in a footnote. Such selectivity obviously compromises
the effort of the book at objectivity. Second, I have tried to
keep my own critical appraisals short, while at the same time not
leaving the volume bereft of some critique of the works covered.
Likewise, the conclusions of each part and of the volume represent
brief observations from my own perspective on the status of scholarship.

Each of the three parts is centered about one major concern
in the interpretation of the fourth gospel. The first involves
the questions of the origin and present literary condition of the
document. How may one account for the apparent disorder of the
gospel (e.g., 6:1 read in the light of chapter 5) and its allegedly
contradictory ideas (e.g., 5:24 and 28)? How is the relationship
between the synoptic and fourth gospels to be understood? How did
the gospel originate? These questions are taken to be concerned
with the matter of the literary problems of the gospel, for the
most part, and to be associated with the theories having to do with
the original production of the gospel. Hence, Part One will survey
those theories which propose a view of the composition of the gospel.

Simply expressed, Part Two is then concerned with historical
questions about the gospel. That is, the questions of the identity
of the originator of the gospel and the date of his work are
concerns of the strictly historical probings of the gospel. In
addition, there is the endeavor to isolate the ideas which most
clearly influenced the evangelist and to describe the specific
conditions which may have occasioned his production of the document.
While the division between "literary" and "historical" questions
is a simplistic one, that division for the most part is represented
in the first two parts.

Part Three then takes as its subject the investigations of the
evangelist's thought. What were the evangelist's views of some of
the themes which are given expression in his document (e.g.,
eschatology, signs, dualism)? In short, the three parts divide the
concerns of johannine criticism in terms of the three major areas
of biblical research--literary, historical, and theological.

PART ONE:

THE EVANGELIST
AND
HIS TRADITION

One of the most creative advancements in the study of the
synoptic gospels in the twentieth century has been the refinement
of the method of redaction criticism (or more precisely, redaction
history). It has provided the scholar with a tool by which to
distinguish with varying degrees of certainty between the traditions
(both oral and written) behind the present gospels and the contributions of the evangelists themselves working with those traditions
to produce the final form of the gospels. With the help of source
hypotheses (source criticism) and theories of the pre-literary
history of the synoptic materials (form criticism or history),
redaction criticism has been able to detect the manner in which the
evangelist handled the traditions at his disposal--his organization
of the materials, the deliberate changes he effected in the content
of the traditions, and his insertions of an editorial and interpretative kind. From the body of material isolated as the work of
the evangelist, the critic has been enabled to describe in at least
a tentative fashion the theological stance of the evangelist, deduce
some descriptive elements concerning the setting in which the
evangelist lived and wrote, and write as it were the concluding
chapter in the history of the synoptic tradition. While far from
a completed undertaking, redaction criticism of the synoptic gospels
has yielded immensely rich conclusions for our understanding of the
first three gospels and the history of the Christian communities
of the first century.[1] It is an over-simplification to say that
redaction criticism has succeeded only because of a generally
conceded set of hypotheses having to do with the sources and the
pre-literary history of the synoptic materials; but it is

---

[1]Examples of some of the most influential redaction critical
studies on the synoptic gospels available in English include: Willi
Marxsen, *Mark the Evangelist* (New York: Abingdon Press, 1969);
James M. Robinson, *Mark's Understanding of History* (Edinburgh:
Oliver and Boyd, 1956); Hans Conzelmann, *The Theology of St. Luke*
(New York: Harper and Row, 1960); Gerhard Barth, Heinz J. Held, and
Günther Bornkamm, *Tradition and Interpretation in Matthew* (Phila-
delphia: Westminster Press, 1963); Karl Kundsin, "Primitive
Christianity in the Light of Gospel Research," *Form Criticism*,
F.C. Grant, ed. (Chicago: Willett, Clark, and Co., 1934). For an
overview, cf., Joachim Rohde, *Rediscovering the Teachings of the
Evangelists* (Philadelphia: Westminster Press, 1968).

indisputable that redaction criticism has taken its stand upon the shoulders of source and form criticism.[2]

A comparable development in redaction criticism on the fourth gospel has been retarded by a number of problems. First, it has not been the case that a source hypothesis for the fourth gospel has emerged in scholarly debate with any such consensus as supports the two-source theory for the synoptic gospels.[3] This is indeed not surprising since the basis for the initial insights into the synoptic sources was facilitated in part by the possibilities of comparing the first three gospels. Comparisons of the fourth gospel with the synoptic materials have not provided a method of source analysis nearly as successful as that employed in the early stages of the synoptic source quest. The uniqueness of the fourth gospel among the canonical gospels presents the source critic with a more complicated problem. Furthermore, source criticism of John was for some time retarded by the assumption that the fourth evangelist had depended upon one or more of the synoptic gospels and that it (or they) constituted his source(s). Finally, the application of form critical techniques to the johannine materials has been far more difficult than in the case of the synoptic gospels. This has been due in part to the peculiar style of the fourth gospel; the entire document is pervaded by a distinctiveness which makes analysis of passages in terms of pre-literary history most difficult (and some would say, unnecessary).

While comparisons of selected bits of the johannine gospel with materials in the synoptic gospels aided by the results of a form critical analysis of those relevant synoptic bits have yielded some interesting results,[4] it is not unfair to say that such undertakings have not been met with widespread support in the scholarly world. Discussions of the theology of the fourth evangelist, the community of which he was a member, and its place in relationship to the wider Christian community of the first century have been

---

[2] See the useful introduction to redaction criticism by Norman Perrin, *What is Redaction Criticism?* (Philadelphia: Westminster Press, 1969).

[3] There is, of course, a new questioning of this theory. See for example, William R. Farmer, *The Synoptic Problem, A Critical Analysis* (New York: Macmillan, 1964) and his edition of a synoptic gospels parallel, *Synopticon: The Verbal Agreement Between the Greek Texts of Matthew, Mark, and Luke Contextually Exhibited* (Cambridge: University Press, 1969).

[4] E.g., C.H. Dodd, *Historical Tradition in the Fourth Gospel* (Cambridge: University Press, 1963) and Bent Noack, *Zur johanneischen Tradition, Beitrage zur Kritik an der literarkritischen Analyse des vierten Evangeliums* (Copenhagen: Rosenkilde, 1954).

without the benefit of a finely honed criticism of the kind developed on the synoptic gospels. The consequence has been that such discussions have been fatally diverse and mortally debatable. The efforts at something like a "scientific" argument for the sources and traditions of the fourth gospel and the evangelist's use of them seem doomed to charges of subjectivism and speculation. Fourth gospel research seems at a stalemate unless the questions of the sources and traditions of that writing can somehow be laid bare.

Research in recent years has seen the emergence of three major types of critical enterprises related to the sources and traditions behind the fourth gospel. First, a significant effort at isolating and establishing the signs source which was employed by the evangelist has been made. At the same time, other theories of the composition of the gospel have been advanced, some of which propose hypotheses of a developing johannine tradition and some of which build upon views of the relationship of the fourth gospel to the synoptics. Finally, on the basis of either a signs source theory or some other view of composition, pioneering work in johannine redaction criticism has been done.

CHAPTER I

RECENT SIGNS SOURCE ANALYSIS

In spite of the absence of those conditions which would
facilitate source criticism of the fourth gospel, scholars have
responded with various kinds of source proposals to some of the
difficulties posed in the text of the gospel--for example, the
abrupt breaks in the narrative materials (e.g., 6:1), the apparent
contradictory theological ideas of the gospel, and the discontinuity
between chapters 20 and 21, to cite but a few.[1] Their proposals
seem to be of three kinds: First, theories which have to do with
the evangelist's alleged use of the synoptic gospel(s);[2] second,
theories which conjecture an original gospel left incomplete by the
evangelist and completed with more or less success by a pupil;[3]
and, third, theories which posit at least one extensive source which
has become the basis of the present gospel by the work of the
evangelist. It is useful to distinguish within this third type of
solution two variations. First, some scholars have attempted to
isolate one main source which by a process of expansion was gradually
redacted to take the form of the present gospel.[4] Others have argued

---

[1]For a summary of the major older theories see W.F. Howard,
The Fourth Gospel in Recent Criticism and Interpretation, 297-305.
[2]E.g., E.K. Lee, "St. Mark and the Fourth Gospel," *New Testament Studies*, 3 (1956-57), 50-58; S. Mendner, "Zum Problem 'Johannes
und die Synoptiker'," *New Testament Studies*, 4 (1957-58), 282-307.
[3]E.g., M.-E.Boismard, "Saint Luc et la rédaction du quatrième
évangile (Jn 4:46-54)," *Revue biblique*, 69 (1962), 185-211; Pierson
Parker, "Two Editions of John," *Journal of Biblical Literature*, 75
(1956), 303-314.
[4]E.g., Wilhelm Hartke who argues that a basic signs source was
first expanded into an "ur-John" before reaching the evangelist who
revised and enlarged the work to its present form. *Vier urchristliche
Parteien und ihre Vereinigung zur apostolischen Kirche* (Berlin:
Akademie Verlag, 1961).

instead for a multiple source theory which proposes a number of
sources incorporated together with the evangelist's own work into
the present gospel.[5] The history of such efforts is beyond the
scope and purpose of this survey of contemporary scholarship,[6] but
suffice it to say that from the mid-nineteenth century to the middle
of this century source theories for the fourth gospel were numerous
but widely divergent and singularly unsuccessful in meeting with
extensive scholarly acceptance! Many seemed to have shared an
opinion recently issued on the source criticism of the fourth gospel:
"...[It] indeed often becomes so hypothetical that no one but the
critic himself believes it."[7] Yet, it is interesting to note that
these early critical pioneers were in some cases not far from those
proposals which have recently become more successful.[8]

A decisive turning point in source-redaction criticism was the
appearance of Rudolf Bultmann's monumental commentary on the fourth
gospel, *The Gospel of John*, the first edition of which dates in
1941.[9] Summaries and critiques of Bultmann's proposal for the
sources of the gospel and how the evangelist utilized them are
numerous and easily available, so that only a brief summary of that
proposal will suffice for our purposes. Bultmann argued that by
means of a number of different methods of analysis the evidence of
sources could be detected in the present form of the gospel. By
marked stylistic differences among passages Bultmann claimed to
detect the distinctive literary styles of (1) three sources, (2)
the evangelist, and (3) the work of a later redactor who further
contributed to the gospel (style criticism). The distinctive
theological ideas of each of the contributors to the gospel--sources,
evangelist, and redactor--also aided in the delineation of the
source materials (content criticism). Bultmann argued, however,
that incongruities in the relationship of a passage to its context
are the basic means of detecting the sources, the evangelist, and
the redactor (context criticism).

---

[5]E.g., G.H.C. Macgregor and A.Q. Morton, *The Structure of the Fourth Gospel* (Edinburgh: Oliver and Boyd, 1961); Edwin C. Broome, Jr., "The Sources of the Fourth Gospel," *Journal of Biblical Literature*, 63 (1944), 107-121.

[6]The best survey of the history of the material is Howard M. Teeple, *The Literary Origin of the Gospel of John* (Evanston, Illinois: Religion and Ethics Institute, Inc., 1974), 1-116.

[7]W. Nicol, *The Sēmeia in the Fourth Gospel* (Leiden: Brill, 1972), 4.

[8]The proposal of a "signs gospel" was made as early as 1915 by J.M. Thompson, "The Structure of the Fourth Gospel," *Expositor,*10 (1915), 514, 523. Compare Robert T. Fortna, *The Gospel of Signs. A Reconstruction of the Narrative Source Underlying the Fourth Gospel* (Cambridge: University Press, 1970).

[9]English translation by Beasley-Murray (Oxford:Blackwell, 1971).

By use of these critical methods Bultmann claimed to distinguish among four primary sources utilized by the evangelist: First, from a *signs source* the evangelist drew a number of the narratives of Jesus' miraculous actions. This source, Bultmann conjectured, was a collection of a large number of miracle stories quite distinct from the synoptic traditions; it was written in Greek but with strong semitic influences. References to the ennumeration of the signs in the source are present in the gospel at 2:11 and 4:54. Second, the evangelist drew freely from a collection of *discourses* in which a gnostic redeemer figure speaks his revelatory words for the enlightened to hear. These speeches came into the hands of the evangelist in a poetic Aramaic from a group which can only generally be described as an oriental gnostic community similar to the later Mandaeans. Bultmann thought he found close parallels in the johannine discourses with the *Odes of Solomon*. Third, the *passion and resurrection stories* of the gospel are indebted to a source which was independent of the synoptic traditions regarding the final events in the life of Jesus. Bultmann alleged that such a source came to the evangelist in a semitized Greek. Finally, Bultmann alludes to but does not sharply distinguish certain *miscellaneous* sources utilized by the evangelist. These four major sources were main ingredients which went into the gospel along with the careful work of the evangelist himself; but Bultmann further conjectures the work of a later redactor who added to the evangelist's work in the interest of the church of the redactor's day and most particularly the orthodox faith of that church.[10]

Bultmann's extensive source analysis was met with lively and prolonged debate. It is fair to say that the debate was most concerned with the proposal of a signs and a discourse source. While the proposal of a signs source was greeted with some agreement, the alleged discourse source was the subject of more negative than positive criticism.[11] Of course, Bultmann was not the first to suggest a signs source behind the gospel,[12] but his formulation of

---

[10]Dwight Moody Smith, *The Composition and Order of the Fourth Gospel* (New Haven: Yale University Press, 1965) presents a careful summary and analysis of Bultmann's source theory.

[11]One of Bultmann's students has attempted a more extensive and persuasive argument for a discourse source: H. Becker, *Die Reden des Johannesevangeliums und der Stil der gnostischen Offenbarungsreden* (Gottingen: Vandenhoeck, 1956). His labors, however, have not evoked significant adherence to the theory. See, however, the following works: Broome, "Sources of"; Octave Merlier, *Le Quatrieme Evangile: La question Johannique XI* (Paris: Presses Universitaries de France, 1961); and Teeple, *Literary Origin*.

[12] He actually depends heavily upon observations and arguments advanced by A. Faure, "Die alttestamentliche Zitate im 4. Evangelium und Quellenscheidungshypothese," *Zeitschrift fur die neutestamentliche Wissenschaft und die Kunde der alteren Kirche*, 21 (1922), 107ff.

the source and his efforts to exegete the gospel text specifically
with the signs source hypothesis gave the theory its most influential
expression in the mid-twentieth century. The result was a significant scholarly assent.[13]

The most decisive attack upon Bultmann's source theories came
in the form of an analysis of the style criticism he had employed
as a basis for the separation of the sources. First, Eduard
Schweizer[14] and then E. Ruckstuhl[15] investigated the style characteristics of the fourth gospel and each concluded that there was, on
the basis of style criteria, no evidence on which to advance a
distinction among either the proposed sources and the work of the
evangelist, on the one hand, or the work of the evangelist and an
alleged redactor, on the other hand. Their combined studies seemed
to point toward the conclusion amply expressed in the title of
Ruckstuhl's monograph, "the literary unity of the gospel of John."
As the scholarly world assimilated the results of their work, there
seemed little basis for a source analysis of the gospel. While
many scholars continued to maintain a general assent to the proposed
signs source in some form, no serious source criticism was undertaken for nearly two decades. The Schweizer-Ruckstuhl challenge
to the whole project of source criticism of the fourth gospel was
not seriously answered.[16]

Notwithstanding the powerful assault of the Schweizer-Ruckstuhl
criticism, the hypothesis of a signs source (or gospel) has gained
prominence, at least in some circles, within the recent decade.
This is due in part to the appearance of three major investigations:
Robert T. Fortna's *The Gospel of Signs: A Reconstruction of the
Narrative Source Underlying the Fourth Gospel*, W. Nicol's *The Semeia
in the Fourth Gospel--Tradition and Redaction*, and Howard Teeple's,
The Literary Origin of the Gospel of John.[17] In addition, one major

---

[13]To mention only a few, Hartke, *Vier urchristliche Parteien*;
Hans Conzelmann, *An Outline of New Testament Theology* (New York:
Harper and Row, 1969); Willi Marxsen, *An Introduction to the New
Testament* (Philadelphia: Westminster Press, 1968); Reginald H. Fuller,
Interpreting the Miracles (Philadelphia: Westminster Press, 1963).
    [14]Eduard Schweizer, *Ego Eimi* (Gottingen:Vandenhoeck, 1939).
Even though Schweizer's study was first published before Bultmann's
commentary appeared, his argument for the stylistic unity of the
gospel has been employed against Bultmann's source analysis.
Schweizer himself, however, in the second edition of his work in 1965
acknowledges that source criticism of the prologue and the miracle
stories is not ruled out by his contention for the style unity of
the gospel(p. vi).
    [15]E. Ruckstuhl, *Die literarische Einheit des Johannesevangeliums*
(Freiburg: Paulus, 1951).
    [16]See, however, J. Becker's work which undertakes, in part, a
response to the arguments for stylistic unity.
    [17]See notes 6, 7, and 8.

commentary has employed the signs source hypothesis, that of the
Roman Catholic scholar, Rudolf Schnackenburg;[18] and an article by
Jürgen Becker, primarily concerned with the redactional study of the
fourth gospel on the basis of a signs source, reconstructs and
revises Bultmann's signs source.[19] We will summarize the findings
of these five works and demonstrate their interrelatedness by
looking first at the methods employed by the authors, then at the
content and character of the sources they propose; finally some
criticism of their collective enterprise will be offered.

A. *The Methods of the Source Analyses*

In general the methods of the three major investigations--
Fortna, Nicol, and Teeple--are considerably distinct. Teeple's
undertaking is the most ambitious and his hypothesis the most
thorough and daring, for his solution to the difficulties of the
fourth gospel involves an elaborate four-source proposal. The so-
called "S" document is only one part of the pre-johannine material
to be detected in the gospel. Moreover, Teeple is confident enough
of his hypothesis that he is able to label, at least tentatively,
each portion of the gospel in terms of the literary strand employed
at that point.[20] Fortna's study attempts only to isolate the
narrative signs source, but, as the title of his monograph suggests,
he attempts to reassemble from those passages the source as it is
transmitted to us through the fourth gospel. He attempts with the

---

[18]Rudolf Schnackenburg, *The Gospel According to St. John* (New
York: Herder and Herder, 1968) vol. I; *Das Johannesevangelium*
(Freiburg: Herder, 1971), Band II. A less extensive commentary has
also employed a signs source hypothesis: Siegfried Schulz, *Das
Evangelium nach Johannes* (Göttingen: Vandenhoeck und Ruprecht, 1972).

[19]Jürgen Becker, "Wunder und Christologie," *New Testament
Studies*, 16 (1969-70), 130-148.

[20]Teeple, 143-147. While we will not give major attention to
the other sources which the evangelist employed, according to Teeple,
it is necessary to describe briefly Teeple's total source theory.
It is important at least because it is the first major multiple
source theory for the gospel of John advanced since Bultmann. Teeple
proposes in addition to the "S" source the evangelist's use of "G"
which roughly parallels Bultmann's proposed discourse source.
According to Teeple, "G" was for the most part a collection of speech
materials, which originated in the milieu of a "semi-gnostic",
hellenistic Christian mysticism. The two sources, "S" and "G", were
the primary strands in the evangelist's production of the first form
of the gospel; the evangelist's own work ("E") was instrumental in
giving the gospel a somewhat gnostic orientation similar to that
found in "G". Finally, a redactor ("R") added to the first form of
the gospel his own interests which grew up out of the problems of
the church in the second century. He dates the "G" source about 90,
the work of the evangelist about 95, and the final redaction, 125.
Generally, the source analysis undertaken by Teeple is careful and
scholarly, although his basic method seems to fault his proposals.
(See below.)

greatest precision to isolate the source material from the rest of
the gospel, and his detailed analysis even leads him to include as
an appendix to his study the possible text of the proposed source.[21]

Nicol's work is a broader undertaking in some ways and attempts
an initial redaction critical study on the basis of his hypothesis
regarding a signs source, as well as the explication of that
hypothesis itself. Nicol's study moves through three stages. He
first undertakes a separation of the signs traditions from the
redactional work of the evangelist; then, by use of the tools of
form criticism, examines those passages he has isolated in order to
describe the character of the signs tradition prior to the evangelist;
and finally Nicol turns to the redaction critical task. His proposal
for a signs source is as cautious as Teeple and Fortna's are bold.
Nicol seems to want to correct what he deems the excesses of the
"older" source criticism of the fourth gospel by a more modest
claim for his results. His undertaking is deliberately a "separation"
of the source and not a "reconstruction," which places him in a
position quite different from that of Fortna's deliberately
reconstructive endeavor. Moreover, it is not Nicol's claim that the
entirety of the source can be isolated from the evangelist's
redactional work; he freely admits that he may have isolated only
a portion of the tradition employed by the evangelist. Nicol further
qualifies his results by suggesting that the precise and detailed
separation of the source may have been rendered impossible due to
the method by which the evangelist worked with that source. "The
source was probably his 'Gospel' from which he had preached for
years, thus more or less knowing it by heart. When he finally
started writing his own Gospel, he probably wrote down the traditional
miracle stories from memory." The words and style of the evangelist
may naturally have "infected" the purity of the source's style and
language.[22]

Before the appearance of the studies by Teeple, Fortna, and
Nicol, Rudolf Schnackenburg, writing in the introduction of his
multiple-volumed and as yet incomplete commentary on the Gospel of
John, gives his assent to a theory of a signs source for the gospel.
Although cautious, he concludes, "The use of a written '*sēmeia*-source'
may be maintained with some probability."[23] Although his discussion
is necessarily brief and in some cases too indecisive for clear
explication, his proposal of a signs source is significant because

---

[21]Fortna, 235-245.   [22]Nicol, 5-6.
[23]Schnackenburg, *Gospel*, vol. I, 72.

it represents a use of the thesis in a commentary and because it comes from a Roman Catholic scholar.

Another brief but important summary of a proposed signs source appears in a recent article by Jürgen Becker. It is important for our purposes for it demonstrates the continued influence of the Bultmannian proposal for a signs source. Becker essentially utilizes a summary of Bultmann's arguments for the *sēmeia* source as the foundation of his isolation of the source and epitomization of its character. While Becker's reconstruction of the source does not allow for an investigation of his method and the reconstruction it-self is briefly summarized, his effort to describe the character of the source and how it was used by the evangelist is an important example of contemporary criticism of the fourth gospel.

In each of these studies a major criterion for separating the source material from the evangelist's material is proposed. Teeple's proposal leans heavily upon stylistic variations within the gospel material as the means of detecting the use of various sources. In particular, Teeple maintains, it is syntax which is the most import-ant clue to source detection, and his study includes an appendix which demonstrates the syntactical variations among the four proposed strands of the gospel. In the case of the "S" source, vocabulary figures significantly along with syntax. For example, "In John only S uses *te* for 'and' or 'both', 'after this' at the beginning of a sentence, and *hōs* in the sense of 'about' with numbers." The Schweizer-Ruckstuhl claim of the stylistic unity of the gospel is due entirely, Teeple thinks, to their faulty selection of style characteristics. The style characteristics which occur most frequently in the gospel naturally tend to be those which are typical of more than one of the sources; it is the less frequently appearing style features which should be studied, for they signal the presence of individual sources.[24]

For Fortna it is the analysis of the aporias (difficulties) of the narrative which yields the primary basis for source separation. "It has always been clear that difficulties present themselves in the narrative portions of [John], but it is not recognized that they themselves contain the means to their own solution."[25] These breaks or discontinuities in the narrative are the data which when scrutinized indicate the breaks between the source and the work of the evangelist.

Nicol's basic methodological criterion seems to be a form analysis. He detects a unique form in certain of the miracle stories

---

[24]Teeple, 118-119, 145-146, quote, 145.   [25]Fortna, 19-20.

of the fourth gospel. In contrast to the more ordinary narrative
form of the gospel, which is long, dramatic, and carried on by
lively dialogue, one finds in a number of miracle stories a form
which is more typical of the synoptic gospels: A short account
which follows the standard synoptic sequence discernible in the
miracle stories of the description of the illness, the healing, and
the demonstration of the healing. (Compare, for instance, the
narrative form of chapter 7 and that of 2:13ff).[26]

Schnackenburg's method of delineating the boundaries of the
signs source is not explicitly stated, but he seems to value most
highly the indications of a tension between the "tradition" and the
"redaction" as the starting point for source isolation. He argues
that the evangelist was attempting faithfully to transmit a tradition
which had come to him and at the same time develop his own theological
statement. The result is a telltale "tension" between the two.[27]
Becker grounds his reconstruction of a signs source for the most part
on Bultmann's arguments. But the disharmony which exists in the
gospel as it now stands between the signs and the statements which
minimize the importances of signs (e.g., chapter 11) is the leading
criterion for separating source and redaction.[28]

In addition to these major criteria for separating source and
redaction, the critics propose supporting criteria which may test
the initial separation achieved by the application of the first
criterion or may simply add cumulative evidence for the proposed
separation. Teeple will recognize only syntactical and vocabulary
criteria as sufficient to isolate the "S" source, but he acknowledges that what he calls literary structure (aporia, catchwords,
etc.) and thought content may be employed to bolster the findings
of the stylistic evidence.[29]

Fortna suggests that, in addition to attention to the aporias
of the gospel (which he calls the "contextual criterion" for source
isolation), stylistic and ideological criteria must be employed.
Fortna has responded to the arguments of Schweizer and Ruckstuhl
for the literary unity of the fourth gospel by shifting the stylistic
criteria for source isolation to a secondary and supportive place
in his methodology. Stylistic criteria prove to be inconclusive,
he argues, for a number of reasons: First, the evangelist may
imitate the style of his source either deliberately or accidentally.
Second, the source and the evangelist may share a number of stylistic

----

[26]Nicol, 14-16.
[27]Schnackenburg, *Gospel*, vol. I, 59, 64-67.
[28]J. Becker, 132-134.   [29]Teeple, 118.

characteristics due to a common milieu.[30] Third, the evangelist
may have been expected to redact his source in the process of using
it and may have inserted words or phrases of his own to substitute
for the source's style. It is true that stylistic features provide
confirmation of a source hypothesis but they cannot become the
foundation of any such hypothesis. Therefore, "the discouraging
results of the stylistic tests as applied to earlier source reconstructions do not *per se* argue against a new attempt."

Similarly, ideological criteria are not sufficient ground in
and of themselves for source analysis, Fortna contends. They are
far too subjective and are diminished in significance by the fact
that a single author, especially a subtle theologian like the
fourth evangelist, may in fact contain within his writing ideas of
differing and even contradictory nature. The most such ideological
data can do in an argument for source separation is provide "a kind
of cumulative force in the argument."[31] The heart of Fortna's
method, therefore, lies not in the application of stylistic or
ideological criteria to the text but in what he calls "contextual
criteria."

Having established a reconstruction of the source by means of
contextual criteria, Fortna then attempts to test it for stylistic
integrity and ideological uniqueness. While Teeple rejects entirely
Ruckstuhl's style characteristics of the gospel, Fortna utilizes
Ruckstuhl's list of fifty style characteristics which are peculiar
to the fourth gospel and finds that sixty-four percent of those are
not found in the isolated signs source. More important, he claims,
is the fact that individual words and phrases which are rare or
lacking entirely in the New Testament except in the fourth gospel
are in the source passages alone, not in the rest of the gospel.
The proposed source does have a unique style, Fortna concludes.
"What all this means is that we have uncovered, however inexactly
in detail, a pre-Johannine stratum which had already a distinctive
literary character imposed upon it." In a less exact manner, Fortna
similarly attempts to show that his proposed source has a unique
theological character about it which can be distinguished from the
theological emphases of the evangelist. He understands the so-called
"Signs Gospel" to claim that Jesus demonstrated his messianic identity

---

[30]These two observations Fortna draws from Emmanuel Hirsch's
response to Schweizer's book. "Stilkritik und Literanalyse im
vierten Evangelium," *Zeitschrift für die neutestamentliche
Wissenschaft*, 43 (1950-51), 129-143. Fortna, 203, 211.
 [31]Fortna, 212, quotes, 19 and 17 respectively.

by his marvelous acts.[32]

Nicol similarly understands that stylistic and ideological differences in the text may be taken as supporting and testing evidence for the source separation. In spite of his suggestion that the evangelist may have reported the source through the medium of his own style and language, the critic finds that there is stylistic evidence of the uniqueness of those synoptic-like miracle stories. Testing these passages with the style characteristics of Ruckstuhl's list plus thirty-two additional characteristics which are distinctive of the fourth gospel as a whole, he concludes that "the Johannine characteristics are evenly distributed in the Gospel, with the exception of some short synoptic-like pericopes, mostly miracle stories." There is, then, stylistic evidence for the separation of these stories, and Nicol believes that this refutes the Schweizer-Ruckstuhl contention of the stylistic unity of the whole of the gospel. Another indication of the traditional character of these stories is the aporias encountered in their relationship to the context in which they appear. Nicol relegates to a supportive position these aporias which in Fortna's study are the basic means of isolating the source. Finally, Nicol maintains that the ideo-logical tension between the content of these stories and the rest of the gospel supports their isolation as source material. In these stories one encounters an understanding of miracle as an acceptable basis for Christian faith (e.g., 2:11; 4:53), while the gospel else-where urges that faith founded merely upon a response to miracle is yet an inadequate or immature faith (e.g., 4:48; 14:11).

These four indications of the presence of a source--form, style, aporias, ideological tension--allow the careful critic, Nicol main-tains, to separate the traditional material. But that separation must further be tested by whether or not the historical existence of such a source is plausible. It is incumbent upon the source critic to suggest a convincing historical character and setting for the proposed source as well as a feasible way of understanding how the evangelist utilized that source in his own work.[33] Nicol, there-fore, contends, in contrast especially to Teeple's project, that form criticism (the study, in this case, of the character of the source materials before their incorporation into the gospel) and redaction criticism are integral parts of the task of source criticism. The latter cannot be done apart from the further evidence adduced from the other.

---

[32]*Ibid.*, 205-11, 215-217, 228ff, quote, 217.
[33]Nicol, 25, 30-40, 7, quote, 25.

Schnackenburg's primary criterion for separating source and redaction is the detection of the "tension" between the two, but he adds to this basic means of detection a second which seems to correspond to Nicol's primary criteria, namely, the evidence of a synoptic-like form in certain of the miracle stories in the fourth gospel. Between these synoptic-like johannine materials and the synoptic gospels themselves there are enough similarities to suggest that the former were associated with a synoptic tradition; but the differences between these narratives and their synoptic counterparts are too striking to allow for an alleged use of the synoptic narratives themselves as a source for the evangelist. Furthermore, within these miracle stories one is impressed by the absence of special johannine characteristics (e.g., 5:2-9). Finally, his method seems to value the similarities among the isolated passages. That similarity (sometimes of form, sometimes of content) suggests to the critic that these passages shared a place in a common tradition. An example of note to which Schnackenburg points are the parallels between the healings reported in chapters 5 and 9: In both cases a chronic illness is healed at a pool in Jerusalem.[34]

Becker's article does not explicate a methodology beyond that which has been summarized above, but he does argue against the stylistic criterion as a decisive means of separating source and redaction. In what is obviously an attempt to counter the arguments for the stylistic unity of the gospel as a foil against source analysis, he contends that style statistics do not solve the aporias of the gospel and only suggest that the total johannine materials-- the sources and the work of the evangelist--share a single community of faith. In other words, if the source materials do not have a distinctive style of their own, it is due to the fact that they arose from the same community tradition as did the ideas and language of the evangelist.[35] While Teeple, Nicol, and Fortna all attempt to rescue style criticism as a method of source separation from the hands of their opponents, Becker concedes the stylistic unity of the gospel and surrenders the use of style as means of source analysis.

An overview of these methods of source analysis demonstrates that johannine criticism has not devised universally acceptable means of source detection. Among the three major attempts to do a source analysis in the last decade there is no agreement as to which of the possible criteria for source detection ought to play the major role and which should function as supportive criteria.

---

[34]Schnackenburg, *Gospel*, vol. I, 64-67.
[35]J. Becker, 132-133.

While Fortna gives pre-eminence to the aporias as both the problem
of the gospel and its solution in source criticism, Nicol gives
that function to form analysis and relegates Fortna's major method
to a supportive role. Teeple elevates style criteria and will give
context criticism a minor role and form analysis none at all! If
we can understand what Schnackenburg means by tension between
tradition and redaction to be primarily ideological (which
seems the most likely interpretation of his brief exposition of
method), then we can conclude that both Becker and Schnackenburg
give the ideological criteria the major role in source separation,
since the conflict between the ideology of the proposed source and
the evangelist seems to be Becker's practiced method.

If Fortna, Nicol, and Schnackenburg all agree in the use of
stylistic criteria as a supportive testing of the separated source,
Becker dissents by eliminating that criterion entirely from the
procedure, and Teeple claims it is the only objective means of
source criticism. Fortna, Teeple, and Nicol all agree to use the
ideological tensions only for the accumulative force of the argument for the isolated passages. Schnackenburg would seem to agree
with Nicol that form is important in source analysis, but uses
form criticism in a supportive rather than primary way. Teeple and
Fortna, on the other hand, make no explicit use of form analysis at
all in their projects. To these differences among the critics on
the method of source analysis we must add the disagreement as to
whether the goal of such analysis is reconstruction (Fortna) or
only separation (Nicol and Teeple and by implication Schnackenburg
and Becker).

Of all these critics, only Teeple believes that his method
can be applied to the gospel in a thorough manner and render not
only the passages drawn from the signs source but the other sources
as well. Teeple alone ventures a multiple source theory for the
gospel. Finally, only Nicol seems to be concerned with what might
be called a "wholistic" method--one which combines the tools of
form and redaction criticism with source analysis. While one
would not want to press these differences too far, it would seem
fair to conclude that the method of source criticism of the fourth
gospel is somewhat in shambles. Still, it is a contribution of
recent johannine criticism that such efforts at source analysis
should be taken up with such seriousness at all.

B. *The Content of the Source Analyses*

When one turns to the question of the proposed content of the
source isolated by these critics, there is somewhat more consensus
evidenced, although we are still far from being able to talk about
a clearly defined signs source. The summaries of the proposed
contents of the signs source represented in the chart on the
following page suggest the similarities and the differences among
the four source theories. (It should be noted that the representations of Teeple and Fortna's reconstructions do not attempt to
recount their reservations about specific words and phrases within
certain verses, and suggest only the general results of their
findings. Verses in parentheses are those whose place in the source
is not as certain as the others.)[36]

Several general comments are called for: First, the categori-
cally different nature of Fortna's reconstruction is to be noted.
He has been so bold as not only to isolate those passages which he
thinks properly are to be understood as source material but to
rearrange the isolated passages into an order which represents
something of what Fortna argues might have been their original order
in the source document.

Furthermore, it is striking that the reconstruction Fortna
proposes is not simply a collection of narratives about Jesus but a
gospel in its own right; that is to say, it has all of the characteristics of the canonical gospels with the exception that it lacks
teaching material, which exclusion, Fortna concedes, relegates the
signs document to the status of a "rudimentary" or "narrow" gospel.
But the inclusion of the passion and resurrection accounts, along
with its connected narratives, producing a continuous account,
surely qualifies the reconstruction as something more than a
collection of materials.[37] Teeple's source, too, appears to have
some of the features of a full gospel, although it is important that
he does not attribute any resurrection material to his hypothetical
"S" source. Still, Teeple and Fortna agree that passion materials
were drawn by the evangelist from this source.

It is evident from the summary of Nicol's proposal for the
contents of the source that he has not limited his source separation

---

[36]For the separation of source and redaction in chapter 11
Schnackenburg cites with approval the results of Wilhelm Wilkens,
"Die Erweckung des Lazarus," *Theologische Zeitschrift*, 15 (1959),
22-39. *Gospel*, vol. 1, 66.

[37]Fortna, 221-222.

THE PROPOSED CONTENTS OF THE SIGNS SOURCE/GOSPEL

TEEPLE (Pages 166-248)	FORTNA (Pages 235-245)	NICOL (Pages 30-40)	SCHNACKENBURG (Pages 64-67)	BECKER (Page 35)
	Introduction:			I. Galilean Works of Jesus:
Baptist's Testimony--1:19-21, 24-26, 31, 35-42	Exordium--1:6-7			Baptist--1:19ff
Conversion of First Disciples --1:43-45, 47 (mixed with "E")	Baptist's Testimony--1:19-21, 23, 26-27, 33-34	*First Disciples--1:35-50		Calling of Disciples--1:35ff
	Conversion of First Disciples --3:23-24, 1:35b-50			
Water into Wine--2:1-9, 11	The Signs of Jesus:	Water Changed into Wine-- 2:1-11 (except for a few phrases in 4,6,9,and 11)	Marriage Feast at Cana--2:1-11a	Cana Miracle--2:1-11
Cleansing Temple--2:13b-16	1. Water Changed into Wine-- 2:1-3,5-11 (except for a few phrases in 4,6,9,and 11)			
A Pharisee--3:2,22,25-26a				
Samaritan Woman--4:3-6, 16-19, 25-29,31-32,40,42-43	2. Nobleman's Son Healed-- 2:12a; 4:46b-47, 49-54	*Jesus and Samaritan Woman --4:5-9, 16-19, 28-30, 40	Healing at a Distance--4:46-54	Jesus and Samaritan Woman-- 4:1ff (Basic content of conversation drawn from source.)
Nobleman's Son Healed--4:46b, 47b, 49-50a, 51-53a, 54	3. Miraculous Draught of Fish --21:2-8, 10-12, 14	Nobleman's Son Healed-- 4:46-47, (49), 50-54		Healing of Nobleman's Son-- 4:46-54
38-Year Illness Healed-- 5:5-9a, 14, (16)	4. Multitude Fed--6:1-3, 5 7-14	Healing at Bethesda-- 5:2-9b	Multiplication of Loaves-- 6:1-15	Feeding of 5,000--6:1-15
Feeding Miracle--6:1a, 5b, 7, 9-14	Interlude--Walking on Water and Miraculous Landing-- 6:15b-22, 25 (67ff)	Feeding of 5,000 and Walking on Water--6:1-3, 4-21 (except for last four words of 12 and last five of 14)	Walking on Water--6:16-21	Walking on Water--6:16-25
Walking on Water--6:16-21, 22b,24b-25,60,66-67,70	5. Dead Man Raised; A Samaritan Woman--11:1-3,7,11,15; 4:4-7,9,16-19,25-26,28-30, 40,(42); 11:17-20,28,32- 34,38-39,41,43-45			II. Judean Works of Jesus:
Feast in Jerusalem--7:3, 6a, 9-10, 32b, 40-49			Miracle at Bethesda--5:2-9	Healing at Bethesda--5:1-9
Man Blind from Birth Healed --9:12, 6-7, 8-12, 16b-17	6. Man Blind from Birth Healed --9:1-3a, 6-7, (8)	Man Born Blind--9:1-3a, 6-7	Healing of Man Born Blind-- 9:1, 6f	Healing of Man Born Blind-- 9:1ff
Raising of Lazarus--11:1a, 3- 4,6-8a,11b-15,19-21,23-27 35-36,39-41a,43b-44,46-50, 54-55, 57	7. A 38-Year Illness Healed-- 5:2-3, 5-9, (14)	Raising of Lazarus--11:1-3, 6,12-19, (28-32), 33-39, 43-44	Raising of Lazarus--11:1a, 3, 17, 33-34, 38, 39a, 41a, 43-44	Resurrection of Lazarus-- 11:1-44

Anointing at Bethany--12:1-
2a,3-5,7-9a,11b-14,18b-21a
Triumphal Entry--12:11b-14,
18b-21a
Arrest--18:3, 4b-5a, 6a, 10b,
12, 13b, 19,22

Trial--19:1-5a, 12-13a

Crucifixion and Burial--19:
14b-17a, 18-19, 21-24a, 25b,
28-30, 40-42

Conclusion--20:30

The Death and Resurrection:
Cleansing of Temple and Death
Plot--2:14-16,18-19,47a,53
Anointing at Bethany--12:1-5,
7, (8)
Triumphal Entry--12:12-15
Last Supper--fragments in 12
Arrest--18:1-4, 10-12
In High Priest's House--18:13,
24,15-16a, (19),20,(21),22-23,
16b-18, 25b-28a
Before Pilate--18:28b, 33, 37-
38; 19:15; 18:39-40; 19:6,
(12), 13-14a, 1-3, 16a
Crucifixion and Burial--19:
16b-19,(20),23-24,28-30,25,
31-34,36-38;(3:1),19:39-42
Resurrection--20:1-3, 5, 7,
8-12, 14, 16-20

Peroration: 20:30-31

Conclusion --20:30-31a

*Regarded as other possible
source materials

Conclusion--20:30 (uncer-
tain)

Conclusion--12:37-38;
20:30-31

to those miracle stories which have a synoptic-like form (e.g.,
the healing at Bethesda) but has found what he apparently takes to
be "broken" forms of such stories within an enlarged johannine
context (e.g., the raising of Lazarus). Nor has he separated out
only those miracle stories which he understands to have a sense of
unity by their similarities, but additionally finds it likely that
the calling of the first disciples and the discussion with the
Samaritan woman were a part of the signs tradition. In a comparable
manner Schnackenburg seems to contend that the signs source consisted
of a number of short miracle stories which have either been incorporated into the fourth gospel essentially in their original form
(e.g., 5:2-9) or broken up and worked into an expanded johannine
narrative (chapter 11). Becker's proposal is distinctive in that
he perceives in the source material a simple two-fold geographical
division between the Galilean and Judean works of Jesus.

Putting aside differences over specific verses, a number of
interesting similarities and differences emerge from our comparison
of the proposed contents of the source. First, all five critics
agree that seven "sign" narratives came to the evangelist through
his source (the miracle at Cana, the healing of the nobleman's son,
the feeding of the multitude the walking on water, the healing at
Bethesda, the healing of the man blind from birth, and the raising
of Lazarus). Moreover, all five agree that 20:30 and perhaps 31
comprised the conclusion of the source, although Schnackenburg is
somewhat reserved at this point. Teeple, Fortna, Nicol, and Becker
agree together in including some portion of the narratives regarding
the calling of the first disciples and Jesus' encounter with the
Samaritan woman. Becker, Teeple, and Fortna further agree that the
account of John the Baptist in the fourth gospel depends upon source
materials.

In disagreement with the others, Fortna finds evidence for
attaching the resurrection stories to the source and for including
portions of chapter 21 in the source's narrative. Teeple is alone
in attributing portions of the narratives concerning the conversation
with a Pharisee ("S" did not name him Nicodemus, Teeple believes),
and the schism over Jesus among the Jews at the feast (chapter 7)
to the proposed source; hence, his hypothetical "S" is a fuller
narrative document than any of the others excepting, of course,
Fortna's "signs gospel." Like Fortna, Teeple finds evidence for
believing that portions of the temple cleansing narrative were part
of the source. Only Becker is convinced that 12:37-38 was part of
the signs source. Therefore, without anything approaching unanimity,

the critics nonetheless have reached a consensus concerning the
main body of the narrative source used by the fourth evangelist.

C. The Character of the Proposed Source

Beyond the bare contents of the source, what do these critics
propose to have been the character of the document? It originated,
Fortna deduces, in a Jewish-Christian milieu, since its Jewish
characteristics are evident. It may have come into existence in
either a Palestinian or Syrian environment at a time either before
or after the Jewish war--Fortna is not able to support a decision
on the question of a date. As to the intent of the gospel more
can be ventured. It seems to have been written as "a missionary
tract with a single end, to show (presumably to the potential Jewish
convert) that Jesus is the Messiah....It is, among other things,
this unifying purpose that differentiates the source from a mere
collection of stories." It presented the evangelist with a tradition which had close contacts with the synoptic traditions, and it
is the use of this source, Fortna believes, which supplied the fourth
evangelist with his only knowledge of the synoptic tradition.
(Fortna thus believes his hypothesis resolves the debate over
whether John knew the synoptic gospels in some form.) The tradition
represented in the signs gospel, however, is a relatively "developed"
one; that is, its picture of the historical Jesus has been blurred
by the influences of a Christian community and its interests. Its
missionary purpose shaped the christology of the signs source
significantly, with the result that the narratives of Jesus'
actions are presented as demonstrations of his messiahship; most
especially are the passion and resurrection stories given this
meaning: The last and greatest sign of his authority is his death
and resurrection.[38]

Teeple contends the author of "S" was familiar with Jewish
Christianity, reflects a semitic background in a number of ways,
and even writes in a semitized Greek. However, the author was
not a Jewish Christian, Teeple argues, because a Jewish Christian
would not have written about "the Jews" as the author of "S" does
(e.g., 11:19; 19:14-16). While Teeple disagrees with Fortna on
the background of the author of the source, he agrees that the
source was influenced by Mark and Matthew. It was surely written
after 75, since 11:48 alludes to the destruction of the temple, and

---

[38]*Ibid.*, 221-234, quote, 225.

it represents a later and Gentile state of the Christian tradition
as is evidenced, Teeple thinks, by its "deification" of Jesus. The
source was produced shortly after the Jewish council at Jamnia which
officially excluded Christians from the synagogue, and like the
Gospel of Matthew it represents the Pharisees as the major opponents
of the Christian movement. Its purpose was to present Jesus as a
worker of signs (20:30) which evoked faith, on the one hand (2:11;
4:53), and hostility on the other (7:32a). It is probable, but not
certain, that the miracle stories of "S" were originally post-
resurrection accounts which the author has placed back into the
context of the earthly ministry of Jesus.[39]

Nicol's explication of the character of the signs tradition is
done in a form-critical manner in the second major section of his
study. He concludes that the purpose of the proposed *sēmeia*
tradition was to present Jesus as the expected Jewish Messiah to
prospective Jewish converts. It is likely that it was a written
tradition arising among Jewish Christians. "The sole aim of [the
signs source] is that all should see the miracles as authenticating
signs (*sēmeia*) of the Messiah and believe."[40] In this tradition
Jesus is represented as taking the initiative in his miraculous acts
as opposed to the synoptic tradition in which Jesus is often made to
respond to requests for healing; likewise, his acts are not demonstrations of compassion or pity as is sometimes the case in the
synoptic tradition, but always demonstrations of his power. The
secrecy motif is absent as is the concern for the miracles as
indications of the presence of the kingdom of God; the miracles
openly declare Jesus' messiahship; and Jesus and his power, not the
kingdom, is the central point of the acts. Moreover, there is no
concern for an explication of the nature of Jesus' messiahship, only
the unadulterated proclamation of that messiahship.

Nicol argues that such a tradition represented in the signs
material is a restrained development within the church beyond the
synoptic tradition. That is, it presents us with features which
can best be explained as evidence of a tradition later than that
witnessed in the synoptic gospels. The absence of the kingdom idea,
for instance, is due to theological developments in the church
brought about by the gradual diminishing of the hope for an imminent
parousia. The tradition reflects a development best explained, he
emphasizes, by the continuing influence of Jewish, not hellenistic,
thought upon the Christian community. He contends that the miracles
of Jesus in the signs source are not so reminiscent of the *theios*

---

[39]Teeple, 143-147.   [40]Nicol, 44.

anēr (the divine man, a wonder worker) of the hellenistic world [41]
as they are the effort of Christians to fashion a convincing portrayal of Jesus as the mosaic prophet of Jewish expectation who is
authenticated by his wonderous acts; it is, then, for a Jewish
audience and out of a Jewish-Christian community that the source
evolved. This hypothesis is confirmed, Nicol believes, by virtue
of the numerous Jewish characteristics of the isolated material:
The knowledge of Palestinian geography and customs, Aramaic words
and sentence structures, and distinctively Jewish ideas such as
the concept of *sēmeia*. (The LXX translates *'ot* with *sēmeia* and
Moses authenticates himself with his signs.) Likewise the messianism
of the signs material is thoroughly Jewish:

> [The signs source] could use the miracles of Jesus to proclaim
> them as *sēmeia*...because [the Jews] had many ideas about a
> (final) prophet authenticated by signs, and these ideas had
> the inherent possibility of being connected to Jewish Messianic
> expectations.

The christology of the signs materials isolated by Nicol comprises
its strongest theological motif and that christology is one of a
divine Jesus. legitimating his messiahship with his miraculous acts.[42]

Schnackenburg's characterization of the proposed source is brief
and cautious: The source doubtless contained many more such stories
than the seven the evangelist has chosen to include in his gospel.
The source was concerned to recount "straight-forward miracle stories"
with no theological elucidation. Those stories were understood in
the source as signs which revealed the "hidden glory of the incarnate
Logos." Schnackenburg would seem to believe that the signs concept
has Jewish affinities rather than hellenistic.[43]

While Becker's reconstruction offers us little basis upon
which to observe his methodology and few details of reconstruction,
his epitomization of the christology of the source is richer. Jesus
was portrayed, thinks Becker, in this hypothetical source as a
miracle worker after the fashion of the hellenistic wonder worker
(*theios anēr*)whose miracles evoke faith in the worker himself and
hence christological recognition. It is the epiphany character of

---

[41]This is the position of a number of scholars who understand
the heightened miraculous character of the acts of Jesus in the
fourth gospel and/or signs source as evidence of the tendency to
portray Jesus as a *theios anēr* to Gentiles in the hellenistic world.
See, for example, Fuller, *Interpreting the Miracles*, 89ff; Helmut
Koester, "One Jesus," *Harvard Theological Review*, 61 (1968), 232ff;
Luise Schottroff, *Der Glaubende und die feindliche Welt* (Neukirchener
Verlag, 1970), 257ff.
[42]Nicol, 42-91, quote, 84.
[43]Schnackenburg, *Gospel*, vol. I, 526, 527, quote, 67.

the signs and the revelation which the recognition of their worker
brings that is the main purpose of the signs source. The dialectic
between this christology of the signs source and that of the
evangelist himself is what produces the general confusion over the
christological statements of the fourth gospel as a whole.
Redactional analysis of the gospel in the light of the theology of
the signs source is, believes Becker, the means of understanding
the perplexing johannine christological problem.[44]

All five of these scholars would seem to concur that the source
was above all a christological document. Moreover, all would agree
that in some way or another the signs are represented in the source
as performing a christological function. They are variously described
as demonstrations (Fortna) or authentications (Nicol) of Jesus'
identity. But moving beyond these general descriptions, the consensus among the critics begins to dissolve. Fortna, Nicol, and
Schnackenburg subscribe to the view that the source arose out of a
Jewish-Christian milieu, but Becker and Teeple hold out for a
hellenistic setting (although Teeple acknowledges the evidence of
Jewish-Christian influence on the source). Fortna and Nicol further
agree with one another in describing the source as a missionary
document for potential Jewish converts.

As strongly as Nicol tries to maintain that the tradition
crystallized in the source was free from the influence of the
concept of the hellenistic *theios anēr*, Becker is equally insistent
that it is precisely this model of the divine man which shaped the
portrayal of Jesus in the signs source. (Fortna maintains a careful
reserve on this question, suggesting that *theios anēr* influence is
possible but not certain.) While Teeple, Fortna, and Nicol view
the tradition in the source as a "developed" one (implying thereby
that it could not be earlier than the synoptics), they disagree
regarding the possible contact of the signs tradition with the
synoptic tradition--Fortna and Teeple contend that it had close
contacts with the synoptic tradition; Nicol stresses the fundamental
differences between the two traditions. Whereas Teeple, Nicol,
Fortna, and Becker all seem to discern a rather thorough, if somewhat naive, theology in the source, Schnackenburg wants us to
believe that it was essentially without theological coloration.
Again, one might venture to generalize: There is a common direction
in what the scholars claim concerning the general character of the
proposed source, but beyond that, divergence rather than convergence

_____

[44]J. Becker, 136-143.

seems to characterize their positions.

D. *A Critical Appraisal of the Source Analyses*

The critical appraisal of these efforts to isolate a signs source or gospel behind the fourth gospel must be made on each of several levels. First, there is the fundamental question as to whether or not source analysis of the fourth gospel can be profitably undertaken at all given the peculiar character of that document.[45] Some scholars, of cource, would raise a simple but important question: Are there not less complex solutions to the literary problems posed by the fourth gospel (especially the aporias) than that of source hypotheses, and should not these solutions be preferred in part just because of their greater simplicity?[46] There is no doubt that the source hypotheses here reviewed are complex and tenuous, and there is no doubt that the criteria for fourth gospel source analysis are at best tentative. Still, the growing evidence of the widespread use of source (and/or traditional) materials in New Testament documents should persuade us that we must not shy away from the possibility that the fourth evangelist too availed himself of written materials in the tradition known to him. Moreover, the rich results of the pursuit of the source hypotheses are encouraging. That is, the early efforts at redaction criticism on the basis of the signs source hypothesis demonstrate, at least to my satisfaction, that source analysis may provide keys to a number of the forbidden chambers of johannine thought and history. In a word, the simpler solutions offered by some may be appealing but they may also be easy detours around the hard and admittedly dangerous work of source analysis.

Once we have put to one side the general sort of critical response which depreciates the entire effort at johannine source analysis, we come upon more specific types of critical matters.[47] The endeavors of Teeple and Fortna, for instance, at a thorough and

---

[45]See for example the summaries of criticisms of source theories in D.M. Smith, *Composition*. Cf., Francis Williams, "Fourth Gospel and Synoptic Tradition. Two Johannine Passages," *Journal of Biblical Literature*, 86 (1967), 311-319; C.K. Barrett, *The Gospel According to St. John* (London: SPCK, 1958), 17.

[46]J.H. Crehan, review of Fortna, *Theological Studies*, 31 (1970), 757-759.

[47]For a general discussion of method in source criticism written from one perspective, see Howard M. Teeple, "Methodology in Source Analysis of the Fourth Gospel," *Journal of Biblical Literature*, 81 (1962), 279-286.

detailed source isolation (and, in Fortna's case, reconstruction) seem most vulnerable at the point of their ambition. Fortna's claim to have reconstructed the signs gospel (in a tentative fashion, to be sure) is perhaps the most regrettable feature of his work; for it necessitates that he become too speculative, and his otherwise careful scientific method passes over into imaginative reconstruction. Barnabas Lindars' criticisms of Fortna are the most persuasive of the several critical responses to the signs gospel hypothesis, and Lindars among other things faults Fortna's basic assumption that the evangelist took over the proposed signs gospel almost in its entirety. Is it likely that such a creative thinker and writer as the fourth evangelist would incorporate into his work a complete source in such a manner as to make its reconstruction from his gospel a possibility?[48]

Teeple has not attempted to reconstruct the "S" source in its essential features, as Fortna has the signs gospel, but he shares with Fortna the conviction that this hypothetical source contained a passion story, at least in an adumbrated form. I find Teeple and Fortna's arguments less convincing once they move beyond the simpler "signs" material and begin to incorporate other narrative materials into their proposed sources.[49] Lindars has suggested that Fortna's hypothesis suffers the problem that his proposed "signs gospel" supposes the existence of a kind of document for which we have no evidence in the early Christian movement, i.e., a purely narrative source comprised of miracle stories and the passion narrative. "One cannot help feeling even more sceptical about the whole reconstruction when so much of what is common to all the early Christian literature is missing from the source."[50] Lindars

[48]Barnabas Lindars, *Behind the Fourth Gospel* (London: SPCK, 1971), 32-33.
[49]The critical response to Fortna's work has generally been similar. Positive response has been wide-spread: D.M. Smith, review of Fortna, *Journal of Biblical Literature*, 89 (1970), 498-501. Smith writes, "[Fortna]...has made a strong case for the literary character of the tradition [employed by the evangelist]." Johnson, "Another Primitive Literary Source?", *Encounter*, 33 (1970), 393-399; J. Louis Martyn, "Source Criticism and *Religionsgeschichte* in the Fourth Gospel," *Jesus and Man's Hope* (Pittsburgh: *Perspective*, 1970), vol. I, 247-273. On the other hand, Fortna's contention that the source included a passion and resurrection narrative has drawn dissent from among many of those who would otherwise concur with his proposal: Smith, review, 501; James M. Robinson, "The Johannine Trajectory," Robinson and Helmut Koester, *Trajectories Through Early Christianity* (Philadelphia: Westminster Press, 1971), 247-249; Lindars, 30.
[50]Lindars, 36. J. Louis Martyn, Fortna's teacher and generally an adherent to the "signs gospel" hypothesis, recognizes that Fortna's proposed gospel amounts to an odd piece of first century Christian literature. "Source Criticism," 253.

may be making too much of this point, particularly in the light of
the fact that we may know far less than we think about the sorts of
Christian literature which existed in the first century, but his
point is well made. A collection of signs would seem to have some
greater degree of historical likelihood than does a collection of
narrative materials which includes signs materials along with a
passion account. In this sense the narrower (and more modest)
hypotheses of Nicol, Becker, and Schnackenburg are to be preferred
to those of Teeple and Fortna.

Finally, the methodological basis of source analysis must be
viewed critically. The use of style characteristics is perhaps the
most debatable and dangerous of the various criteria employed by
these scholars. In addition to the critiques of style criteria by
Fortna and Nicol mentioned above, the use of style characteristics
tends to become circular, that is, they are used to separate the
source materials and then to verify the integrity of the proposed
source. Fortna may be charged with that tendency upon occasion,
perhaps in his enthusiasm to isolate and reconstruct the entire
signs gospel.[51] Teeple, too, fails to guard himself against the
danger of this circularity, and in his case it seems particularly
fatal due to the centrality of style criticism in his entire method.
He seems less than sensitive to this danger and that insensitivity
contributes another reason for one's suspicion of his work. Nicol,
on the other hand, has taken such care not to employ the stylistic
criteria in a circular manner that he has failed to use the criteria
in a successfully supportive manner.[52]

Style criteria are the most complex and dangerous of the criteria to employ, it seems to me, and only those studies which have
used the criteria in a supportive way and with the greatest of care
should be trusted; that excludes the work of Teeple and casts some
doubts upon portions (but only portions) of the work of Fortna.
Teeple's application of the stylistic criteria seems to illustrate
one of the formidable problems of this method. If one were to
accept the syntactical basis of the Teeple study, it would involve
the judgment that the fourth evangelist was possessed of such a
wooden style that he could effect few variations from the style the
critic assigns him. Teeple's attention to such matters as the
arthrous and anarthrous use of personal names (that is, the use or

---

[51]Nicol (in criticism of Fortna), 18, 27; Leo McMorrow, review
of Fortna, *Irish Theological Quarterly*, 39 (1972), 308.
    [52]Fortna, review of Nicol, *Journal of Biblical Literature*, 93
(1974), 120.

absence of the definite article before the personal name) and the
difference between two connectives (*de* and *kai*) seems paramount to
pushing the stylistic criteria to their breaking point. Style
characteristics must, it seems to me, remain broad enough to recognize the validity of variation in the work of the source or the
evangelist.[53]

The ideological criteria must also be viewed with a certain
suspicion, for they entail among other difficulties the question
of why the evangelist would have used a source which held such
different views from his own.[54] The employment of ideological
criteria must produce evidence for a viable proposal regarding the
motives for the evangelist's use of the source. Teeple fails to
do this, but Fortna and Nicol are both successful in their attention
to this matter. Contextual criteria are subject to the charge that
the source hypothesis requires the belief that the evangelist
was a sufficiently clumsy editor as to leave the aporias in his
text. It is this question which most seriously plagues Fortna's
admirable attention to the aporias of the text as the key to the
solution of the literary puzzle of the book. How can one believe,
on the one hand, that the evangelist was an astute enough theologian
to sense the weaknesses of his signs gospel and subtly correct them
and yet, on the other hand, was such an inferior editor that he
left glaring flaws in the simple readability of his document?[55]
Until that contradiction can be resolved, it seems that the value
of the contextual criteria will be seriously impaired.

---

[53]Robert Kysar, review of Teeple, *Journal of Biblical Literature*, 93 (1974), 310. To this extent the observations of Edwin D.
Freed are helpful. Freed points out examples of the wide-spread
variation in language (names, Old Testament quotations, etc.) and
ideas (the glorification of Jesus, judgment, life, and truth) and
even highlights some conflicting ideas (e.g., Jesus baptizing
believers). Freed asks, "Could it be that the writer was more
concerned with the art of sheer variation than with historical
accuracy and theological consistency?" "Variations in the Language
and Thought of John," *Zeitschrift für die neutestamentliche
Wissenschaft*, 55 (1964), 167-197, quote, 197. While I would not
want to suggest that such variation makes source analysis unnecessary or impossible (which Freed does not attempt to argue), it
does seem that such an element of variation is realistic and must
be taken into account with the use of any of the criteria for
source separation.
[54]McMorrow, 308. Lindars, 37. Lindars writes, "It seems to me
very strange that John should take over a source, fully approving of
its rather special character as an appeal to wonder, and yet at the
same time should make it the major purpose of his own work to subject
the source to a radical criticism...Why reproduce verbatim a source
which is so grievously inadequate?"
[55]Robert Kysar, review of Fortna, *Perspective*, 11 (1970),
334-336.

Nicol's form critical method has been only marginally effective. Even though it constitutes his primary means of source identification, the explication of that method is given only two pages in his text. Moreover, it is questionable whether Nicol has not extended himself beyond his method when he claims to isolate the signs material by detecting synoptic-like forms but then includes as source material those johannine accounts in which the form is not clearly evident or is present only by means of the critic's reconstruction to it (e.g., chapter 11). Still, the use of form critical methods in source soundings in the depths of the gospel is, I believe, a fascinating and promising enterprise. Among the criteria employed by the five scholars we have been discussing, it is perhaps the one which is least successfully employed yet most seductive in its possibilities. Schnackenburg's conservative insistence that the similarity of the isolated materials is a necessary validation of the source separation is a commanding proposition to be emulated by future source seekers in the fourth gospel.

CHAPTER II

OTHER RECENT THEORIES OF THE COMPOSITION OF THE GOSPEL

Although the signs source hypothesis has gained significant
support in recent years, there is clearly no consensus for such a
source analysis, and new understandings of the composition of the
fourth gospel have been proposed and older theories restated.
Risking an overgeneralization, it may be said that two kinds of
alternatives to the signs source hypothesis have found considerable
adherence among johannine scholars. The first of these consists
of a number of ways of understanding the present form of the gospel
as a result of a process of development. The second is theories
concerning the relationship of the fourth gospel to the synoptics.

A. *Developmental Theories of Composition*

The critics who advocate a signs source theory for the fourth
gospel agree that the source was in some sense "pre-johannine."
By that they mean that the signs material took a literary form
prior to the fourth evangelist's life and work and in all likelihood
in an environment in some way significantly different from that of
the fourth evangelist's. In this case, the author of the gospel
as we know him was not responsible for the shaping of the signs
source document, and it represented views quite distinct from his
own. The source came from a hand and perhaps a community allegedly
pre-johannine. A number of other scholars understand the history
of the traditional material in the fourth gospel in quite a
different manner. They argue that that tradition originated from

an apostle who himself was an eye-witness of the historical Jesus
and who nurtured the tradition through several stages of development into its present gospel form. They opt for understanding the
tradition and the gospel as one continuous process. Hence, they
argue that the johannine community stretches back into the pre-
markan and apostolic period and that the evangelist was not a
second or third generation Christian but a member of the original
circle of the followers of Jesus.[1]

The first such theory for the use of johannine traditions in
the fourth gospel is explicated by Raymond E. Brown in his impressive
two-volume commentary on the Gospel of John in "The Anchor Bible"
series.[2] Brown not only spells out his theory in the introduction
of his commentary but continually refers to it and offers strength
to its plausibility in the course of his exegesis of specific
sections of the gospel. The popularity of the commentary and the
admiring respect with which it has been received in the scholarly
world as one of the most exhaustive and informative commentaries
since Bultmann's work assure us that his theory of the development of the gospel will be widely embraced and discussed. Brown's
theory of the composition of the gospel has been hailed as his
"most original contribution" and deemed highly plausible.[3]

Brown recognizes three major difficulties in the gospel which
point in the direction of some theory of tradition and redaction:
First, there are stylistic differences evidenced for example in
chapters 1 and 21. Second, breaks and incongruities in the narrative flow are experienced in a number of passages (e.g., 14:31ff;
20:30ff). "It appears that in John we have on the one hand the
elements of a planned and cohesive outline...and on the other,

---

[1]M.-E. Boismard has proposed a developmental theory of the
composition of the fourth gospel which seems to have provided something of a precursor of the more recent attempts of this kind. He
argues on the basis of the tension between the realized and futuristic eschatology of the fourth gospel that there were at least two
different editions or strata in the composition of the gospel. The
futuristic eschatology represents the first edition, the realized
eschatology the later. These earlier editions were dependent upon
the work of John, the son of Zebedee. Then, a final redaction was
effected by the evangelist Luke at a later time, which is evidenced
by the lukan characteristics of chapter 21 and insertions into the
prologue. "L' Evolution du theme eschatologique dans les traditions
johanniques," *Revue Biblique*, 68 (1961), 507-524, and "Saint Luc et
la redaction du quatrième évangile."

[2]Raymond E. Brown, *The Gospel According to John*, "The Anchor
Bible," (Garden City, N.Y.: Doubleday, 1966), 2 vols.

[3]E.C. Blackman, review of Brown, *Canadian Journal of Theology*,
13 (1967), 284.

elements that seem to indicate alterations, insertions, or re-
editings." Third, some materials seem clearly repetitious of
earlier passages (e.g., 5:19-25 and 5:26-30) and other passages
seem to intrude into the movement of the gospel (e.g., 12:44-50
when seen in relation to 12:36).[4]

These problems, Brown believes, can best be accounted for by
positing a five-stage development of the gospel. At *stage one*
there existed a body of traditional material having to do with the
words and works of Jesus. This body of material existed independent
of the synoptic tradition, although the two were similar to one
another and probably influenced one another. The memories of the
actual historical Jesus were reflected in this tradition due in
large part to the fact, Brown suggests, that it may have had its
source in John, the son of Zebedee. This material was developed
into "johannine patterns" in the course of its oral transmission
(*stage two*). Narratives were given dramatic shape, words of Jesus
woven into longer discourses, sign narratives joined with relevant
discourse materials, and peculiarly johannine features such as
misunderstanding and irony introduced.

These developments were the work of a "school" rather than
one individual, that is, a community of thought and expression.[5]
Consequently, the literary style (insofar as oral traditions become
"styled") of these materials was varied (e.g., chapter 21). John,
son of Zebedee, should be regarded as the principle figure in the
tradition, but Brown suggests that in this second stage a disciple
of John played an increasingly important role. It is this disciple
too who was responsible for the *third stage* of development--the
organization of this oral tradition into a consecutive gospel. This
organization and writing (probably in Greek) gave the materials a
basic cohesiveness which continued down into the final form of the
gospel. Some of the "johannine" traditions, however, which lived
in the school were not included in this first edition of the gospel.

The *fourth stage* saw the production of a second edition of
the gospel by the same evangelist (a disciple of John, the son of
Zebedee). Although Brown does not venture to suggest a concrete
setting for this second edition, he proposes that some new problems
had confronted the johannine community and new goals for the
written document became necessary. 9:22-23, for instance, seems
to adapt the healing of the man blind from birth to the new
situation of the Christians after they had found themselves

---

[4]Brown, vol. I, xxiv-xxv, quote, xxv.
[5]For a comparable concept see Krister Stendahl, *The School of
St. Matthew* (Philadelphia: Westminster Press, 1968).

excommunicated from the synagogue.

The *final stage* of the writing of the gospel is the further redaction of the document by a friend or pupil of the evangelist. He incorporated johannine materials which had been in existence for years (from stage two) into the gospel, even though those materials had not been included in the first and second editions of the gospel. The result was, then, a fuller representation of the johannine tradition. Brown confesses that it is sometimes difficult to distinguish between those materials added to the first gospel by the evangelist's revision (stage four) and those later introduced by his pupil (the fifth stage). It does seem to Brown, however, that the final redaction accomplished a number of things: Much of the last supper discourse (e.g., 16:4-33) was added along with chapters 11 and 12; the cleansing of the temple narrative was shifted from its original place just before 10:42 to its present position in chapter 2; eucharistic words were shifted from the last supper setting into chapter 6 for what Brown calls "liturgical" reasons; some sacramental themes were made more explicit than they had been in earlier editions; and chapter 21 and the prologue were added.

These additions, shifts, and explications on the part of the "friendly" redactor are indicated by a number of factors in the text of the gospel. The intrusiveness of a passage in a context is one such indicator. Another is the inclusion of duplicate material (e.g., 6:51-58 and 6:35-50). Still another is the presence of discourse material appended to a narrative scene which seems complete in itself (e.g., 3:31-36 and 12:44-50). A final indicator mentioned by Brown is the different meaning attached to the same term (the meaning of "the Jews" in chapters 11 and 12, for instance, as compared with elsewhere in the gospel).

With this theory Brown proposes to account for the literary and stylistic unity of the gospel stressed by Schweizer and Ruckstuhl, but at the same time to explain the presence of seemingly different styles, duplicate discourses, interruptive passages, and the apparent disorder of some of the scenes. Further, his view accounts for the influences of the synoptic tradition without calling for any literary dependence of the evangelist upon the synoptics. But Brown is appropriately modest in presenting his proposal. He confesses that it is not conclusively proven, nor does it present itself without implicit difficulties.[6]

> All that we pretend to have done is to have given a working
> hypothesis for the study of the Gospel, a hypothesis that
> combines the best details of the various theories [for the
> composition of the Gospel]... and avoids the more obvious
> difficulties.[7]

It is appropriate, following the review of Brown's theory,
to look at another proposal for the development of the fourth
gospel out of a strictly johannine tradition. We refer to the
proposal of Wilhelm Wilkens, *Die Entstehungsgeschichte des vierten
Evangeliums,* first published in 1958.[8] Even though this work falls
outside of the period we are attempting to survey, Wilkens has
been a persistent proponent of his original proposition even into
recent years[9] and has done one of the redaction critical studies
of importance in our decade.[10] Since his recent redaction study
is based upon his 1958 investigations essentially unaltered, it
is fair to say that Wilkens' initial proposal is a live option on
the contemporary scene for understanding the history of the composition of the gospel even though it must be confessed that his
theory has received only limited assent. The examination of
redactional studies later in this chapter will give due attention
to his recent work. Therefore, it is necessary here to examine
his original theory for the history of the formation of the fourth
gospel.

There are a number of striking similarities between Wilkens'
earlier proposal and that adopted by Brown in his commentary, and
Wilkens has appealed to Brown's theory as a general confirmation

---

[6]Brown, vol I, xxxiv-xxxix. Brown's proposal calls to mind
another view of the development of the fourth gospel suggested by
M. Làconi (and known to me only indirectly). He contends that the
gospel went through six stages of development: (1) The material
was present in early catechisms of the church.   (2) It took on
certain johannine characteristics and developed into small units
(e.g., the "I Am" sayings) while being transmitted orally. (3) The
apostle, John, developed narratives and discourses as a result of
meditating on Jesus' words and deeds. (4) Gradually the material
was grouped together. (5) The evangelist, the apostle, began
writing the gospel but died leaving it incomplete. (6) His disciples
finished it, inserting early johannine material, and completed it
by the end of the first century. "La critica letterarie applicata
al IV Vangelo," *Angelicum,* 40 (1963), 277-312. Làconi's theory
has not received wide discussion or acceptance.

[7]Brown, vol. I, xxix.

[8]Wilhelm Wilkens, *Die Entstehungsgeschichte des vierten
Evangeliums* (Zollikon: Evangelischer Verlag, 1958).

[9]Wilkens, "Das Abendmahlszeugnis im vierten Evangelium,"
Evangelische Theologie, 18 (1958), 354ff; "Die Erweckung";
"Evangelist und Tradition im Johannesevangelium," *Theologische
Zeitschrift,* 16 (1960), 81-90.

[10]Wilkens, *Zeichen und Werke* (Zurich: Zwingli Verlag, 1969).

of his own.[11] Like Brown, he understands that the present gospel
is a result of a process of formation, the decisive stages of which
can be detected and isolated. Further in agreement with Brown, he
understands that process of formation to have been shaped by one
principle figure, an apostolic figure. In general methodology,
like Brown, he demurs before the task of source analysis and
believes it is not sources one detects in the process of formation
but different movements of editing. (Brown, however, does not
respond favorably to Wilkens' proposal and does not appear to want
his own theory linked with that of Wilkens--see below.)

The first step in Wilkens' method of reconstructing the history
of the gospel's formation is the isolation of what he calls a
Passover framework apparent in the gospel. This framework is built
around a series of Passover formulas (i.e., temporal allusions to
the Passover season) found throughout the gospel (e.g., 2:13;
6:4; and 11:55). By means of a combined content and literary
analysis he believes he has discerned the contours of such a
Passover framework which can be lifted out of the gospel to reveal
an earlier form of the document. The narratives which are introduced by the formulas at 2:13, 6:4, and 11:55 do not seem to be
appropriate to their introductions, for they do not contain the
Passover themes promised by these opening verses in each case.
Wilkens concludes that the narratives were not originally in their
present place in the gospel and that the introductory passages are
contrived to give the gospel a Passover motif which was not ini-
tially prominent in it. But he contends that a still earlier
version of the gospel can be discerned. By literary analysis he
claims to have recognized the earliest form of the gospel which
was predominantly narrative material. His method is not fully
explicated, but it does seem that Brown is correct in observing
that, by Wilkens' analysis, at each stage of the formation of the
gospel one does not expect to find a rewriting of the previous
material but only a rearrangement and expansion of it.[12]

Wilkens proposes, therefore, a three-fold development of the
gospel and reconstructs the contents and order of the document at
each of those stages. At the foundation of the tradition he finds
a "basic gospel" (*Grundevangelium*) which was a signs gospel. It
was comprised of three principle parts which may be roughly
represented as follows:

---

[11]*Ibid.*, 6.

[12]Brown, vol. I, xxxiii.

I.   A Galilean Signs Ministry

> The Witness of the Baptist (1:6, 7a,c, 19-21, 25-26, 27 (?))
> Calling of the Disciples (1:35-42, 43-51)
> Four Galilean Signs
>> Miracle at Cana (2:1-11)
>> Healing of the Nobleman's Son (4:46-54)
>> Feeding the Multitude (6:1-3, 5-15)
>> Walking on Water (6:16-21, 23, 24-27)

II.   A Judean Signs Ministry

> Three Judean Signs
>> Healing at Bethesda (5:2-3, 5-9)
>> Healing of the Man Born Blind (9:1-3, 6-7, 24-41)
>> Raising of Lazarus (11:1, 3-4, 11-15, 17,32, 38-39, 41-57)
> The Triumphal Entry (12:12-19, 37-41)

III.   The Passion

> Cleansing of the Temple (2:14-22)
> The Last Supper (13:21-38)
> Arrest (18:1-8, 10-11)
> Jesus' Appearance Before Annas and Caiaphas (18:12-27)
> Trial Before Pilate, Crucifixion, Burial (18:28-31, 33-38; 19:7-30, 38, 41, 42)
> Resurrection(20:1, 11-29)

Conclusion (20:30-31)[13]

This signs gospel predates both the gospels of Matthew and Luke, although Wilkens will not venture a date more precise than that. It was the work of the "beloved disciple" as was also its first redaction. This first redaction left the basic gospel intact but added to it extensively with discourse materials. The discourse materials attached in the process of this first expansion can be distinguished from those added at the final stage by a critical assessment of the relationship of the speech material to the narratives. In the first redaction, the discourse material is added in such a manner that its coherence with the narratives is much stronger than in the case of the speeches added at the final stage of redaction. The later speech material is not as closely integrated with the narrative material. Wilkens holds that speeches on various themes were attached to the narratives of the basic gospel at the first stage of redaction: "living bread" (ch.6), judgment (chs. 5, 7, and 8), "light" (portions of chs. 8, 10, and 12), "resurrection and life" (ch. 11), "the Greek speech" (ch. 12), "the farewell speech" (ch. 14), and the prologue (1:1-18).[14] The result was that the narrative materials of the first gospel were

---

[13]Wilkens, *Entstehungsgeschichte*, 92-93.
[14]*Ibid.*, 174, 94-122.

enriched by discourse materials which were doubtless traditional
but which were dependent upon the mind and memory of the beloved
disciple, not a written source.

The final editing of the gospel brought a rearrangement of
the existing materials and the addition of materials with strong
paschal themes, the effect of which was to reshape the entire
work into a Passover gospel. It is at this final stage of redaction,
for instance, that the temple cleansing narrative was relocated in
the earlier part of the gospel. A number of additions were made
to the gospel:

1. Journey to Jerusalem (3:22-30; 4:1, 3, 44-45)
2. Speech of the Feast of Tabernacles (7:14, 25-30, 37-44)
3. Footwashing (13:4-5, 12-17, 20, 34)
4. Nicodemus conversation (2:23-25; 3:1-21, 31-36)
5. Conversation with the Samaritan woman (4:4-43)
6. Division among the disciples (6:60-71)
7. Division among the hearers (7:31-32, 45-52; 12-42f)
8. "Children of Abraham" speech (8:30-59)
9. "Shepherd" speech(10:1-18)
10. Temple cleansing (10:22-39)
11. Warning concerning Judas (11:7-10)
12. Footwashing of Peter (13:6-11)
13. Farewell speech (chs. 15 and 16)
14. "High Priestly prayer" (ch. 17)
15. Race to the tomb (20:2-10)
16. Resurrection appearance of ch. 21

The expansion and rearrangements produced the Passover gospel in
its present form. The completed work dates from 100 and represents
the mind of the "beloved disciple" over a period of two or three
decades.

There is, Wilkens believes, evidence of a mounting polemic
against docetic tendencies in these three stages of formation. It
is that anti-docetic motivation, plus a general concern for the
preservation of traditional material, which led to the original
composition of the signs gospel and its subsequent redactions.
Wilkens is of the general persuasion that the fourth gospel is
the source of some accurate historical information about the
career of Jesus of Nazareth (e.g., the johannine dating of the
crucifixion on the 14th of Nisan), although he recognizes as
well schematic tendencies in its representation of the movements
of Jesus and chronology.[15] On the issue of the possibilities of
the gospel's being a source of historical information about Jesus
Wilkens and Brown seem once again congenial.

Thus far the impression has been given that developmental
theories for the composition of the gospel necessarily involve

_____

[15]*Ibid.*, 127-164, 171-174.

arguments that the process of composition was the unfolding of a strictly "johannine" tradition and that, consequently, such theories always carry with them arguments for the apostolic quality of the tradition embedded in the gospel. Brown and Wilkens clearly employ the theory with just such correlative proposals. But proposals of a developmental kind need not be weighted with such claims.

Barnabas Lindars has become the proponent of a theory of the composition of the fourth gospel which recognizes the evolving of the gospel materials through a number of stages, but he avoids some of the difficulties which are evident in the Brown-Wilkens type of hypothesis. Like Brown and Wilkens, Lindars finds evidence of the use of traditional materials in the composition of the gospel and, like them, posits two editions of the gospel itself. But unlike Brown and Wilkens, he understands that the evangelist utilized traditional and "pre-johannine" material which was passed on to him from the wider Christian community and that the gospel underwent a "post-johannine" redaction. Most important, perhaps, Lindars nowhere argues for the apostolic status of the fourth evangelist and concludes rather that we must regard the evangelist as an anonymous Christian preacher and writer. "The Beloved Disciple is not the author, nor even a person who could have supplied eye-witness information, in spite of 21:24."[16] We examine Lindars proposal in more detail below because it represents an important variant on the developmental hypotheses of Brown and Wilkens and because it has already been hailed as "a genuinely modern approach to the Gospel, ...casting a flood of light on hitherto obscure parts and features of it."[17]

Lindars is led to propose his theory for a rather complex process of composition because of a number of factors: First, the aporias of geographical, temporal, and thematic kinds point in the direction of a process of composition. Second, different literary forms are discernible in the gospel and suggest that the writing of the gospel has involved the connecting of some of these, e.g., synoptic-type narratives, discourses, and editorial links. Finally, ideological differences may witness to the composition process,

---

[16]Barnabas Lindars, *The Gospel of John*, "The New Century Bible," (London: Oliphants, 1972), 34. See review by P. Joseph Cahill, *Catholic Biblical Quarterly,* 36 (1974), 271-273.

[17]Nigel M. Watson, "Barnabas Lindars' Approach to John," *Australian Biblical Review*, 1973, 43. Another positive appraisal is expressed in P. Joseph Cahill's review, *Catholic Biblical Quarterly*, 35 (1973), 102-103.

although Lindars shies away from the use of such differences as
the basis for a theory of composition, since the discernment of
such differences is highly subjective. "The effect of these various
approaches to the literary character of John is to confirm the
impression that the Gospel is the end-product of a complex process,"
Lindars concludes.[18]

Although Lindars does not summarize his proposed process of
composition in stages, it might be well for our review to do so
and thus show more clearly the relationship of his theory to those
of Wilkens and Brown. He denies the success of source analysis on
the fourth gospel and is particularly critical of Fortna's efforts
in that direction. His denial arises out of the conviction that
the evangelist's use of sources is barely perceptible to the critic.
The most one can suppose for the *first stage* of composition is the
existence of a great many unrelated traditions and/or short collections. The numbered signs (2:22 and 4:54) suggest that one of
the collections contained those two narratives (the Cana miracle
and the healing of the nobleman's son) and perhaps more, but any
reconstruction further than this generalization is unwarranted.
These traditions of narratives and short sayings were, Lindars
thinks, synoptic-like, but independent of the synoptic tradition
itself. Moreover, the evangelist doubtless received a connected
passion narrative. The evangelist employed the sources/traditions
in a very creative manner. That the miracle stories seem to give
the impression Jesus was a wonder-worker is probably the evangelist's
own doing, in order that he could use that impression as a foil to
unfold a much more profound understanding of Jesus. Lindars makes
the suggestion that this use of wonder-faith is comparable to the
evangelist's use of the misunderstanding motif in the discourses,
again as a means by which he could push the reader to a deeper
understanding of the subject matter. Whatever the sources behind
the fourth gospel, Lindars insists, what we recognize in the gospel
is that they have been so creatively employed, so reworked, that
their original form is nearly lost to the evangelist's redaction.[19]
"...the creative composition places the precise underlying traditions
beyond recovery."[20]

The *second stage* of composition, in which much of the creative
composition took place, is the weaving of traditional materials into
homilies. The evangelist used sayings and narratives as the basis

---

[18]Lindars, *Behind the FG*, 14-18, quote, 18.
[19]*Ibid.*, 38-41; Lindars, *Gospel*, 47-48.
[20]Lindars, *Behind the FG*, 54.

for sermons in which he expounded the traditional segment, little
by little, piece by piece. His early written pieces were then of
a homiletical nature, and emotional effect was as important as logic.
"...the Fourth Gospel began life as separate homilies, which John
subsequently used as the basis for a continuous Gospel."[21] 8:31-58
is an example of such a homiletic bit. These homilies were addressed
to the community of which the evangelist was a member in the midst
of its spirited dialogue with the synagogue which Lindars dates in
the 80s. [22]

Lindars believes that the first form of the gospel (*stage three*)
was produced in response to the request for a more permanent form
of the evangelist's sermons. Perhaps not unlike the manner in
which a successful contemporary preacher may be asked to publish a
collection of his sermons, we might add. But since the evangelist
had seen the gospel of Mark (although he was not dependent upon it),
he chose the gospel genre as a means by which to present his sermons
to the community in written form. Lindars suggests that the first
edition of the gospel attempted to explore the meaning of Jesus for
faith and looked something like this:

I.   The Ministry of Jesus

          The Witness of the Baptist--1:6-7a

          Narratives and Discourses--1:19-5:47 and 7:1-10:42
          (The unexpected allusion to the Baptist in 10:40-42
          brings the reader back to the beginning of the gospel
          and constitutes a sort of neat *inclusio*.)

II.   The Passion and Resurrection
          Triumphal Entry (12:12-19)
          Death Plot (11:47-53)
          Temple Cleansing (2:13-22)
          Anointing at Bethany (12:1-8)
          Encounter with Greeks (12:20-36a)
          Last Supper and Discourse (chs. 13-14)
          Gethsemane (ch. 18)
          Remainder of the Passion and the Resurrection Appearances
          (chs. 19-20)

A second edition of the gospel (*stage four*) was called for in
the light of the new danger the church experienced, threatened as
it was by Jewish persecution; and that edition was designed to
foster faithful discipleship in troubled times (in the 90s). Since
the evangelist was at the center of a Jewish-Christian debate, it
was only natural that he should rework his gospel in response to
developments in that debate. The second edition of the gospel,
according to Lindars, brought the addition of a number of passages:

---

[21]*Ibid.*, 47.
[22]*Ibid.*, 43-60; Lindars, *Gospel*, 51-54.

the prologue (1:1-5, 7b-18), the narrative and discourse of chapter
6, the raising of Lazarus (11:1-44), and the supper discourse (chs.
15 and 16) and prayer (ch. 17). Two narratives were moved to
accomodate the new purpose of the gospel and the additions made for
that purpose: the temple cleansing from its location in the passion
account to its present position in chapter 2, and the anointing at
Bethany from after to before the triumphal entry to bring it into
closer proximity with the Lazarus narrative. Finally, (*stage five*)
Lindars isolates some "post-johannine" additions--7:53-8:11,
chapter 21, and 19:35.[23]

In addition to those comparative remarks with which Lindars'
theory was introduced above, it is necessary to try to draw the
three proposals for a developmental composition of the gospel into
closer relationship with one another. On the question of the methods
upon which each theory is advanced, only variety is witnessed in the
survey of these three proposals. Between Brown and Lindars there
is a common concern for the aporias of the gospel; but while Brown
invokes stylistic differences, Lindars clearly believes that the
evangelist has produced a generally homogeneous style throughout
the gospel. Where Lindars understands repetition as one of the
evangelist's own rhetorical devices, Brown understands it to be an
indication of the process of composition. Neither Brown nor Lindars
appreciates the supposed importance of the Passover references upon
which Wilkens bases his entire theory. Perhaps the only point at
which these three scholars agree is in their common distrust of
source criticism as a tool for johannine investigation!

When we turn to the proposed stages of development offered by
Wilkens, Brown, and Lindars there are some more interesting comparisons. A synopsis of their respective stages is perhaps helpful as
a basis upon which to draw some conclusions:

Wilkens	Brown	Lindars
	1. Oral Traditions	1. Traditions and Sources
1. "Basic Gospel"	2. Traditions developed into johannine patterns	2. Homilies
2. Discourses added	3. First edition of gospel	3. First edition of gospel
3. Passover edition	4. Second edition of gospel	4. Second edition of gospel
	5. Additions of "friendly redactor"	5. "Post-johannine" additions

---

[23]Lindars, *Behind the FG*, 62-78; *Gospel*, 51.

Lindars and Brown together understand that the early form of the
material was given shape in the hands of the evangelist--for Brown
that process occurred while the material was circulating orally in
the "johannine school," and for Lindars it took place as the evangelist fashioned homilies around traditional materials. Wilkens seems
in no way really comparable. Brown and Lindars' two editions are
somewhat parallel, since both understand that the gospel went
through two stages of writing before it reached a form essentially
that of the canonical gospel. Then, each understands that a few
additions were later made to the essentially completed gospel. In
contrast, Wilkens contends that the first and second forms of the
gospel can be neatly distinguished as narrative and discourse (a
distinction Lindars explicitly denies as possible)[24] and that the
final stage of the gospel brought a more drastic transformation.
Little consensus can be deduced from this comparison beyond the
most general sort of suggestion that the present gospel is the
result of a process which involves two or three different editions.

The developmental, non-source theories of Brown, Wilkens, and
Lindars are attractive alternatives in some ways to the precarious
and oft-times speculative character of source analysis. The
evolutionary models offer comprehensive ways of resolving the
literary problems of the gospel with appealing ease. Brown's
form of the theory commends itself, since it encompasses the pre-
literary (oral) history of the tradition both before the first
edition of the gospel and (for some of the materials later incorporated into the document) alongside of the written document.
Lindars likewise takes into account the probability of the evangelist's receiving a number of traditions, both oral and written;
and his form of the hypothesis is striking for its emphasis upon
the creativity of the fourth evangelist. Wilkens along with Brown
and Lindars makes the entirely plausible suggestion that the evangelist did not once write a gospel and put it down; but having
produced the document came back to it, not once but twice, to
improve upon his work in the light of changes in his own thought
and in the dynamic experience of the church.

Still, such proposals as Wilkens, Lindars, and Brown's are
fraught with difficulties. It has been charged that Wilkens'
method is faulty since his own theological persuasions are not
suspended for the sake of objectivity and that he "is too anxious
...to defend the gospel's place in the center of normative

---

[24]Lindars, *Behind the FG*, 41.

Christianity."[25]   That charge might be leveled against Brown as
well, although with admittedly less justification.   There is a
sense, however, in which one feels that Wilkens and Brown are
both overly concerned to protect the apostolic quality of the
tradition embedded in the gospel.   Wilkens does this by maintaining firmly that the apostle, John, son of Zebedee, is the sole
figure responsible for the gospel.   Brown accomplishes the same
purpose with his more believable picture of a "school" of tradition
originating with the disciple, John, and preserved and nurtured by
his students.

Now, the apostolic authorship of the gospel is a defensible
thesis (as we will see in Part Two); but a theory of composition
must not be propagated in order to justify and protect such a
thesis.   It must, rather, arise out of the internal evidence of
the gospel itself--stylistic, contextual, and ideological.   Wilkens
does not seem to suspend his view of the apostolic authority of the
document long enough to examine the bare evidence, and his developmental theory tends to appear at least partially as an effort to
defend a view of its authorship.   Brown's case is less clear, but
there too one is suspicious that the proposal of the development
of the tradition within the johannine community may be somewhat
influenced by the conviction that the gospel represents a purely
"johannine" (meaning John, son of Zebedee) document.   Brown's
stages of development could account for the gospel evidence more
completely, I believe, were they to acknowledge the possible
contributions of early "pre-johannine" origins which were not rooted
in the witness of the son of Zebedee.   Hence, Lindars' proposal is
at least in this way preferrable to Brown and Wilkens'.

Other questions concerning Wilkens' method must be asked.   Is
it legitimate to use the outline of the resultant document (the
"basic gospel") to establish its isolation, rather than simply to
test it for internal integrity once it has been isolated by other
means?   Wilkens seems to use a projected image of the outline,
flow, and direction of his proposed signs gospel as part of the
argument for isolating certain parts of it from later stages of
composition; such a procedure produces a circular argument.[26]
Further, is it feasible to conceive of the editing process as Wilkens

[25]Robert T. Fortna, "Wilhelm Wilkens' Further Contribution to
Johannine Studies," *Journal of Biblical Literature*, 89 (1970),
457, 461.
[26]James M. Robinson, "Recent Research in the Fourth Gospel,"
Journal of Biblical Literature, 78 (1959), 245.

does? Is it likely that the evangelist's editing of his earlier
work would not involve any rewriting of what he had earlier produced but only an expansion and sometimes reordering of portions
of his work?[27] Such a concept of the evangelist's editing process
does indeed make it convenient for the critic, but seems an arti-
ficial way of understanding the editorial work of the evangelist.

Wilkens may be further criticized for a number of his propositions. His thesis in general seems too schematic. It is so
neat as to suggest contemporary interests with its precise divisions
of narrative and discourse material. Such a division seems contrived
once again more for the convenience of the critic than for the sake
of historical understanding.[28] The anti-docetic motivation for the
whole composition process is too sweeping. It is perhaps beyond
the evidence available in the gospel to posit such an anti-docetic
polemic, and it is too simple to read the entire gospel as concerned
only with intra-church matters.[29]

Finally, is the Passover theology of the final stage of editing
plausible? Schnackenburg dislikes the "progressive theology"
foisted upon the evangelist by Wilkens' hypothesis and justifiably
wants to know how he can be so sure that the interest of the
evangelist in Passover theology was late.[30] Moreover, is it not
dangerous to put so much weight upon the temporal allusions of
three verses (2:13, 6:4, and 11:55); for it is they alone in the
final analysis which demonstrate the Passover orientation of the
final stage of editing. In this same connection, "why did this
passover theology assert itself [only] through radical rearrangement and never state itself theologically?"[31] For the most part,
Wilkens' project lacks a convincing methodology and commands little
adherence. It is far too simplistic and schematic, it seems to me,
to be persuasive.

Brown's five-stage theory of composition, while perhaps preferable to Wilkens', seems supremely imprecise. While Wilkens
might be charged with trying to delineate the stages too specifically, Brown's work does not go far enough in that direction. He
does not lay down a sufficient basis for a study of the redaction

---

[27]Brown, vol. I, xxxiii. Teeple criticizes Wilkens' entire
single author-redactor scheme and shows rather effectively the
weakness of the proposal that the gospel was redacted by the
evangelist himself. *Literary Origin*, 101.
   [28]Schnackenburg, *Gospel*, vol. I, 69.
   [29]Fortna, "Wilhelm Wilkens," 462.
   [30]Schnackenburg, *Gospel*, vol. I, 69.
   [31]Robinson, "Recent Research," 245.

process at the various stages and is unable to provide an adequate method for separating materials introduced into the gospel at the various stages. Furthermore, Brown claims that the process of the development of the tradition allows for the probability of its being a source of historical knowledge of Jesus' ministry and teaching. But is it really possible to unearth that historical knowledge from the complex editorial process Brown envisages?[32]

Lindars has freed himself of this charge as well as a number of other possible criticisms by denying the apostolic character of the johannine gospel and its value as a source for historical knowledge of Jesus.[33] Of the three, Lindars' form of the developmental hypothesis seems least encumbered with difficulties. However, I wonder if Lindars' sole claim to persuasion does not lie in the simple, common-sense plausibility he gives his proposal. And if that is the case, is adherence to that theory not a concession that scientific evidence cannot be amassed to support a theory of composition and that one has only the rather subjective appraisal of plausibility upon which to rely?

This suggests another but related kind of criticism of Brown and Lindars' developmental theories. They are provocative and imaginative but essentially unprovable. That is, they offer the student a rather ingenious way of accounting for the present gospel, but if one were to press for anything approaching proof for these developmental theories, they would be found wanting. It is fair to say that they provide historical models by which to view the gospel in its present form and, as such, work rather well to account for the evidence in the gospel; but the evidence itself in no way suggests or dictates these sorts of theories.

My point is that the theories advanced by Brown and Lindars are such that no amount of analysis of the gospel materials will ever produce convincing grounds for them. If the gospel evolved in a manner comparable to that offered by Brown and Lindars, it is totally beyond the grasp of the johannine scholar and historian to produce even tentative proof that such was the case. Perhaps the same charge may be leveled against the source analysis discussed above; but the difference is that the source analyses seem more closely anchored in the gospel evidence and less prone to fanciful flights of imagination. Moreover, one can optimistically believe

---

[32]C.K. Barrett, review of Brown, *Journal of Biblical Literature*, 85 (1966), 484.

[33]Lindars, *Gospel*, 54-56.

that with more precise methods the evidence can be made to support or refute the source theories; but the same hope cannot be held out, it seems, for the Brown-Lindars developmental schemes. The latter must believe that such a theory makes sense without any hope of eventually being able to demonstrate this conclusively.

Finally, one is still left with the johannine literary puzzle, even after the advancement of these three process theories of composition: Why does the gospel in its final stage still present its reader with incongruities, intrusions, and breaks in narrative? Wilkens proposes a basic gospel which flows nicely. As he reconstructs it, it is logical and consecutive. But the final form of the gospel is not like this, which must mean that the redactions process on the basic gospel had the effect of spoiling its literary structure. "We must suppose that as time went on the evangelist's grasp of logic and construction weakened, so that he spoiled his own work."[34] Brown and Lindars' theories are faced no less with the same problem--why after the long process of editing did the gospel not emerge as a polished work?

B. *Theories of the Relationship of the Synoptic Gospels and the Fourth Gospel*

The tradition utilized by the fourth evangelist bears some resemblance to those traditions which have come to us by way of the synoptic gospels, while at the same time differing markedly from the synoptics. Along with the question of how the evangelist received and used that tradition is the further question about the relationship of that tradition to the synoptic gospels. Some would propose that correctly answering the second question resolves the problem of the quest for sources behind the gospel of John and to some degree the question of the process of composition, as well. Hence, it would seem that the issue of the relationship of the fourth gospel to the synoptics is an integral part of the general concern for source and tradition criticism. If, indeed, the evangelist utilized the synoptic gospels themselves in the composition of his work, the puzzle of the sources is thereby solved and redaction criticism could then proceed by examining how it was the evangelist employed the synoptic accounts. But, alas, that simple solution does not seem to be the case!

Scholarship on the question of the relationship of the fourth

------

[34]C.K. Barrett, review of *Entstehungsgeschichte*, *Theologische Literaturzeitung*, 84 (1959), 829.

gospel to the synoptics has recently produced two important movements which must be seen as sort of complementary tendencies in
the criticism of the fourth gospel. On the one hand, the past
decade has witnessed the near demise of the proposition that the
fourth evangelist was dependent upon one or more of the synoptic
gospels. Percival Gardner-Smith's epoch-making study, *Saint John
and the Synoptic Gospels*, in 1938 shattered efforts to demonstrate
John's literary dependence upon any one of the synoptic gospels.[35]
It is almost as if the force of his argument over the intervening
years has gradually but surely eroded any continuing efforts to
salvage such theories of dependency; until it could be concluded
that the question was nearly closed or at least that the burden
of proof was heavily upon any who dared to suggest that John did
utilize one of the synoptics.[36] It is illustrative of the impact
of this wave of disproof of the synoptic dependence theories that
the last major commentary to build upon any such theory was that
of C.K. Barrett in 1955 and his work was severely criticized precisely at that point.[37]

As a counterpoint movement in this period, there emerged a
growing tendency to understand the apparent contacts between the
synoptic gospels and John not on the basis of a literary dependence
but by means of cross influences between the synoptic and johannine
traditions at their pre-literary stage. Gardner-Smith himself
had pointed out that such oral influences were most likely to
account for synoptic-John similarities. In 1954 Bent Noack
published his thorough study, *Zur johanneischen Tradition*, which
attempted to show that the johannine materials had a pre-literary
history as oral tradition and that it was in oral form that the
synoptic traditions influenced the johannine and vice versa.[38]
It was the persuasiveness of Noack's investigation which convinced
Bultmann beyond doubt that one could not contend for a synoptic
dependency at any point in the fourth gospel.[39]

These two movements--the demise of efforts to demonstrate
literary dependence of John upon the synoptics and the rise of

---

[35]Percival Gardner-Smith, *Saint John and the Synoptic Gospels*
(Cambridge: University Press, 1938); cf., "St. John's Knowledge of
Matthew," *Journal of Theological Studies*, n.s. 4 (1953), 31ff.
    [36]D.M. Smith, "John 12:12ff and the Question of John's Use
of the Synoptics," *Journal of Biblical Literature*, 82 (1963),
58-64.
    [37]C.K. Barrett, *The Gospel*.
    [38]Bent Noack, *Zur johanneischen Tradition*.
    [39]Rudolf Bultmann, "Zur johanneischen Tradition," *Theologische
Literaturzeitung*, 60 (1955), 524.

interest in the pre-literary history of the johannine material--
have been working their way through to their conclusions in recent
years. We will see that where critics were once inclined to argue
for literary dependence at points of similarity between John and
the synoptics, they are increasingly favorable to explaining such
similarities on the basis of pre-literary contacts between the
traditions. Moreover, if there was once a propensity to attribute
large segments of the peculiar content of the fourth gospel to the
creativity of the evangelist, there is an ever-increasing tendency
to see that material, too, as having a history, that is, as arising
out of a tradition.

Our survey must, first, note an example of the remaining
scholars who cling to an effort to demonstrate some degree of literary dependence upon the synoptics. Then we will pay heed to a
number of suggestions in the past decade regarding the theory of
John's dependence upon an oral tradition. Finally we will survey
a number of scholars who are undecided on the delicate issue of
whether the similarities between John and the synoptics suggest
literary or pre-literary contact, but who stress the independence
of the tradition represented in the fourth gospel.

The one most careful study which concludes that John did know
and used one of the synoptic gospels was published in 1963 by
John A. Bailey.[40] Bailey's study is concerned with those apparent
contacts between the gospels of Luke and John and more particularly
those passages in which the gospels of John and Luke appear to
agree with one another but disagree with Mark and Matthew. (Bailey
also holds but does not try to prove that John used the gospel
of Mark.) He proceeds to examine each of eleven passages carefully
and tries to discern in which cases it is likely that there was a
literary dependence of the fourth evangelist on the gospel of Luke.
Bailey is also concerned to assess the historical value of each of
the passages he examines. He concludes that there is indeed
evidence to support the contention that the fourth evangelist
utilized the third gospel and that in general there is a high
degree of historical value in such passages. His method of detecting a contact between Luke and John depends upon isolating passages
in one or the other which appear to be intrusions into the narrative
or discourse movement. When such occurs and there is a parallel in
the other gospel, Bailey claims some borrowing has taken place. In
the following passages he believes it is evident that John drew

---

[40]John Amedee Bailey, *The Traditions Common to the Gospels of
Luke and John* (Leiden: E.J. Brill, 1963).

elements of his account from the gospel of Luke:

>The anointing of Jesus (Lk 7:36-50/Jn 12:1-8)
>
>Certain parts of the Last Supper, the Last Discourse, and the High Priestly Prayer (Lk 22:14-38/Jn 13-17)
>
>Arrest of Jesus (Lk 22:39-53a/Jn 18:1-12)[41]
>
>Trial Before Pilate (Lk 23:1-25/Jn 18:29-19:16)
>
>Crucifixion, Death, and Burial (Lk 23:25-56/Jn 19:19-42)
>
>Resurrection Appearances in Jerusalem (Lk 24/Jn 20)

But Bailey believes that the quality of the agreement of John and Luke in some other passages dictates that the relationship in those cases was not a direct literary one; and so he proposes that while some of the points of agreement are best explained by assuming that John used the gospel of Luke, other passages suggest that related traditions came to each of the evangelists independently. Similar but distinct written accounts were used by each of the evangelists, for instance, in their narratives concerning Jesus' approach to Jerusalem (Lk 19:37-40/Jn 12:12-19). The same oral account of aspects of the last supper (its chronology and Jesus' assuming a servant role) was allegedly used. A common written source underlies Jesus' examination before Annas (Lk 22:53b-71/Jn 18:13-28), according to Bailey.

Other materials which show that they were carried in related traditions to the respective evangelists include the question of the identity of the Baptist (Lk 3:15/Jn 1:19, 27), the fishing miracle (Lk5:1-11/Jn 21:1-14), the charge that Jesus claimed to be a king (Lk 23:2c/Jn 19:12), two disciples coming to the empty grave (Lk 24:24/Jn 20:3-10), and the words of the risen Christ to Peter (Lk 24:34/ Jn 21:1ff). Bailey concludes, "What characterizes the instances of related material is, indeed, the variety of the means by which the relationship came about...the evidence of our analysis points to the existence in the Church at the time both evangelists wrote of many isolated written and oral traditions... on which ...the two writers drew."[42]

It is one of the strengths of Bailey's study that he is not concerned to see the relationship between the gospels of Luke and

---

[41]Bailey's thesis on John 18:1-12 received general support from G. Richter, "Die Gefangennahme Jesu nach dem Johannesevangelium (18:1-12)," *Bibel und Leben*, 10 (1969), 26-39. Richter argues that the fourth evangelist was dependent upon synoptic material for his account of the arrest of Jesus and that he reshaped the synoptic material to apologetic ends, namely, to refute Jewish charges against the messiahship and sonship of Jesus. It is clear to Richter that John did not use an independent tradition here but was dependent upon the literary form of the other gospels.

[42]Bailey, 115.

John in a monolithic way and recognizes that in addition to a
literary dependence of John upon Luke, there were a number of other
means of contact between the traditions prior to the writing of
the gospels. Such a complex theory of the relation of the fourth
evangelist to the gospel of Luke, the sources for Luke, and oral
tradition, however, seems implausible. Is it possible that John
would use the completed gospel of Luke on one occasion, but then
prefer a lukan source on another? "One wonders whether such a
reconstruction is humanly probable."[43] And just this effort to
see a multiplicity of relationships also raises the methodological
problem which is the soft spot of the theory of the literary
dependency of John on one or more of the synoptics: How can the
critic discern between a similarity which is accountable only by
means of a literary contact and a similarity which may be due to
pre-literary (or pre-gospel) contact? This methodological problem
is intensified by the question of the verbal exactitude of oral
tradition. That is, if some scholars are correct in their understanding of the nature of the pre-literary history of the gospel
material,[44] it is possible that exact verbal agreement between two
passages could be due to common use of a very precise oral tradition.
Although this is not likely the case, such considerations do open
wider the possibility of understanding the relationship of John and
the synoptics of a purely pre-literary basis.

A proposal which attempts to salvage the theory of literary
dependence, however, and avoid claiming the use of oral tradition
is that of Josef Blinzler. He seems to have recognized the difficulties in deducing any theory of the relationship of the gospels
from apparent points of contact between John and the synoptics,
and has been influenced both by Gardner-Smith and Noack as well as
the classical theories of literary dependence. His conclusion is
both remarkable and ingenious:

> The findings of literary criticism do not allow the
> conclusion that the fourth evangelist had before him
> one of the synoptic gospels as a source for the com-
> position of his gospel and constantly looked into it.

---

[43]Pierson Parker, review of Bailey, *Journal of Biblical
Literature*, 85 (1966), 508.

[44]The most radical argument for the verbal exactitude of the
oral transmission is found in the works of Bierger Gerhardsson,
e.g., *Memory and Manuscript: Oral Transmission and Written Trans-
mission in Rabbinic Judaism and Early Christianity* (Lund: C.W.K.
Gleerup, 1961); cf., Harald Riesenfeld, *The Gospel Tradition*
(Philadelphia: Fortress Press, 1970), 1-30. But see Morton Smith,
"A Comparison of Early Christian and Early Rabbinic Tradition,"
Journal of Biblical Literature, 82 (1963), 169-176.

> Everything points much more to the fact that he had know-
> ledge of the content of Mark (and perhaps Luke), parts of
> which he produced by memory and in a more or less trans-
> formed shape worked into his representation.[45]

Blinzler's suggestion stimulates the imagination and provides a
means of understanding the varying degrees of exactitude in the
johannine parallels to synoptic materials by appeal to the degree
of the precision of the fourth evangelist's memory. Moreover, it
parallels the proposal that the fourth evangelist used Old Testament
citations in his work by appeal to memory.[46] Still, one wonders
how such a theory as Blinzler's could be proved--his presentation
is more a suggestion than a proof; it seems to lie outside of the
realm of scientific demonstration and can only be tested by appeals
to plausibility. On that score, one must ask if other theories
are not backed by stronger evidence and equally, if not higher,
degrees of plausibility. His proposal appears as an effort to
maintain the older theory of literary dependence in the face of
mounting evidence for its abandonment.

A remarkably novel proposal for the composition of the fourth
gospel, which attempts to account especially for the synoptic-
related materials in John, has been recently advanced by Günter
Reim. In the course of his explorations of the use of the Old
Testament in the fourth gospel, Reim found what he claims to be
evidence for a two-stage process of composition. The first form
of the gospel was shaped by the evangelist out of a signs source
and prologue materials. The result was that in its first and
earliest form the gospel of John was a collection of signs stories
with a commentary that fostered belief in Jesus on the basis of
his deeds. It included some narratives regarding John the Baptist
and some speech materials (e.g., 5:19ff and the good shepherd
speech) but no passion narrative.

Reim conjectures that the gospel originally ended with the
prayer of Jesus in chapter 17. Then the evangelist drastically
transformed his gospel by incorporating into it large blocks of
material which he took from a synoptic gospel. This synoptic
gospel is one unknown to us and was probably written earlier than
any of our canonical gospels. From this "fourth synoptic" the
evangelist drew materials which included the whole passion narrative,
the healing at Bethesda, and the discourse with the Samaritans.

---

[45]Josef Blinzler, *Johannes und die Synoptiker* (Stuttgart:
Katholisches Bibelwerk, 1965), 59.
[46]Edwin D. Freed, *Old Testament Quotations in the Gospel of
John* (Leiden: E.J. Brill, 1965), 6, 130.

Since the materials employed from this fourth synoptic were, for
the most part, passion episodes, the synoptic related narratives
in the present gospel of John are more numerous in the latter half
of the document. The radical transformation effected in the first
form of the gospel by the insertion of the contents of the fourth
synoptic resulted in the disorder and "historical inaccuracies" of
the existent gospel of John. Reim points out that in the gospel,
"where the original order of the text is disturbed, synoptic
material has caused this disturbance."[47]

Reim's innovative hypothesis does a number of things: It
accounts for the basic evidence for a signs source behind the
gospel; it explains the aporias of the current text; and it solves
the problem of the synoptic-related materials in the johannine
gospel. In sum, it is a kind of *total* hypothesis for the composition of the gospel. But Reim's proposal gains its success at
terrible expense. Doubtless the greatest hurdle in accepting this
theory of composition is Reim's claim for the existence of a "fourth
synoptic" gospel. For that claim the scholar can offer no evidence,
only fanciful speculation. It may be an indication of the desperate
state of scholarship on the relation of the fourth gospel to the
synoptics that it includes even the proposal that the evangelist
employed an unknown synoptic gospel. Surely, such fantastic, extra-
evidential conjectures are not necessary to resolve the question of
the composition of the gospel.

But it is not only this radical proposal of a fourth synoptic
gospel that prevents assent to Reim's hypothesis. A number of his
claims must be tested with a greater degree of care than he expends.
For instance, is it indeed the case that *every* contextual difficulty
in the gospel of John is caused by the intrusion of synoptic related
material? It is interesting that Reim is not able to substantiate
this claim without resorting to a significant qualification: The
disturbance is caused by synoptic material--not necessarily the
synoptic material we know through the first three gospels, but
subject matter which might be unique to Reim's hypothetical fourth
synoptic! Finally, one may wonder why the revision and expansion
of his gospel was accomplished with such carelessness by the evangelist. Why did he spoil the literary structure of the first form of
his gospel when he incorporated the synoptic materials? Perhaps
the best we can say for Reim's proposal, other than to commend its

---

[47]Günter Reim, *Studien zum Alttestamentlichen Hintergrund des
Johannesevangelium* (Cambridge: University Press, 1974), 214-216,
233-246, quote, 238-239.

novelty, is to point out that his reconstruction of the first form
of the gospel adds further confirmation of the use of a signs
source and particularly one which did not include a passion narrative.

The possibility of understanding the relationship of John and
the synoptics on a purely pre-literary base was taken up by C.H.
Dodd in his second massive volume on the fourth gospel, *Historical
Tradition in the Fourth Gospel*.[48] Published the same year as
Bailey's monograph, Dodd's work is a meticulous attempt to lay bare
the traditional material in the fourth gospel by a comparative
analysis of that material with the synoptic gospels. He begins
with those johannine passages with the clearest relation to the
synoptic gospels, namely, the passion narratives. Then, he moves
his analysis through the materials where there are fewer and fewer
apparent synoptic contacts: the narratives of Jesus' ministry,
those regarding the Baptist and the first disciples, and finally
the discourse materials. He searches out synoptic materials and
finds some interesting parallels (e.g., Jn 3:8 and Mk 4:27). He
unearths "parabolic forms" in the johannine discourses. But he
asserts and rather persuasively demonstrates that "John is not
dependent on the Synoptic Gospels, but is transmitting independently
a special form of the common oral traditions."

He concludes that "behind the Fourth Gospel lies an ancient
tradition independent of the other gospels, and meriting serious
consideration as a contribution to our knowledge of the historical
facts concerning Jesus Christ." That tradition was synoptic-like,
in many ways, even though most of the characteristics of the
tradition have been veiled in the fourth gospel by the manner in
which they were shaped by the evangelist. The johannine tradition
is susceptible, Dodd claims, to the same sort of categorizing by
form as has been done by form criticism on the synoptic materials
and he offers a summary of the salient features of the johannine
tradition.[49]

What is impressive about Dodd's work in this case is the manner
in which he was able to make plausible the existence of a common
oral tradition out of which both the synoptic and johannine evangelists drew their material. His detailed analyses point toward the

---

[48]Dodd's earlier and important work was *Interpreting the Fourth
Gospel* (Cambridge: University Press, 1953). For a similar kind of
effort to argue for an independent and historically reliable tradition
behind the fourth gospel, cf., A.J.B. Higgins, "The Words of Jesus
According to John," *Bulletin of John Rylands Library*, 49 (1966-67),
363-386.
    [49]Dodd, *Historical*, 366-387, quotes, 349 and 423 respectively.

likelihood that much of the fourth gospel had a pre-literary history
which involved contact and even integration with the synoptic
materials. What is disappointing about his study is that this whole
effort carried with it a presupposition that "traditional" means
historically accurate. That is, Dodd was concerned not only to
show that the johannine materials had a pre-literary history in
relationship with the synoptic materials but also to prove that the
johannine materials contain a great deal of information about the
historical Jesus, his activities and his teachings. Such a narrow
understanding of "tradition" places an undue amount of weight upon
the historicity of the material, but more important it simplifies
the whole concept of tradition. "Primitive tradition" need not
mean   "Jesus"; for, as form criticism has shown indisputably, the
history of the tradition brought developments, additions and
deletions, transformations and numerous reapplications of whatever
may have been the historical kernel of the original piece of
material.

> The whole reservoir of primitive tradition, narratives
> and sayings, upon which the four gospels are built had
> already been radically reshaped by the translation of the
> earliest witness into various expressions and forms of
> Christological piety and faith.[50]

But strangely enough others have criticized Dodd for not
attempting to establish the reliability of the johannine Jesus as
a source of knowledge for the historical Jesus![51] Consequently,
Dodd's suggestion of linking the tradition to Jesus himself seems
to be damned from all sides! What Dodd has done has been to break
through a long-standing prejudice which held the synoptics alone
to be a potential resource for the question of the historical Jesus.
On this score, it can be concluded that thanks to the discovery of
the tradition behind the fourth gospel, that gospel now stands on
an equal footing with the synoptics; but whether *any* of the four
gospels can provide an avenue to the historical Jesus is still
another question.

Dodd's understanding of the oral tradition has dissatisfied
some of his critics. In spite of Dodd's stature as a New Testament
researcher and a pioneer in johannine studies, his monograph on
the johannine tradition was met with considerable reserve. First,
it was argued that Dodd does not show the source of the contacts
between the fourth gospel and the synoptics to have been at the

---

[50]Amos N. Wilder, review of Dodd, *Journal of Biblical Literature*,
83 (1964), 306.
[51]John Bligh, "C.H. Dodd on John and the Synoptics," *Heythrop
Journal*, 5 (1964), 276.

pre-literary stage, and to the contrary, the data he exhibits leads some to the quite opposite conclusion that the evangelist knew and used one or more of the synoptics.[52] The opinion is inescapable, however, that such a criticism of Dodd only reveals the critic's own predisposition to the literary dependence theory.

That Dodd's conception of the oral tradition is too simple has correctly been charged by some. Where Dodd imagines a rather simple continuous tradition, it is more likely that primitive oral transmission was a far more dynamic movement.[53] Where Dodd sees a johannine tradition running parallel to and independent of the synoptic tradition but with significant overlap with that tradition, others prefer to conceive of the johannine form of the oral transmission as an offshoot from a single common tradition, perhaps supplemented by both a smaller independent tradition and a possible literary contact between the fourth gospel and one of the synoptics.[54] The latter view would seem to bring us back to the complexities and accompanying problems of a thesis similar to Bailey's. The criticism of Dodd's work exhibits the disarray of critical conceptions of the tradition behind John, notwithstanding the growing recognition of the existence of such a tradition.

On the point of the recognition of such an oral tradition, Dodd has found considerable support in more recent johannine research. A lengthy doctoral dissertation, published in 1972, investigates the history of the traditional material found in John 18:1-19:30 and the johannine understanding of the passion narrative. The author, Anton Dauer, concludes that the tradition of the passion account which the fourth evangelist used was an independent tradition, even though it had been influenced by the synoptic accounts of the passion. The written tradition of the synoptic gospels exerted influence upon the still oral johannine tradition; and the reverse seems also to have been the case. While the author contends that the synoptic influences reached the johannine tradition while it was still oral and that it is likely that the fourth evangelist availed himself of it while it was still unwritten, he does recognize the possibility that it may have come to the

---

[52]Allen Wikgren, "A Contribution to the New Quest," *Interpretation*, 20 (1966), 238.

[53]Reginald H. Fuller, review of Dodd, *Journal of Bible and Religion*, 32 (1964), 271.

[54]John Bligh, 287-292. See also M.I. Williams, "Tradition in the Fourth Gospel—A Critique of Professor C.H. Dodd," *Studia Evangelica*, F.L. Cross, ed., (Berlin: Akademie, 1968), vol. IV, 259-268.

fourth evangelist in written form.[55]

An increasing number of other critics are coming down on the side of the dependence of the synoptics and John on common sources or traditions. These proposals sometimes tend to beg the question of whether the common traditions were oral or written or both at the time they were influential in shaping our canonical gospels. What is important is that there were such traditions and that the fourth gospel stands as much indebted to them as do the synoptics --a view which was not popular earlier in this century.

One such highly respected scholar is Ernst Haenchen, whose essay, "Johanneische Probleme," deals with the question of the relationship of selected johannine passages (4:46-54; 6:1-21; 2:14-22; 5:1-14) to their synoptic parallels. Haenchen agrees that literary dependence has been ruled out, and he concludes instead that the contact with the synoptic gospels in these passages is only a general one which suggests a common tradition. The comparison of the gospels, however, does augur for John's use of a later, more developed, and isolated form of the tradition than the synoptics.[56]

A similar conclusion was reached by Edward Siegman and Rudolf Schnackenburg's investigations of John 4:46-54. The evangelist found a form of the story in a source and adapted it for his purposes.[57] Others have equivocated on the question of a written or oral source which supplied the johannine-synoptic account but agree that there was such a common source.[58] Recent commentaries seem to bear out our conclusion that theories of literary dependence are being displaced by theories of a common tradition.[59] A recent

---

[55]Anton Dauer, *Die Passionsgeschichte im Johannesevangelium* (Munich: Kosel, 1972), 335-336. See J. Edgar Bruns' review, *Catholic Biblical Quarterly*, 35 (1973), 374-376.

[56]Ernst Haenchen, "Johanneische Probleme," *Gott und Mensch* (Tubingen: J.C.B. Mohr, 1965), 78-113.

[57]Edward F. Siegman, "St. John's Use of the Synoptic Material," *Catholic Biblical Quarterly*, 30 (1968), 182-198; Schnackenburg, "Zur Traditiongeschichte von Joh 4, 46-54," *Biblische Zeitschrift*, 8 (1964), 58-88.

[58]E.g., David Hill, "The Request of Zebedee's Sons and the Johannine *Doxa*-theme," *New Testament Studies*, 13 (1966-67), 281-285. Cf., Riesenfeld's earlier suggestion concerning the johannine tradition and the synoptic parables, *The Gospel Tradition*, 139-169.

[59]Brown, vol I, xlv; Schnackenburg, *Gospel*, vol. I, 42; J.N. Sanders and B.A. Mastin, *A Commentary on the Gospel According to St. John* (New York: Harper and Row, 1968), 12; Leon Morris, *The Gospel According to John* (Grand Rapids, Michigan: Eerdmans, 1971), 52; cf., Morris, *Studies in the Fourth Gospel* (Grand Rapids, Michigan: Eerdmans, 1969), 15-63. But in contrast see Norman Perrin's assertion of a literary dependence. *The New Testament: An Introduction* (New York: Harcourt, Brace, Jovanovich, 1974), 229.

study of the contacts of the gospels of Luke and John has added
further weight toward the theory of a common tradition and has
offered an intriguing variation on such theories. After a thorough
survey of the contacts between Luke and John, F. Lamar Cribbs
proposes that:

> Luke was influenced by some early form of the developing
> Johannine tradition in the writing of his gospel rather
> than vice versa...perhaps one of Luke's motives in his
> seeking to write a "vita Jesus" was his attempt to reconcile
> the differing Markan/Matthean and Johannine traditions
> ....[60]

Cribbs' thoughtful proposal suggests how far scholarship has come
on the question of the johannine tradition. Not only is it thought
that such an independent tradition existed and had contact with
the synoptic traditions, but now it is even argued that that
tradition was influential enough in the early church to motivate
its harmonization with synoptic traditions! The importance of a
tradition behind the fourth gospel has now come into its day.[61]

In summary of these efforts to discern an oral tradition behind
the fourth gospel and relate it to the synoptic traditions, it must
be said that they offer interesting possibilities while at the same
time raising serious difficulties. Dodd's investigation goes a
long way toward enabling one to understand the relationship of the
synoptic and fourth gospels in a new and more convincing way. Still,
his view is plagued by his overly simplistic understanding of
"tradition" and the nature of the pre-literary history of the gospel
materials. Another way of putting this point (and more modestly)
is to suggest that Dodd's proposal along with others like it raises
anew the persistent questions about the nature of the early
Christian traditions—questions which must be answered before
proposals such as Dodd's can prove very helpful. For example,
exactly how rich and creative was the pre-literary history of the
gospel materials? How varied and numerous were the traditions?
How localized were they? Some of these questions are being dealt
with, especially with regard to the synoptic traditions,[62] and

---

[60]F.Lamar Cribbs, "A Study of the Contacts That Exist Between
St. Luke and St. John," *Society of Biblical Literature, 1973
Seminar Papers* (Cambridge, Mass.: Society of Biblical Literature,
1973), vol. II, 92.
[61]A persistent critic of these efforts to speak of an oral
tradition behind the fourth gospel is Howard Teeple, *Literary Origin*,
64-73 and "The Oral Tradition That Never Existed," *Journal of
Biblical Literature*, 89 (1970), 56-68.
[62]E.g., E.P. Sanders, *The Tendencies of the Synoptic Tradition*
(Cambridge: University Press, 1969).

the results of those findings should help us to better understand
the possibility of the fourth evangelist's use of oral tradition;
but until then the proposals are only partially helpful.

Finally, we must again suggest that as fascinating as these
proposals are they seem unprovable. That is, Dodd, Haenchen, or
others are not able to establish with any certainty the "traditional"
nature of this or that bit of johannine material. What is needed,
it seems to me, is a more highly developed method of johannine form
criticism; and until such methodology can be developed, our efforts
in this regard may satisfy little more than the fancy. Dodd began
an effort toward the development of a johannine form critical
method, but that method still remains essentially primitive and
crude years after his initial endeavors.

CHAPTER III

REDACTION CRITICISM OF THE FOURTH GOSPEL

With a grasp of the contours of the tradition which came to the evangelist and an understanding of the character of that traditional material, critics can move on to engage in redactional studies of the gospel. That is, they are able, having once satisfactorily separated the tradition/source and the work of the evangelist, to study how the evangelist treated his source--how he revised it, how he affirmed or corrected its theology, and how he supplemented it. Moreover, critics can venture suggestions on the basis of the conclusions regarding the evangelist's handling of the tradition as to what the situation of the evangelist was. These suggestions have to do with the sense in which the conditions of the community of faith have been altered by events occurring between the writing of the traditional material and the writing of the gospel and with how such events and changing conditions have necessitated new theological concerns.

How the individual critic does redactional studies is determined by his or her persuasions concerning the nature of the traditional materials. Is it the author of the "source" himself who is doing the redaction of the tradition (e.g., Wilkens)? Was the source a full gospel (e.g., Fortna) or just a collection of miracle stories (e.g., Becker)? Is he dealing with a tradition which although used by his community is not a product of that community? These questions all bear upon the direction and the nature of the redaction criticism undertaken by the scholar. Since source analysis has been the more precise in its isolation of the traditional material, it is not surprising that redaction criticism has proceeded from source theories. Therefore, our survey in this

section returns to consideration of the work of the source critics,
for the most part.

The redactional work on the fourth gospel can be summarized
under three major topics: The content of the redaction, the theological motifs of the redaction, and the situation of the redactor.

A. *The Content of the Redaction*[1]

General consensus has been reached on at least one issue: The
dialogue and discourse material in the fourth gospel has in most
cases arisen from the redaction. This is not to overlook the
efforts in earlier decades to argue for the evangelist's use of a
source containing speech material; it is however, to observe that
none of those efforts has been given credence among current source
and redaction studies.[2] Of the works we have examined, all with
the exception of Teeple would seem to concede that the discourse
material, for the most part, came into the gospel after the first
stage of its developments. Second, it appears that the conclusion
that the evangelist was responsible for rearranging some of the
signs seems fairly well established. Fortna, Becker, Schnackenburg,
and Wilkens all grant that the miracles in chapters 5 and 6 seem
to have been reversed in the source (see above). Fortna and Wilkens
would further see evidence of the evangelist's reordering of the
temple cleansing narrative, and Lindars and Brown similarly understand that the narrative was moved in one of the editings of the
gospel.[3] J.L. Martyn concurs in this judgment.[4] Third, of course,
all would seem to understand that the evangelist commented upon the
signs in the course of including them in his gospel; that is, he
added explanatory insertions within the narratives and appended to
them.

What remains quite uncertain is whether or not the evangelist
combined the signs narratives with a passion account. Such a
question is of fundamental importance for understanding the theological motivation of the evangelist and for understanding the

---

[1]For this section I am indebted to an unpublished paper by
Reginald H. Fuller.
[2]Robert Kysar, "The Source Analysis of the Fourth Gospel--A
Growing Consensus?", *Novum Testamentum*, 15 (1973), 151. Notwithstanding the most recent proposal that the evangelist used a speech
source, namely, Teeple, *Literary Origin*.
[3]Brown, vol. I, 118.
[4]J.Louis Martyn, "Source Criticism," 262-263. Martyn general-
izes about the place of the temple cleansing narrative in John,
"it is a re-location on virtually any theory of tradition history."

meaning he attached to the miracle stories. But, unfortunately, we find the critics divided, and it is fair to say that redaction criticism of the gospel will be seriously divided so long as consensus on this question is not obtained. What is involved in the question, from the viewpoint of the history of the literature, is the origin of the gospel genre. Assuming that there was no literary dependence of either the source document or the gospel itself upon the synoptics, is it feasible that both Mark and either the author of the signs gospel (Teeple, Fortna, and Wilkens) or the fourth evangelist independently originated the gospel genre? Or are we to suppose some influence of the markan gospel upon the creation of the source (as Lindars suggests) or vice-versa? An important issue for the writing of a history of the literature of the New Testament remains unresolved just because of the failure of source critics to reach a conclusion on the relation of signs and passion narratives prior to the fourth evangelist.[5]

B.   *The Theological Motifs of the Redactor*

One of the points upon which a great deal of attention has been focused in current redaction study is the role of *miracle faith* for the evangelist. It appears relatively certain that the evangelist knew and used a tradition which held that the miraculous acts of Jesus evoked faith on the part of those who witnessed them, and such faith seems to have been highly regarded by the tradition (Lindars dissenting.) It is obvious, however, that the fourth evangelist is not comfortable with that understanding of the role of miracle in producing faith and undertakes either to correct or supplement that idea with his own view (or in Brown and Wilkens' view, the evangelist supplemented his own position). Two different understandings of how the evangelist accomplished this are held.

On the one hand, it appears to some that the evangelist wanted to distinguish between two levels or stages of faith. The faith evoked in witness to the miraculous acts of Jesus is a first stage of faith--a preliminary or as yet immature faith--but nonetheless a positive faith response to Jesus. Both Fortna and Nicol argue that it is this sort of supplementary revision that the fourth evangelist effected of his source. Nicol argues that the evangelist wants to say that faith founded solely upon the miracles of Jesus is not a mature, exemplary faith, but neither is it unbelief. It

_____

[5]Robinson, "The Johannine Trajectory," 266-268.

is a step toward more acceptable faith, and as such the signs are
a concession to human weakness, as Bultmann suggested some years
ago.[6] "Belief" in Jesus on the basis of miracles denotes only an
"interest" in Jesus (8:30f), which the evangelist goes on to have
tested by the "hard words" of Jesus (8:30f). Nicol argues that
the evangelist "intensified" the meaning of the signs so as to
make proper response to them more than mere belief in Jesus
because of his wonderworking powers.[7] In a similar manner, Fortna
has contended that the evangelist wanted clearly to delineate
between a believing response to the signs and pure faith. The
latter--believing without seeing (20:24-29)--is the superior of
the two. The evangelist is particularly critical of requests for
signs (4:48) and understandings of them as mere wonders (6:26).[8]
Brown and Lindars hold comparable interpretations of the evangelist's
view of miracle faith.[9]

On the other hand are those critics who perceive that the
evangelist has gone still further and discredited signs-faith
altogether. Such faith is on the side of death and darkness,
according to Becker's work. Signs are not legitimations of Jesus
for the fourth evangelist and are entirely disavowed by him in that
function (chapter 11). Signs are wholly ambiguous and occasion
only schism among the witnesses, just as the words of Jesus do
(e.g., 4:48). Genuine faith for the evangelist roots in a response
to Jesus' words.[10] Wilkens, too, sees the evangelist opposed to
signs-faith. The evangelist depreciates any turning to Jesus strictly
for the sake of his gifts. The signs are given deeper meaning in
the expanded gospel; they are concerned with the revelation of
Jesus' *doxa*. Hence, the proper response to them is not a faith in
Jesus' miraculous power, but a positive response to the glory of
the Christ. Signs, therefore, occasion both faith and unbelief;
they produce a crisis, a schism among the witnesses (2:11; 11:25,
29). As such, they are the occasion for the first development of
faith, in that they necessitate an initial decision vis-a-vis Jesus
(9:8-41). But word-faith is the end goal which the evangelist has
in mind for his readers.[11]

---

[6]Bultmann, *Gospel*, 209.
[7]Nicol, 99-106.
[8]Robert T. Fortna, "Source and Redaction in the Fourth Gospel's Portrayal of Jesus' Signs," *Journal of Biblical Literature*, 89 (1970), 156-165.
[9]Brown, vol. I, 196; Lindars, *Gospel*, 203.
[10]J. Becker, 145-146.
[11]Wilkens, *Zeichen*, 44, 59.

Two other critics hold that John's redaction of the story of the healing of the nobleman's son (4:46-54), which came to him in the source, in effect turns the role of miracle-faith upside down. Franz Schnider and Werner Stenger understand that the fourth evangelist wanted to stress that faith in the word of Jesus is a presupposition for "seeing the sign" in the acts of Jesus. "One does not believe because one has seen; but one sees because he believes and because one sees believingly, one believes." They propose the following as a diagramatic representation of the evangelist's view of the relationship of faith and experiencing the miraculous acts of Jesus:

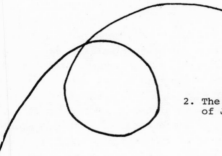

3. The believer then "knows" and believes more deeply.

2. The believer "sees" the signs of Jesus.

1. Faith is rooted in a response to the word of Jesus.

Hence, signs are given a secondary role, reinforcing and deepening faith, in the gospel and are not the primary beginning experience out of which faith grows.[12]

A somewhat different reading of the material finds its proponent in Luise Schottroff who argues that there is an irresolvable contradiction in the fourth evangelist at the point of the role of signs-faith (e.g., 7:13 and 4:48). The evangelist has combined two traditions, one which understands signs as having a legitimating function, and another which has Jesus refusing to grant signs as a means of initiating faith. The view of the evangelist is that it is the quality of the perception of the sign which distinguishes

---

[12]Franz Schnider und Werner Stegner, *Johannes und die Synoptiker. Vergleich ihrer Parallelen* (Munchen: Kosel, 1971), 83. This volume is actually a study of three pericopes--the temple cleansing, the healing of the nobleman's or centurion's son, and the feeding of the multitude and walking on the water--and how each is redacted by the several evangelists who received the narrative through their traditions and included them in their gospels.

true and false faith. At the hand of the evangelist, the signs
have been expanded in their meaning to refer to the heavenly origin
of the actor. It is a matter of perceiving the signs as either the
acts of an earthly miracle worker *or* a heavenly revealer. For
example, "the sign in 4:48 is an innerworldly miracle and therefore
a false sign; the correct sign is not the miracle but the heavenly
reality of the revealer." John criticizes not the legitimating
role of signs but signs seen in a this-world context. True and
false faith are to be distinguished by their objects: True faith
has as its object the heavenly revealer, Jesus, who is in but not
of this world (6:40; 9:37; 20:30); while false faith is directed
toward Jesus as a wonderworker, bringing salvation in this world's
term--the *theios anēr*, the Messiah, and king of this world (6:14,
26; 3:2).[13]

The views of Nicol and Fortna seem to be borne out by the
evidence of the gospel. The radical rejection of signs-faith
altogether or its diametrical and irreconcilable relation to
genuine faith are views which exaggerate certain bits of gospel
evidence and ignore others. While this is no place for an exegetical
study of 4:48, Jesus' rebuke there of the request for a sign does
not appear as general as Becker would understand it, but should be
read as a resistance to faith that requires signs for its sustenance.[14] Moreover, the view that the evangelist wanted only to
distinguish a higher level of faith from that of signs-faith accounts
for his use of the signs material. He is not including in his
gospel a view of faith which he wants essentially to repudiate, but
only one he wants to supplement. Further, it seems reasonable that
the evangelist, writing as he does for a community of second and
third generation Christians, would feel the need to supplement a
faith understanding which necessitated an eye-witness experience
of Jesus with one which transcends that necessity (20:29). But
Schnider and Stenger are also correct in the proposal that the
evangelist wants to point out that "seeing the sign" already presupposes an embryonic faith, and hence the sign opens the schism
between those who believe in this initial way and those who do not.
The result of the evangelist's redaction is to supplement the signs-
faith motif of his source by, first, insisting that the sign is
perceived only by those already possessed of an initial faith and,

---

[13]Luise Schottroff, *Der Glaubende und die feindliche Welt*
(Neukirchener Verlag, 1970), 247-257, quote 355.
[14]I am indebted at this point to, although not in full agreement with, an unpublished paper by Paul Meyer, "Seeing, Signs,
and Sources in the Fourth Gospel."

second, by showing how faith at its most mature level moves beyond signs. In neither case, however, is signs-faith repudiated, only embellished.

Christology is the second concern of much current redaction criticism and is obviously closely related to the concept of signs-faith. It is commonly held that the evangelist wanted to deepen and criticize the view of Jesus which he found in his source or which he himself produced in the earlier form of his work. Whether that source (or basic gospel) contained a simple "divine man" (*theios anēr*) or some other form of a christology focused upon Jesus' extraordinary works, the redaction critics sense that the full gospel gives Jesus a more sophisticated and "higher" explication. The nuances of differences among the critics in their articulation of the christology of the fourth evangelist are subtle, and all those subtleties need not concern us here. It is perhaps enough to say that there are three emphases in the christological redaction found by the critics.

Certainly a great deal of attention is given to the importance of the concept of the glory (*doxa*) of Jesus by the evangelist. Nicol finds this to be the primary motif of the evangelist betrayed by his handling of the signs source. For him Jesus is the glory in flesh. The signs christology is taken by the evangelist as the fleshly history which the evangelist exegetes in order to make obvious the presence of the glory in that fleshly history (e.g., 11:40f). Under the guidance of the Paraclete (14:26), the evangelist takes it upon himself to deepen and articulate the meaning of the historical events represented in the miracle stories. The hermeneutic principle of the evangelist involves these two elements and their relationship--history (the miracles enacted in the flesh) and meaning (the glory of Jesus).[15] It is interesting to note that Nicol utilizes the dichotomy of event and meaning in trying to grasp the theological dimensions of the redaction of the source. The theme of glory finds emphasis in Wilkens' examination as well. He argues that the evangelist wants the reader to perceive the glory of Jesus in the signs, which in turn suggests the identity of Jesus. The signs are explicitly connected with the "I am" sayings (*Ego Eimi*, e.g., ch.11) in the first expansion of the gospel to make that point clear and to demonstrate to the reader that this Jesus is no simple divine man (*theios anēr*). In revealing the glory of Jesus the signs point to his death and resurrection (2:4). The passion is already present in the signs and the signs are already part of

---

[15]Nicol, 125-137.

Jesus' final act--the supreme expression of his glory, his
exaltation.[16]

Less clearly, Fortna believes that the evangelist wanted to
recast the signs narrative with the result that they pointed to the
meaning of Jesus' messiahship, his sonship, and his glory, the
supreme expression of which is his death on the cross. Fortna
contends that whereas the gospel of signs climaxed in the resurrection (understood as the final sign which proves Jesus' messiahship), the fourth gospel is a gospel of salvation which climaxes
in the crucifixion as the exaltation of Jesus which gives life to
the believer (3:14f; 12:32).[17]

Only slightly different in emphasis is Becker's contention
that the fourth evangelist wanted to deepen the source by stressing
the epiphany character of the signs. This was to suggest that
Jesus was no exemplary man, as the source would have it, but the
incarnate logos. Attention is shifted in the gospel from the
miraculous works of Jesus to the cross and resurrection (which by
Becker's reconstruction did not find a place in the source).
The speeches are attached to the signs to show Jesus' divine
identity (chs. 5 and 6). He is the obedient Son, not the divine
man (*theios anēr*) of the source (1:50). The evangelist is concerned
to polemicize against the christology of the signs material, not
just to supplement or deepen it.[18]

Schottroff sees a comparable radical departure from the signs
christology in the fourth gospel. The divine man christology of the
source is transformed in the dualistic setting of the fourth evangelist. Jesus is the heavenly revealer from another realm of reality
present for a time in this world. Faith must see Jesus as more
than a man--which the source fails to do; indeed, it must perceive
him as the revealer from another world, although he is for the time
being a human.[19]

Once again the views of Becker and Schottroff exaggerate the
gulf between the evangelist and his source. Much more convincing
are proposals of Fortna and Nicol. The evangelist seems to have
had in mind the deepening, the expansion, and the enriching of the
christology of his source. Becker is probably right, however, that
the view of Christ in the source was a rather unsophisticated
divine man christology; and the evangelist's redaction simply

---

[16]Wilkens, *Zeichen*, 49-57.
[17]Fortna, "Source and Redaction," 152-155, 165-166.
[18]J. Becker, 144-147.
[19]Schottroff, 267, 274-276.

affirms that the divine man of the signs is actually the Son of
the Father in whom the divine glory may be perceived. If we are
correct in our conviction that it is more likely that the source
did not contain a passion narrative, then the union of the signs
material with the revealer discourses and the passion narrative
has the effect of vastly enriching the christology of the source.

A word might be added here regarding Nicol's rather strange
resistance to the proposal that the source contained a "divine
man" christology. Nicol's view on this matter can only be regarded
as an unfortunate "blind spot" in his otherwise commendable study.[20]
An examination of the isolated signs source material surely indicates
that Christ is viewed there as some sort of divinely gifted man
whose wonderful deeds evoke faith. The evangelist did not reject
that view but improved upon it, in effect by saying Christ is indeed the divine man but much more. That he does this by means of
an interpretative scheme of event and meaning, as Nicol points out,
is surely the best way of understanding the johannine redaction of
the christology of the signs source.

Finally, Fortna has attempted to picture the difference between
his proposed signs source and the fourth gospel on the question of
soteriology. (His discussion of this theme is the only one, to my
knowledge, done in recent redaction criticism of John.) In the
signs gospel, as Fortna has reconstructed it, there is little
development of the theme of salvation. Salvation is a simple matter
of believing that Jesus is the Messiah. The signs themselves imply
that salvation involves an "overabundance of Christ's sustenance,"
health, life, comfort, and teaching. All can avail themselves of
these benefits by a believing response to the signs, especially
the supreme sign worked out in the passion. The fourth evangelist
picked up some of the themes in the signs material and "spiritualized"
them. For instance, while the theme of life was probably meant
literally in the signs material, the fourth evangelist gives it
deeper spiritual significance (e.g., 20:31b) and presents Jesus
himself as that life (e.g., 11:25).

Something similar may have happened with the concept of truth
(see especially the conversation with the Samaritan woman) and
light (suggested to John in the signs account of the healing of the
man born blind). The way in which the evangelist handled the
miracles of abundance suggests that "the physical preoccupation of
the tradition gives way to more symbolic soteriology." The stories

---

[20]Fortna, review of Nicol, 120.

of healing lose their salvific point and become occasions for
controversy between Jesus and the Jews. The resurrection stories
lose their concern with rescuing people from death and emphasize
the revelation conveyed in the act and the faith it calls forth.[21]
Although Brown does not distinguish between the soteriologies of
the early stages of the gospel and later editions, he too understands that in the completed gospel, the signs are made to point
to the spiritual realm of life, sight and judgment.[22]

One need not grant Fortna's contention that the signs source
encompassed a passion narrative in order to affirm his insightful
perception of the manner in which the evangelist had expanded the
conception of salvation found in the source. Again it appears
that the theological content of the evangelist's redaction had the
effect of deepening and enriching a rather simple and perhaps even
crude theology. Signs-faith is supplemented by a more mature
faith; divine man christology deepened by a son christology; and
salvation of abundance ripened by a spiritual view of salvation.
The evangelist seems to have availed himself of a source whose
theology he could affirm as far as it went. He understood his
task, apparently, to show such a theology as found in his source
could be developed into a far more adequate and rich complex of
views.

C. The Situation of the Evangelist

A valuable contribution of redaction criticism is the insights
it renders regarding the setting in which the redactor worked. By
means of redaction critical findings the history of the early
Christian communities can be fleshed out. This is no less true for
the work on the fourth gospel than for the synoptics. Redaction
criticism enables the scholar to work from his knowledge of the
evangelist's handling of his tradition to deduce something about
the situation in which that writer found himself. That situation
supposedly motivated his dealing with the material as he did.
While these kinds of results are not as numerous in johannine as
they are in synoptic studies, some interesting observations have
been made.

Several critics have observed that between the construction of
the signs source and the writing of the fourth gospel some important

---

[21]Robert T. Fortna, "From Christology to Soteriology--A Redac-
tion-Critical Study of Salvation in the Fourth Gospel," *Interpretation*, 27 (1973), 32-45.
[22]Brown, vol. I, 530.

changes in the johannine community occurred. It appears that the
signs material was intended as a missionary document for the Jewish
community,[23] but the fourth gospel seems to have a different
attitude toward the missionary enterprise itself, or toward the
Jews, or toward both. Wilkens understands that when the evangelist
expanded his original gospel he was no longer concerned with the
missionary task among the Jews; for he was in the midst of a
struggle with gnostic docetism within his community. Consequently
he directed his expanded work toward the intra-church situation.[24]
Nicol understands, along with Martyn, that a fundamental shift has
occurred in the relationship between Jews and Christians. The
missionary goal of the source became a polemic in the hands of the
evangelist, for the break between the church and synagogue had been
finalized in the intervening years. "The community from which this
Gospel arose experienced so much hostility from outside that they
isolated themselves from the world and had only a limited missionary
interest."[25] The Christians had been excommunicated from the
synagogue, leaving some Jews in John's town torn between their
traditional faith and Christianity. Preaching miracles was no
longer an effective means of converting Jews, and so those miracles
were subordinated to a more complex but (at least from the evangelist's point of view) more sophisticated faith. The congregation
to which the evangelist addressed his gospel seems surely to have
been comprised of Jewish Christians for the most part.[26]

It is J. Louis Martyn who has most carefully tried to see the
situation of the evangelist from an integration of the perspectives
of redaction criticism, research on the history of religions in the
first century johannine community, and a hypothesis of the development of Christian theology in that century. He proposes that three
questions had been pressed upon the johannine community, particularly
by Jewish opponents, in the years between the composition of the
signs gospel and the fourth gospel: Who is Jesus? Can one follow
Moses and Jesus both? And, what significance has Jesus' death?

On the first question, Christians had been challenged to
show that Jesus is the Messiah, and they had been charged with
being ditheists. The evangelist counters the first by stressing
that Jesus' identity cannot be easily shown (as the signs source
seems to suggest) and that there are no certain bases for faith,

_____

[23]Wilkens, *Zeichen*, 167; Nicol, 142; Martyn, 269; Fortna,
Gospel of Signs, 225.
[24]Wilkens, *Zeichen*, 167-168.
[25]Nicol, 146.
[26]*Ibid.*, 142-149; Martyn, 267-268.

only the guidance of the Paraclete. John introduces his concept
of election precisely to respond to the question of how one knows
that Jesus is the Messiah, and the evangelist's sonship christology
serves to deal with the charge of ditheism.

To the second question, he works out a careful dialectic
between Jesus and Moses which moves directly counter to the Jewish
denial that one can be faithful to both Jesus and Moses (e.g., 9:
28). Because of the experiences of Christian martyrdom at the hands
of Jewish opponents, the significance of the death of Jesus takes
on new importance. Motivated by the crisis, the fourth evangelist
moves the temple cleansing narrative to its present location in
the gospel and places the entire early part of the gospel in the
shadow of Easter and the coming of the Paraclete. The death plot
against Jesus is given new emphasis in his work in the light of
the experience of martyrdom, and it is rooted early in the gospel
(5:18 and elsewhere). The passion account itself is shaded over
with the question of Jesus as the true, Mosaic prophet versus the
false, beguiling prophet (e.g., 18:19). Thus, Martyn is able to
conclude that the fourth evangelist stood over against a Jewish
synagogue which had expelled all Christians and in which there
were treasured traditions about Moses. "[John] belongs in a
dominantly Jewish-Christian milieu....As one views the growth of
the tradition from the [signs gospel] to the [fourth gospel], overt
concerns with Jewish questions become more, not less central."[27]

While Martyn recognizes that some gnosticizing influences
may have colored the thinking of both the fourth evangelist and
his Jewish opponents (especially with regard to their traditions
concerning Moses) and Wilkens believes the evangelist was combating
gnostic tendencies in his own church, Schottroff argues that the
evangelist himself has come under strong gnostic influences. His
basic point of view with regard to Jesus--the revealer from another
realm in the unfriendly and evil world--is certainly gnostic.
But above all, the evangelist for whatever reason originated a
dualism of two realities, which although gnostic in some senses, is
the novel contribution of the fourth evangelist. He adopted a
gnostic dualism to fit the Christian tradition.[28] Unfortunately,
Schottroff does not propose a historical setting in which such

---

[27]Martyn, 254-267, quote, 269. C. Dekker has proposed that much
the opposite was the case. From his analysis of the terms, "the
Jews" and "the crowd," he discerns contradictory uses (compare, for
example 7:1 and 11:42 with 6:41) and concludes that chapter 6 is the
result of a later non-Jewish redactor who inserted his work into an
originally Jewish-Christian document. "Grundschrift und Redaktion
im Johannesevangelium," *New Testament Studies*, 13 (1966), 66-80.
   [28]Schottroff, 229-245, 295-296.

influences and such a creative adaptation could take place.

The situation of the evangelist as it is reflected in his
redaction of the signs source cannot be described in isolation
from the general investigations of the environment of the evangelist to which we will turn in Part Two. Most of the critical
observations appropriate to the subject must be reserved for that
section after the wider field of research has been unfolded.
Suffice it for now to say that Martyn's reading of the implications
of the evangelist's redaction of the proposed signs source commands
my adherence. Martyn has wisely and astutely dealt with the evidence
we have in order to paint a convincing picture of the evangelist
working amid a deteriorating relationship between Christians and
Jews. We will show in Part Two how various forms of research have
converged to add increasing credence to Martyn's proposal.

The gnostic hypotheses of both Wilkens and Schottroff are far
less convincing. They presuppose a degree of prominence to the
gnostic motifs which the evidence of the gospel does not warrant.
While there is little doubt that gnostic-like modes of thought were
present in the milieu in which the evangelist worked, his redaction
of the proposed source does not betray indications that it is those
modes of thought which motivated his revisions of the source. More
likely is the hypothesis that the circumstances of the Christian
outreach among the Jews has been significantly altered.

CONCLUSION OF PART ONE

Our survey of contemporary investigations of the sources and
traditions behind the fourth gospel, their relationship to the
synoptic gospels, the manner in which they were redacted by the
fourth evangelist, and the total process of composition which produced the fourth gospel leaves the clear impression that scholarship has yet to develop a hypothesis in these areas which wins anything approaching universal support. The range of views regarding
the evangelist and his tradition is wide, and the propagation of
those views is vigorous. If the failure to gain any sort of consensus on these matters encourages despair, the enormous amounts
of creative scholarly work spent in pursuit of a better understanding
of the emergence of the gospel can only nurture admiration and hope.
Moreover, it is only a restricted perspective which allows for
discouragement over research on these questions. Seen in a wider
horizon of johannine studies over the past century, recent years

have produced a number of significant advances. A half dozen can
be listed with confidence:

1. Contemporary johannine research has clearly established
that behind the fourth gospel there was a body of traditional
material which became incorporated into the gospel. In what form
(written, oral, or both) that material came to the evangelist, its
relationship to the synoptic traditions, and its specific contents
all remain matters for discussion. But that such a tradition looms
behind the gospel is now nearly indisputable.

2. It is further agreed that the process by which that tradition reached the evangelist and by which it was incorporated into
his work was relatively complex. Again, critics cannot agree on
the outline of that process.

3. Scholars have recently converged on a view of the evangelist as a "creative redactor." This is to say that there is a
common view of the evangelist as one who paid careful and respect-
ful heed to the traditions flowing through the Christian community
to him. He worked with those traditions to preserve them for the
future. At the same time, his work with the traditional materials
was not that of a "scissors and paste" editor--far from it! He
shaped this traditional material in a new way, allowing it to come
to expression in his document but harnessing it as a vehicle of
his own theological views.

4. But the evangelist utilized his traditional materials in
such a creative fashion not alone to give expression to his own
views. That creative work was directed toward the task of addressing
his community with a relevant and timely message. Scholars seem
to agree that the evangelist was speaking through his new gospel
to a troubled community of Christians, perhaps a community faced
with events of crisis proportions. Whatever form the tradition
had taken by the time it reached him, the evangelist felt the
necessity of giving it a new form and enhancing its impact upon the
Christian community; all of this was to allow it to speak meaningfully to his fellow believers.

5. Most critics would seem to emphasize more today than in
previous decades of johannine studies the likelihood that either
the immediate tradition incorporated in the gospel, the gospel itself, or both were set within a community in which Jewish influences
were considerable. We must take up the general question of the
setting of the gospel soon, but for now we must note the degree of
scholarly conviction that the history of the traditional materials
and the composition of the gospel itself was a history of Jewish-

Christian dialogue.

6. Finally, what critics have arrived at again and again through their studies of the relationship of the gospel to its tradition is that the role of the fourth evangelist appears to be more alike than unlike the role of the synoptic evangelists. Where scholars once set the fourth evangelist apart from his synoptic counterparts, where they once saw him as the unique mystic or the theologian among the four gospel writers, they are now portraying his function as exactly the same as that of the synoptic evange-lists: To articulate a Christian tradition in such a manner as to address it with new relevance to a given community.

One final observation must be made before we move on to the question of the historical setting of the fourth gospel. That observation is well expressed by Barnabas Lindars:

> Our assessment of John is bound up with the theory we form about its origins. The effort to get behind the Fourth Gospel is not simply a literary-critical game, but an inescapable task in the process of discovering the real meaning of it in the form in which we know it.[1]

---

[1] Lindars, *Behind the FG*, 22.

PART TWO:

THE EVANGELIST

AND

HIS SITUATION

>All of us are more or less groping in darkness when we are
>asked to give information about the historical background
>of this Gospel, information which would determine our under-
>standing of the whole book and not merely of individual
>details....The evangelist whom we call John appears to be
>a man without definite contours....Historically, the Gospel
>as a whole remains an enigma.[1]

These words of the German scholar, Ernst Käsemann, represent

an honest but somewhat pessimistic appraisal of the quest to under-

stand the historical setting of the fourth gosepl, for it is true

that after centuries of the critical enterprise the crucial histor-

ical questions with regard to the fourth gospel remain essentially

unanswered, notwithstanding individual scholars who may be satisfied

by their own proposals for the solution of these questions. The

evangelist remains, as Käsemann puts it, "a man without definite

contours," and that information so essential to the interpretation

of the gospel remains elusive.

What would it mean to bring the fourth evangelist out from with-

in the shadows of historical uncertainty and illumine him and his

situation? What would it mean to sketch in the definite contours

of his figure? Certainly at least four essential questions would

have to be convincingly answered: First, who was the evangelist?

Second, what was the intellectual milieu out of which he wrote and

which influenced his modes of thought and expression? Third, what

was the concrete historical situation surrounding the evangelist at

the time he wrote and which motivated his work? Finally, when did

[1]Ernst Käsemann, *The Testament of Jesus According to John 17*
(Philadelphia: Fortress Press, 1968), 1-2.

he write? What date can be assigned to the appearance of the gospel?
If these questions could be responded to in some clear and persuasive manner, the pessimism of Käsemann's pronouncement could be
overcome.

We have seen how contemporary scholarship has come to favor
some form of the evangelist's dependence upon a tradition. But
what have been the recent advances, if any, on the questions related
to the evangelist and his situation? Käsemann first wrote these
words in 1966. Has scholarship overcome the state of affairs which
he has so graphically described, or must we still speak of the
evangelist as a man without definite contours. Our survey will
look at each of the four questions suggested above to attempt some
sort of assessment of the accomplishments of recent efforts to
penetrate the darkness surrounding the historical origin of the
gospel.[2]

---

[2]I will not attempt to deal with the question of the location
of the writing of the gospel in this survey, for that question has
more and more become nothing but a deduction from the findings of
research on the intellectual milieu and the concrete situation of
the evangelist. For surveys of proposals for the locale of the
gospel's origin see Paul Feine, Johannes Behm, and W.G. Kümmel,
Introduction to the New Testament (New York: Abingdon, 1966), 175;
Brown, *Gospel*, vol. I, ciii-civ; Schnackenburg, *Gospel*, vol. I,
149-152.

CHAPTER I

THE IDENTITY OF THE EVANGELIST

The question of the authorship of the fourth gospel has been
discussed for centuries within the circles of critical interpreters
of the New Testament. Until the eighteenth century, the traditional
association of the apostle John, son of Zebedee, with the evangelist
was never questioned; but with the advent of critical scholarship
the authorship of the fourth gospel became one of the many literary
questions over which students of the document puzzled.[1] Over the
years unwillingness to accept the ancient tradition of the church
that the author of the gospel was the apostle John increased, and
counter-hypotheses multiplied until it almost seemed that the
scholarly imagination became exhausted with the creation of new
solutions for this old puzzle.[2] Then in the twentieth century
many scholars put aside the question entirely, claiming that it was
hopeless to try to penetrate the mystery of the origin of the gospel.[3]
The attention to such unsolvable questions as the authorship of the
fourth gospel seemed to some to epitomize the theological bankruptcy
of literary historical criticism. They pointed to the variety of
solutions, "sometimes bordering on the bizarre,"[4] as indications of

---

[1]For a history of the problem in modern research see Feine,
Behm, and Kümmel, 139-142, 165-174.
[2]E.g., B.W. Bacon's thesis that Paul was the author of the
gospel, *The Fourth Gospel in Research and Debate* (New York: Moffat,
Yard, and Co., 1910).
[3]E.g., Edwyn C. Hoskyns, *The Riddle of the New Testament*
(London: Faber and Faber, 1931), 183-204; Hoskyns and F.N. Davey,
The Fourth Gospel (London: Faber and Faber, 1940).
[4]Leon Morris, *The Gospel According to John* (Grand Rapids,
Michigan: Eerdmans, 1970), 30.

either the fruitlessness of the whole question or evidence that
the traditional apostolic authorship remained preferable.

In more recent years another reservation concerning the quest
of the identity of the author of the gospel has surfaced. Rudolf
Schnackenburg hints at this reservation in the first volume of his
commentary when he observes that "this work cannot simply be treated
as the work of an author in the modern sense."[5] The reason for this
new reservation, of course, emerges as a consequence of viewing the
gospel as the literary expression of a folk tradition. That is,
when it is recognized that the document before us is the end product
of a process of transmission (beginning in oral tradition, taking
shape in the preaching and teaching ministry of the primitive
church, and emerging finally as the redaction of several earlier
sources and/or traditions only then to undergo still further revision, expansion, and perhaps rearrangement), the question of the
authorship of the gospel becomes at once far more complex, on the
one hand, and significantly less important, on the other. For if
one raises the question of the identity of the author of the fourth
gospel in the light of these new developments in fourth gospel
criticism, what is being sought? Is it the identity of the originator of the tradition eventually embedded in our gospel? Or is
it the identity of the evangelist who may have been the major
redactor of that tradition?

Clearly, the view of the fourth gospel as folk literature
places the question of authorship in a far different light than if
one were to continue to view the document as the work of one single
individual who is solely responsible for the contents of the book
(i.e., "an author in the modern sense"). True, there are some who
in effect reject the whole direction of those movements in fourth
gospel criticism discussed in Part One and continue to treat
the question of authorship in a manner similar to pre-form and
redaction criticism days. Others have only slightly modified a
quest for the author of the gospel in the light of these developments. But the bulk of scholarly work now views the question of
authorship in a radically different manner than their forefathers
in New Testament criticism, and for that reason either puts the
question to one side because it is convinced that not one but a
community of persons is responsible for the gospel, or approaches the
question anticipating a vastly more complex answer than one name!

It is inescapably true, however, that an inquiry into the
historical origins of the fourth gospel, even if it is viewed as

---

[5]Schnackenburg, *Gospel*, vol. I, 75.

folk literature, cannot entirely ignore the question of the identity
and character of those persons primarily responsible for the production of the gospel. Is there evidence of one influential individual in the origin of the tradition? Does the gospel bear the
marks of one mind above the others who contributed to the work?
Albeit in a new context, the critic is still faced with the question
of the identity of the persons who played major roles in shaping
the gospel. The critical efforts on the fourth gospel in recent
years demonstrate that these questions are still with us, even
where they have been tempered by the new approach to the gospel.

Our task for the following pages will not be to survey the
evidence which has ordinarily been involved in questions of the
identity of the evangelist or the originator of his tradition.
Surveys of the external (the witness of the ancient church) and
the internal evidence are readily available to the student.[6]
Rather, let us sketch the kinds of solutions which have been
arrived at by contemporary critics on the question of who was
responsible for the present form of the gospel and thereby demonstrate the major live options and the kinds of approaches to be
found in the literature of the past few years. Because the questions
of the identity of the "disciple whom Jesus loved" (13:23-26; 19:
25-27; 20:2-10; 21:7, 20-23, 24) and sometimes the anonymous
disciple(s) (1:37-42; 18:15-16; 20:2-10) of the gospel are interwoven with the questions of the identity of the evangelist and the
originator of his tradition, brief examinations of studies done on
the former questions will be mentioned in passing.

Recent scholarship has posed four distinct solutions to the
question of the identities of the evangelist and the originator of
his tradition: (a) John, son of Zebedee, is directly responsible
for the present gospel; (b) John, son of Zebedee, is indirectly
responsible for the gospel, since he was the originator of the
tradition which another put in the form of the present gospel;
(c) John Mark is indirectly responsible for the gospel and was the
originator of the tradition embedded in the gospel. (d) An anonymous
person is responsible for the present gospel and the source of his

---

[6]E.g., *Ibid.*, 75-100; C.K. Barrett, *The Gospel According to St.
John* (London: SPCK, 1956), 83-104; H.P.V. Nunn, *The Authorship of
the Fourth Gospel* (London: Alden and Blackwell, 1952). From among
the older but extensive works, see James Drummond, *An Inquiry Into
the Character and Authorship of the Fourth Gospel* (New York: Charles
Scribner's Sons, 1904), 67-514; William Sanday, *The Criticism of
the Fourth Gospel* (New York: Charles Scribner's Sons, 1905), 74-
108; John Donovan, *The Authorship of St. John's Gospel* (London:
Burns, Oates, and Wasbourne, 1936).

tradition is equally unknown.

A. *John, Son of Zebedee -- Author*

That John, son of Zebedee, is responsible for the gospel is,
of course, a view that seems to have first come to clear expression
in the second century in Irenaeus (*Against Heresies*, III, 1).
That view is still championed today in its simplest form among a
number of scholars, the most vigorous of whom is the Australian,
Leon Morris. Morris launches his defense of the traditional view
of authorship by arguing that the author of the fourth gospel was
surely an eyewitness, evidence for which is found throughout the
gospel in features which are admittedly "indirect" but telling.
The kind of evidence Morris values, for instance, are the "unimpor-
tant details" which might be included by an eyewitness but which
would never find their place in a more imaginative account, such as
Jesus' sighs (11:33, 38) and the detailed parts played by Andrew,
Philip, and the young boy in the feeding of the multitude in chapter
6.[7] He links his argument with an attack upon the form critics
and their assumption that the materials found now in the gospel have
an extensive pre-literary history.[8] This eyewitness was, to Morris'
mind, none other than the "disciple whom Jesus loved" mentioned in
the gospel narrative.

Morris' argument includes a popular line of reasoning for his
thesis which is found best expressed, I believe, in an article by
Bruno de Solages. De Solages, after examining the internal evidence,
concludes that the beloved disciple is John, son of Zebedee, because
of the convergence of three facts: First, the fourth gospel's
silence concerning the sons of Zebedee--a strange silence in the
light of their prominence in the synoptic accounts of the disciples;
second, the appearance of the unnamed disciple whom Jesus loved in
intimate relationship with Jesus in the fourth gospel; third, the
parallel between Peter and John in the synoptics and Peter and the
beloved disciple in John.[9] If the intimate trio of disciples--
Peter, James, and John--constitutes the likely candidates for the
identity of the beloved disciple, John must be the obvious choice;

---

[7]Leon Morris, "Was the Author of the Fourth Gospel an Eyewitness?" *Studies in the Fourth Gospel* (Grand Rapids, Michigan:
Wm. B. Eerdmans, 1969), 139-208.
    [8]*Ibid.*, 209-213.
    [9]Bruno de Solages, "Jean, fils de Zébédée et l'enigme du
'disciple que Jesus aimait'", *Bulletin de Littérature Ecclesiastique*
73 (1972), 41-50.

since Peter is named in relationship with the beloved disciple,
and James was martyred early (Acts 12:2), eliminating the possibility
of his being the eyewitness responsible for the fourth gospel.[10]

That the gospel is the result of the work of the eyewitness,
John the apostle, accounts for its clearly Jewish and Palestinian
features, which are obvious to Morris in the accurate topography
of the gospel and its literary style. If there are hellenistic
features to the thought of the evangelist, they are accountable
for in the light of the effect that hellenistic thought had had upon Palestinian Jews by the first century A.D. The evidence of the
Qumran documents and their parallels to johannine thought further
reinforces the Jewish character of the gospel. "The basic reason
for holding that the author was John the Apostle is that this
appears to be what the Gospel itself teaches," Morris claims.
The assertions of eyewitness testimony (21:24; 1:14; 19:35) are to
be taken at face value. The external evidence found in the witness
of the second and third century church only serves to bolster the
testimony of the gospel itself. Morris concludes that there is no
solution to the authorship question which is free of all difficulties
(and in the case of the apostolic solution he attempts to weaken
each of these difficulties as best he can), but he claims that his
solution offers the fewest problems when compared with the alternatives.[11]

Morris' position finds support on the continent in the works
of Werner de Boor and Jean Colson. The former introduces his
commentary with an examination of the question of authorship, and
there argues that 21:24 establishes that the gospel was written by
the beloved disciple and that that disciple can be none other than
John, son of Zebedee. The tradition of the early martyrdom of
John is founded on an erroneous interpretation of Mark 10:39, de
Boor insists. The markan passage refers not specifically to the
sons of Zebedee but to the fate of the disciples of Jesus in
general.[12]

Colson's monograph is more narrowly concerned with the identity
of the beloved disciple and with the refutation of the work of F.-M.
Braun (see below). After surveying the internal evidence for the
identity of the beloved disciple and the tradition in the second
century, Colson puts down to his satisfaction the notion of John's

[10]Morris, *Gospel*, 11.
[11]*Ibid.*, 9-15, 29-30, quote, 9; Morris, "The Authorship of the
Fourth Gospel," 128-276.
[12]Werner de Boor, *Das Evangelium des Johannes* (Wuppertal: R.
Brockhaus, 1971), 1. Teil, 15-20.

early martyrdom. In balance, it appears to Colson that the beloved
disciple is to be identified as John, son of Zebedee. He finds
evidence that this John was a priest and reports the ministry of
Jesus from the perspective of one interested in the sacerdotal
character of Judaism. Furthermore, there is good reason to think
that John was involved in one of the reform movements in Judaism
during the first century--perhaps even the Qumran community. That
he was a disciple of John the Baptist before giving his allegiance
to Jesus is a clear possibility. Hence, he reports with interest
Jesus' involvement with the cultic practices of Judaism and delights
in the accounts of Jesus' discussions with "doctors of the Law"
(e.g., Nicodemus). The prominence of Jerusalem in the johannine
gospel is due to the author's own acquaintance with the temple city.
Moreover, he was the host for the last supper and a witness of the
death and resurrection of Jesus. He wrote his gospel in Ephesus
in collaboration with the presbyters of that city, and it is that
collaboration which accounts for the distinction between the styles
of the gospel and John's later work, Revelation. After his death
at the beginning of the reign of Trajan (ca.98-117), the elders of
Ephesus added the appendix of the gospel, in particular 21:20-23.[13]

Although these three scholars are not to be thought of as a
homogenous group, they share a common concern to demonstrate the
apostolic authority of the gospel. In my opinion, the most serious
criticism to be leveled against each of them is that they insist
upon ignoring the prevailing and clearly established findings of
form and redaction criticism. They continue to operate on the
assumption that the gospel is a new literary work with no pre-
literary history, an assumption which must be proved before their
arguments for apostolic authorship can gain any force. Another
critical observation regards Morris' view of history in particular
but might well be addressed to Colson and de Boor as well. It
is the charge that they operate with an essentially nineteenth

---

[13]Jean Colson, *L'enigme du disciple que Jésus aimait* (Paris:
Beauchesne, 1969). It is interesting that while Colson argues for
the priestly origin of the fourth gospel at the hands of John, son
of Zebedee, another scholar has adduced evidence which points in
quite the opposite direction. In an essay concerned not to identify
the fourth evangelist but to draw conclusions about his characteristics from the gospel itself, Kilpatrick has shown that the contents
of the gospel suggest "the work of a Palestinian peasant, a poor
man in a poor province." While agreeing with Colson that the author
was doubtless Jewish, Kilpatrick analyzes the style of the gospel
and decides that it is as close to "non-literary" Greek as one
could find in writing! He was in effect an uneducated peasant at
the most. G.D. Kilpatrick, "What John Tells Us About John,"
Studies in John (Leiden: E.J. Brill, 1970), 75-87.

century view of history--a view which supposes that history is
discoverable facts to be rehearsed. That history is the product of
minds, "processed" and interpreted by the reporter in accord with
his own historical situation, seems to elude these three. Consequently, they read the gospel and excavate it for their evidence
regarding its author without any regard for the *character* of the
reporting found there. The situation of the evangelist in the life
of the church of his day seems entirely ignored in their quest for
the identity of the author.[14] In both cases--their failure to take
into account the work of form and redaction criticism and their
view of history--they represent critical efforts more at home in
the previous century than the current one and certainly at odds
with the major movements of fourth gospel criticism in the past
decade.

B. *John, Son of Zebedee--Originator of Tradition*

That John, the son of Zebedee, was the originator of the tradition to which another eventually gave expression in the gospel
is a revision of the traditional authorship position in the light
of more recent tendencies in New Testament criticism. This "inter-
mediate solution" argues for the apostolic origin of the tradition
contained in the fourth gospel but holds that the evangelist himself was a later figure. Four such views have come to expression
in the work of Raymond Brown, Rudolf Schnackenburg, A.M. Hunter,
and N.E. Johnson.

On the evaluation of the witness of the early church in favor
of the apostolic origins of the fourth gospel, Brown seems most
inclined to regard that witness with seriousness. "There are some
valid points in the objections raised to this tradition, but
Irenaeus' statement is far from having been disproved."[15] Schnackenburg agrees that the tradition is clear and strongly in favor of
John, the son of Zebedee, but thinks it is plagued with a number of
insufficiencies. It is regrettably late, and doubt may be raised
about the source of Irenaeus' knowledge of John. Moreover, there
might well have been a confusion of "Johns" in the early church.
Add to this the tradition of the possible early martyrdom of John,
and one has sufficient reason for bracketing the external evidence

---

[14]J. Davis McCaughey, "Leon Morris on the Fourth Gospel,"
Australian Biblical Review, 1973, 47-48.
[15]Brown, *Gospel*, vol. I, xcii.

and turning elsewhere.[16]   Hunter cites many of the same reasons
in his far shorter consideration of the external evidence to conclude that it is "indecisive."[17]

   Turning then to the internal evidence, Brown, Hunter, and
Johnson all are impressed by the claims of the gospel to be under-
girded by an eyewitness and the eyewitness character of the material
itself, and all are inclined to account for that eyewitness character
by identifying the beloved disciple as the gospel's source.[18]
Schnackenburg is less certain. He hedges his stand for the eyewitness
basis of the gospel by suggesting that the aporias of the gospel,
the evidence that sources were used in its composition, and that
different traditions were redacted "...all combine to make us less
confident that we have the immediate account of an eye-witness before
us, even though some items of information (such as 19:34f) may go
back to a first-hand account."[19]

   Schnackenburg is likewise the most cautious in identifying the
beloved disciple with John, son of Zebedee. If the beloved disciple
was a concrete historical person in the time of Jesus, he must
surely be synonymous with John, the son of Zebedee; efforts to
identify him with other figures amount to little more than "ingenious
guesswork." But the unsolved question is whether the beloved
disciple represents a historical person in the time of Jesus or a
symbolic figure; and here Schnackenburg does not appear to have
clearly decided.[20] (In a later discussion in this section, we will
consider another position taken by Schnackenburg on the identity
of the beloved disciple which seems to represent at least a partial
shift from the position defended in his commentary.) Brown observes
that the eyewitness disciple referred to himself as "the other
disciple" (1:37-42; 18:15-16; and 20:2-10) while his followers
referred to him as the "disciple whom Jesus loved" (13:23-26; 19:
25-27; 20:2-10; 21:7, 20-23, 24). At 20:2 there is evidence that

---

[16]Schnackenburg, *Gospel*, vol. I, 85-91.
   [17]A.M. Hunter, *The Gospel According to John* (Cambridge: The
University Press, 1965), 12.
   [18]Brown, *Gospel*, vol. I, xcii-xciv; Hunter, 12-13; N.E. Johnson,
"The Beloved Disciple and the Fourth Gospel," *Church Quarterly
Review*, 167 (1966), 278-282.
   [19]Schnackenburg, *Gospel*, vol. I, 94.
   [20]*Ibid.*, 99-100. The argument that the beloved disciple is a
purely symbolic figure with no concrete historical identity has
been advanced by a number of critics in the twentieth century. That
he is a symbol of ideal discipleship is advocated by Alfred Loisy,
The Origins of the New Testament (New York: Macmillan, 1950), 220,
and Martin Dibelius, "Joh 15:13. Eine Studie zum Traditionsproblem
des Johannes-Evangelium," *Festgabe für Adolf Deissmann* (Tübingen:
J.C.B. Mohr, 1927), 169-189. That he represents Gentile Christianity
over against Jewish Christianity symbolized in the figure of Peter
is the contention of Bultmann, *The Gospel*, 484.

the original tradition referred to the "other disciple" and a
redactor has explained that this disciple is the one whom Jesus
loved. Brown then adduces the usual arguments for concluding that
the beloved disciple was John, son of Zebedee, with several additions: 19:25 may suggest that the beloved disciple was related to
Jesus, and John, son of Zebedee, seems the only disciple with
sufficient authority to support the implicit challenge in the
fourth gospel to the petrine tradition of the synoptic gospels.[21]
Hunter concurs, as does Johnson, with the identification of the
beloved disciple with the apostle John, son of Zebedee.[22]

The conclusion reached by each of these four critics is, with
varying degrees of certainty, that the tradition embedded in the
gospel represents the eyewitness testimony of the beloved disciple
(most likely John, the son of Zebedee) and that the evangelist
responsible for the gospel is a later figure who dealt faithfully
with that tradition. Schnackenburg invokes the position of F.-M.
Braun as the basis of his reconstruction of the manner in which the
tradition came into the gospel. Braun argues that the apostle John's
kerygma first developed into small units, and then after a considerable period of time, the apostle gave the main ingredients of his
thought to secretaries and collaborators for writing, allowing them
a great deal of editorial freedom. He then prevailed upon a com-
petent writer of Greek, a Jew living in dispersion, to produce the
gospel. John died before the task was finished, and the author
only generally completed his task, leaving the document with its
troublesome rough spots. It is he, the writer of the gospel, who
acknowledges the source of his material by naming John, the son of
Zebedee, the beloved disciple.[23] Schnackenburg tentatively adopts
this proposal and modifies it only by insisting that the evangelist
surely exercised considerable freedom in editing the recollections
and interpretations of John.[24]

Brown's theory of composition is strikingly similar to Braun's
proposal, although Brown cites no dependence upon Braun. The
apostle John himself is responsible for stage one in Brown's theory
of composition. A disciple of John is, then, responsible for stages
two through four, composing the gospel through these stages while
depending upon John who continued to live in the evangelist's
community. This unknown disciple of John is the "writer" of the

---

[21]Brown, *Gospel*, vol. I, xciii-xcviii.
[22]Hunter, *According to John* (Philadelphia: Westminster Press,
1968), 105; Johnson, 283.
[23]F.-M. Braun, *Jean le Théologien et son évangile dans l'
église ancienne* (Paris: J. Gabalda, 1959), 396ff.
[24]Schnackenburg, *Gospel*, vol. I, 101-102.

gospel in the sense that it is he who gave expression to John's
memories and ideas; while John, son of Zebedee, must be acknowledged
as the "author" of the gospel insofar as he is the originator of
the material found therein.[25]

Hunter's more popularized writings propose a similar view
(independent of Brown). John the apostle was the source of the
ancient tradition behind the fourth gospel, and the gospel itself
was composed out of that tradition by a disciple of the apostle.[26]
Hunter disclaims Brown's theory of composition, however, saying,
"we think that his hypothesis of *five* distinct stages in the gospel's
composition is unduly speculative and complicated."[27] Still, he
goes further than Brown in identifying the writer of the gospel
itself as "almost certainly" John the elder. His certainty for
this identification seems to grow, first, from the knowledge of
Palestinian topography in the gospel and its semitized Greek,
which leads Hunter to believe the author was a Palestinian living
in the diaspora. Second, Hunter claims on the basis of style and
theology that the author of the gospel is the same elder responsible for the three epistles of John (2 John 1:1, 3 John 1).[28]

In 1966 N.E. Johnson, in apparent independence of both Hunter
and Brown, published a proposal that John, the son of Zebedee,
(the beloved disciple) produced his recollections of experiences
with Jesus and that that document (which Johnson call "QJ") was
later incorporated into the gospel by a disciple and friend of
John the apostle. Although Johnson's efforts are directed toward
trying to isolate those passages which might have been included
in the proposed QJ, he also offers his theory as the best solution
to the problem of the apostolic witness of the fourth gospel.[29]

Such "mediate solutions" as proposed by Brown, Schnackenburg,
Hunter, and Johnson offer means of paying heed at once to both the
tradition of the apostolic authorship of the gospel and current
scholarship,[30] and for that reason they commend themselves to the
student. Still, Brown's proposal is deeply interwoven with his
theory of the composition of the gospel which presents problems not

---

[25]Brown, *Gospel*, vol. I, lxxxvii-xcviii.
[26]Hunter, *According*, 104-106; *Gospel*, 12-14.
[27]Hunter, *According*, 118.
[28]*Ibid.*, 106; *Gospel*, 13.
[29]Johnson, 283-291.
[30]Such current scholarship includes both the newer view of the
emergence of the gospel out of a folk tradition and serious attacks
upon the apostolic identity of the evangelist, e.g., Pierson Parker,
"John the Son of Zebedee and the Fourth Gospel," *Journal of Biblical
Literature*, 81 (1962), 35-43.

entirely separable from his proposal for the apostolic origin of
the gospel tradition. (See Chapter Two of Part One for the critique
of Brown's theory of composition.) Much the same kind of reservation must be advanced regarding Braun's theory of composition
upon which Schnackenburg depends. Hunter's hypothesis tries to
avoid the complexities of Brown's theory of composition but becomes
seriously crippled by the identification of the evangelist with
John the elder. Hunter adduces evidence for the identification of
the evangelist which seems to be the very same evidence which
might be used to justify a claim for the eyewitness origin of the
tradition--knowledge of Palestinian topography, Jewish customs,
etc. Further, his suggestion that the same author is responsible
for the gospel and three johannine epistles runs counter to the
evidence which seems to dictate that at least the second and third
epistles (the very ones which claim to be by one who calls himself
"the elder") cannot have come from the same hand as the fourth
gospel.[31]

While Johnson's thesis is suggestive it lacks the refined
source criticism necessary to establish that the passages involving
the beloved disciple came from a document in the hands of the
evangelist. Evidence has been adduced to the opposite effect,
namely, that those passages were added to his tradition by the
evangelist.[32] Notwithstanding the difficulties of his complex
theory of composition, we must conclude that Brown's proposal holds
the greatest promise of the four mediating solutions to the identity
of the originator of the johannine tradition and the fourth evangelist.

C. *John Mark--Originator of Tradition*

Not John, son of Zebedee, but John Mark is indirectly responsible for the gospel, claims the late J.N. Sanders. Sanders brings
together (1) the problems of identifying the gospel with the apostle

---

[31]Rudolf Bultmann, *The Johannine Epistles* (Philadelphia:
Fortress Press, 1973), 1-3; Ernst Haenchen,"Neuere Literatur zu
den Johannesbriefen,"*Theologische Rundschau*, 26 (1960), 1-43, 267-
291,reprinted in Haenchen, *Die Bibel und Wir: Gesammelte Aufsätze,
Zweiter Band* (Tübingen: Mohr, Siebeck, 1968), 235-311; C.H. Dodd,
The Johannine Epistles (London: Hodder and Stoughton, 1946), xlvii-
lvi; Dodd, "The First Epistle of John and the Fourth Gospel,"
Bulletin of the John Rylands Library, 21 (1937), 129-156; J.L.
Houlden, *The Johannine Epistles* (New York: Harper and Row, 1973),
37-38.
[32]Thorwald Lorenzen, *Der Lieblingsjunger im Johannesevangelium:
Eine redaktionsgeschichtliche Studie* (Stuttgart: Katholisches Bibel-
werk, 1971), 12-73. See review by J. Edgar Bruns, *Catholic Biblical
Quarterly*, 36 (1974), 273-274.

John, son of Zebedee, with (2) some evidence for the possible confusion of that disciple with John Mark, and (3) a conviction that
the beloved disciple was Lazarus. With this synthesis he produces
an ingenious, if somewhat speculative, theory of authorship. First,
Sanders poses the problems of linking the gospel with the son of
Zebedee. For example, would a Galilean fisherman be known to the
High Priest in order that he and Peter could gain admittance to the
hearing held on the night of Jesus' arrest (18:15)? Moreover, the
external evidence supporting John, son of Zebedee, as the author of
the gospel is not clear and unambiguous. Therefore, one must look
elsewhere.

Here Sanders links two bits of information: First, it is
Lazarus who is clearly identified as the one Jesus loved (10:5),
and Lazarus' having been raised once from the dead would account
for the rumor that he would never die (21:22). Also, his identity
as the beloved disciple would account for the Judean perspective
of the gospel and the central role in the structure of the gospel
played by the raising of Lazarus. Second, the ancient tradition
of the church that John, son of Zebedee, was responsible for the
gospel seems to have originated among the Valentinian gnostics of
the second century who were looking for apostolic authority to
buttress their understanding of the Christian faith. Hence, the
whole conjunction of the fourth gospel and the son of Zebedee was
erroneous! The truth is that the beloved disciple, Lazarus, left
behind his memoirs which came into the hands of John Mark who
recognized them as the witness of one whom he trusted. He composed
out of these memoirs of the beloved disciple the gospel of John as
we know it. But this John Mark was also an eyewitness of the
historical Jesus, a Jew born about A.D. 15 of a Jewish priestly family
in Jerusalem. He was eventually exiled to Patmos where he wrote
the Revelation, and later returned to Ephesus. 1 John was written
as an introduction to the fourth gospel; and at a later time he also
wrote the other two epistles of John.[33]

The questioning of the dependability of the second century
identification of the fourth evangelist as John, son of Zebedee, is
a valuable contribution to the quest for understanding the persons

---

[33]J.N. Sanders, "St. John on Patmos," *New Testament Studies*,
9 (1962-63), 75-85; Sanders and B.A. Mastin, *A Commentary on the
Gospel According to St. John* (New York: Harper and Row, 1968),
29-52. A similar view is held by J.E. Bruns who produces new
evidence that there was a confusion between John, son of Zebedee,
and John Mark in the ancient church. "The Confusion Between John
and John Mark in Antiquity," *Scripture*, 17 (1965), 23-26, and
"John Mark: A Riddle Within the Johannine Enigma," *Scripture*, 15
(1963), 88-92.

responsible for the fourth gospel, but Sanders' own alternative
solution is burdened with far too many suppositions. On the one
hand, he would have us accept that all the references to the
beloved disciple are explained by a side comment that Jesus loved
Lazarus! On the other hand, he wants us to believe that the
gnostics alone are responsible for attributing the gospel to the
son of Zebedee. Further, his reconstruction again claims the single
authorship of all the New Testament literature attributed to a
"John". Still further, his entire method of arguing seems to overlook that view of the gospel as the result of a long tradition. If
the scholars who maintain the authorship by John, son of Zebedee,
are to be criticized for treating the document as if it were a
modern book owing its existence not to a community but to one mind,
Sanders no less must bear a similar criticism. All in all, while
John Mark must not be excluded from among the candidates for those
involved in the production of the gospel, Sanders' hypothesis seems
unlikely to win support in view of its tenuous foundation in
concrete evidence and its imaginative speculation.[34]

D. Anonymous Source

Finally, a number of scholars have proposed that the identity
of the person(s) responsible for the gospel is beyond recovery.
John Marsh, faced with the evidence for the various solutions to
the authorship question, concludes his brief survey of the matter
with the subtitle,"Splendid Anonymity." The internal evidence, he
suggests, can be used both to support and refute the traditional
identification of the author with John, son of Zebedee; and while
Marsh is willing to concede that the apostle John is the most
likely nominee for the beloved disciple, it is not the case that
one may assume that he is author of the entire gospel. 21:20, 24
may suggest that the beloved disciple was responsible in some way
for that section, perhaps even the entire last chapter; but it is
still another matter to try to assert that the son of Zebedee should

---

[34]It bears mention here that John Mark has recently been
identified as the beloved disciple by two critics working independently of each other. Hugh Schonfield, *The Passover Plot* (New York:
Bernard Geis, 1965), 138-255, weaves this theory into his elaborate
tale. Lewis Johnson, "Who Was the Beloved Disciple?" *The Expository
Times*, 77 (1966), 157-158, set off a lively debate with his proposal that John Mark better fits the internal evidence of the New
Testament for the distinction of the disciple whom Jesus loved than
any other. Cf., J.R. Porter, "Who Was the Beloved Disciple?",
Donald G. Rogers, "Who Was the Beloved Disciple?" (who reasserts
the John, son of Zebedee, solution), and Lewis Johnson, "The Beloved
Disciple--A Reply," *The Expository Times*, 77 (1966), 213-214, 214,
and 380 respectively.

win the title of fourth evangelist.[35]

Barnabas Lindars comes down, too, in favor of the anonymity
of the fourth evangelist. Lindars sides with Sanders in arguing
that the traditional association of the gospel with John, son of
Zebedee, probably originated among the Valentinian gnostics.
"It looks as if the tradition really goes back to the Valentinians,
who themselves derived it from the internal evidence of the Gospel
itself."[36] But Lindars then argues that the internal evidence
supplies little basis for designating John the apostle as the
disciple whom Jesus loved. He undercuts a great many of the
arguments for such a designation by pointing out that the evidence
drawn from the synoptic gospels is totally invalid, for the fourth
gospel omits any mention of the three stories which suggest that
John, son of Zebedee, belonged to the intimate inner circle of the
twelve (the raising of Jairus' daughter, the transfiguration, and
the Gethsemane story). "Thus the identification with John the
Apostle is not only unproven, but also distinctly doubtful."[37]

Lindars' discussion of the identity of the beloved disciple
figures prominently in his argument for the anonymity of the
originator of the johannine tradition; moreover, his treatment of
this subject has some comparable contacts with two other studies
of the beloved disciple recently published, namely, an article by
Rudolf Schnackenburg and a monograph by Thorwald Lorenzen. On the
identity of the beloved disciple all three--Lindars, Schnackenburg,
and Lorenzen--hold the position that he is an anonymous figure.
Lindars believes that he was more than likely one of the original
twelve, but the fourth evangelist wanted the identity of this
disciple whom Jesus loved to remain obscure.[38] Schnackenburg and
Lorenzen, on the other hand, contend that he was not one of the
twelve disciples but a figure in the johannine community. Probably
living in Jerusalem, "he was [the johannine community's] trustworthy
mediator of the tradition, still more a Spirit-illumined proclaimer
and interpreter of Jesus' message, and thus also the ideal disciple
of Jesus."[39]

Lorenzen's study, which is not really an investigation of the

---

[35]John Marsh, *Saint John* (Baltimore, Maryland: Penguin Books,
1968), 21-25.
[36]Lindars, *Gospel*, 29.
[37]*Ibid.*, 33. For a similar view see Siegfried Schulz, *Das
Evangelium*, 2.
[38]Lindars, *Gospel*, 33-34.
[39]Rudolf Schnackenburg, "On the Origin of the Fourth Gospel,"
Jesus and Man's Hope, vol. I, 239-241, quote, 239-240.

identity of the beloved disciple but a redaction historical study
of those passages in which the disciple is mentioned, concludes
that the evangelist projected back into the time of Jesus a figure
active in the contemporary johannine church. He was clearly a
definite person in the community, but for the first time in the
work of the fourth evangelist he is represented as playing a
special function in the life of the community.[40]

All three then argue that the beloved disciple was a concrete
historical person who in the fourth gospel is given an ideal or
symbolic role. Schnackenburg speaks of that symbolic role as a
"paradigmatic significance," and Lorenzen points out that it is
typical of the fourth evangelist that he should assign historical
figures roles in the contemporary situation of the community.[41]
For Lindars, the evangelist has capitalized upon the faceless
quality of most of the disciples in the tradition to make one of
them into the disciple with special discernment and loyalty and
thereby facilitate the presentation of the kerygma through his
gospel.[42] But both Schnackenburg and Lorenzen believe that the
function of the beloved disciple is to represent a position in the
struggle in which the evangelist's own church was involved.
Schnackenburg rejects the thesis that there is a rivalry between
Peter and the beloved disciple in the gospel. He further rejects
the claim that that rivalry symbolizes a conflict between the
ecclesiastical office of the church and the apostolic itinerant
prophetism. (This is a position espoused by A. Kragerud.)[43]
Rather, the association of the beloved disciple with Peter was
intended to enhance the authority of the johannine church, an
authority which was apparently being challenged at the time the
evangelist wrote. The johannine church of the evangelist's day
was struggling to gain recognition for itself among the wider
community of Christians, and the role of the beloved disciple in
the gospel was tailored to advance that recognition.[44] Lorenzen

---

[40]Lorenzen, 76, 79, 82. Jürgen Roloff has compared the
johannine beloved disciple and the teacher of righteousness of the
Qumran literature and has found some intriguing, if perhaps exaggerated, parallels. "Der johanneische 'Lieblingsjünger' und der
Lehrer der Gerechtigkeit," *New Testament Studies*, 15 (1968), 129-
151.
[41]Lorenzen, 80-81; Schnackenburg, "Origin", 234; Lindars,
Gospel, 34.
[42]Lindars, *Gospel*, 34.
[43]Alv Kragerud, *Der Lieblingsjünger im Johannesevangelium* (Oslo:
Universitätsverlag, 1959).
[44]Schnackenburg, "Origin", 233-235, 239-241.

contends with Kragerud, however, that the beloved disciple is intentionally set over against Peter in the fourth gospel. The beloved disciple represents the struggle of johannine Christianity in relation to other Christian groups of the time, and Peter more than likely represents just such a non-johannine group, perhaps conservative Jewish Christianity. "By placing the beloved disciple above Peter, the johannine community is clearly and certainly cautioned to deny Peter's particular conception of Christianity. Thereby it is clear that the person and authority of the beloved disciple, which represents johannine Christianity, go hand in hand."[45]

Lindars concludes, with the implicit support of both Schnackenburg and Lorenzen's studies, that the identities of both the evangelist and the beloved disciple must remain veiled in anonymity and that there is no reason to contend for an eyewitness tradition in the gospel. Such positions as these--especially Lindars'--seem to represent the wisdom of caution in the matter of identifying the originator of the johannine tradition and the evangelist himself. Moreover, Lindars, Schnackenburg, and Lorenzen suggest the manner in which these questions must be approached in the light of the developments in form and redaction criticism. The important thing about their studies is that they are highly sensitive to the likelihood that the evangelist is speaking as much out of the situation of his own community as articulating a tradition. To probe the identities of either the evangelist or the source of his tradition must involve the kind of redactional study Lorenzen has undertaken. While it may be that their specific positions on any detail need considerably more confirmation than is yet available, it is their approach to the problems which seems to me to be in the spirit of recent johannine studies.

---

[45]Lorenzen, 96. A milder anti-petrinism is found by S. Agourides, who thinks it is tempered by the representation of the friendship between Peter and John. "Peter and John in the Fourth Gospel," *Studia Evangelica*, vol. IV, 3-7.

CHAPTER II

THE INTELLECTUAL MILIEU OF THE EVANGELIST

    One's understanding of a text depends in every case upon the
establishment of a context of thought out of which the text has
been written. To interpret properly any written document it is
necessary to have some sort of concept of the world of thought in
which that document was written and hence in the light of which its
expressions and concepts are to be understood. This is true no
less for a modern text than for an ancient one, but the difficulties
in determining what context of thought is to be presupposed for
the interpretation of an ancient text are formidable ones when
compared to a modern document. The task of determining the degree
of affinities an ancient writer has with this or that milieu of
thought has been especially burdensome for the biblical student
since the dawn of the critical era.
    Much historical study has gone into the clarification of this
sort of question in the area of contemporary biblical studies, but
it seems that in the case of the fourth gospel there has been a
disproportionate amount of such research. The intellectual milieu
of the fourth evangelist has posed a continual challenge for the
student of that document.[1] One need only read the appropriate
section of an introduction to one of the standard commentaries to
understand the problem. To read such a survey of the alternative
contexts which have been considered for the interpretation of the
fourth gospel--contexts which all allegedly have affinities with
the gospel--is almost like reading a brief survey of the *whole field*
of religio-philosphical positions extant in the Greco-Roman world

---

[1]See Howard, *The Fourth Gospel*, 144-163.

of the first century of the Christian era! The novice is tempted
to ask, with what intellectual milieu of the first century does
the evangelist *not* have some affinities? As important as the
establishment of such an intellectual context is for interpretation,
the task seems sometimes beyond the scope of modern historical
methods![2]

In the years since the advent of biblical criticism the search
for the intellectual milieu of the fourth gospel continued vigorously.
But in the 1950s the quest was particularly marked by a number of
features. Quite clearly, a dominant concern in research on the
intellectual milieu of the gospel was either the refutation or
defense of Bultmann's controversial proposal that the gospel was
written out of the context of an oriental gnosticism. Did the
gospel's affinities lie with gnostic materials which, although
admittedly post-Christian in literary form, were evidence of a
pre-Christian gnosis?[3]

Bultmann's claims set off a long and fiery debate, focusing
for the most part on the question of the existence of a gnostic
movement before the advent of Christianity. While gnosticism is
known most clearly in its second century Christian form, is it
possible to prove the existence of such a mode of thought prior
to the first century? Is it possible, further, to prove that
gnosticism influenced the formation of johannine Christianity?

Second, as the documents from Qumran gradually became available, the points of similarity between their thought and that of
the fourth gospel were recognized.[4] It then became a preoccupation
of students of the fourth gospel to attempt some sort of explanation
for these affinities. Perhaps on no other portion of the New
Testament did the discovery of the ancient documents have such an
effect, for as Frank Cross observed, "Linguistic and conceptual
contacts between the scrolls and the New Testament are nowhere more
in evidence than in the Gospel of John."[5]

Finally, the search for the intellectual milieu of the fourth
evangelist in the 1950s was increasingly affected by the awareness
that the thought of the entire Greco-Roman world of the first
century tended to be syncretistic. The older efforts to label the

---

[2]Robert Kysar, "The Background of the Prologue of the Fourth
Gospel: A Critique of Historical Methods," *Canadian Journal of
Theology*, 16 (1970), 250-255.

[3]Bultmann, *Gospel*, passim.

[4]Herbert Braun, *Qumran und das Neue Testament* (Tübingen: J.C.B.
Mohr, 1966), Bd. II, 135-144.

[5]Frank M. Cross Jr., *The Ancient Library of Qumran* (Garden
City, N.Y.: Doubleday, 1961), 206.

fourth gospel as "Jewish" or "Greek" were considered to be mis-
leading. There was no Judaism without hellenistic influences and
similarily no hellenism that was potentially untouched by Jewish
modes of thought.[6] These three dominant features of the search up
to the earlier 1960s are still evident in current fourth gospel
research: The debate over the question of a pre-Christian gnosticism has not yet been settled and new evidence seems yet to be
forthcoming. The efforts to appropriate the findings of the Qumran
discoveries for johannine studies go on. And the struggle persists
to define as precisely as possible the perimeters of a proposed
intellectual milieu for the fourth evangelist and still recognize
the syncretistic nature of any milieu of the time.

The arguments for the various milieus in the current literature
have been built around the analysis of a number of johannine themes,
for the most part. For that reason, the following survey of research will be organized around those themes. This form of organization has been chosen in preference over the standard rehearsal
of the proposed backgrounds--Old Testament, rabbinical Judaism,
heterodox Judaism, hellenistic religions, gnosticism, etc.[7] --in
order better to show the manner in which evidence for different
positions is drawn from the same johannine data. Following the
survey of the various themes treated in the search for the evangelist's world of thought, the leading conclusions of recent research
will be summarized.

A. *Johannine Themes Employed in the Search for the Intellectual
    Milieu of the Evangelist:*

1. Old Testament Citations and Allusions in the Fourth Gospel.
Although there are relatively fewer citations of the Old
Testament in the fourth gospel than in the other gospels, the
fourth evangelist's use of the Old Testament materials has been
studied with some interesting results, especially for the question
of the intellectual milieu. It has been claimed that the fourth
evangelist's manner of employing the Old Testament suggests with
considerable force that he was thoroughly trained in the ancient
scriptures. Edwin D. Freed argues that a careful study of the Old

_____

[6]E.g., Morton Smith, "Palestinian Judaism in the First Century,"
Israel: Its Role in Civilization, M. Davis, ed. (New York: The
Seminary Israel Institute of the Jewish Theological Seminary, 1956),
67-81. On the multilingual character of the Palestinians, see
J.A. Fitzmyer, "The Language of Palestine in the First Century A.D.,"
Catholic Biblical Quarterly, 32 (1970) 501-531.
    [7]E.g., Schnackenburg, *Gospel*, vol. I, 119-149.

Testament allusions shows that the evangelist is citing them from
memory,[8] and Schnackenburg concludes that such a study shows "more
clearly how deeply rooted the fourth evangelist was in the Old
Testament and biblical theology."[9] Freed, however, thinks that
the evangelist knew both the Hebrew and Greek forms of the scripture, while F.-M. Braun contends that it is the Palestinian canon
alone which was known to the evangelist (and perhaps a later
redactor utilized the Greek translation of the Old Testament--the
Septuagint).[10] Both Freed and Braun along with Schnackenburg,
however, agree that the evangelist's use of the scriptures was
free; he cited and adapted scriptures to his theological purposes.
Sometimes his citations are direct, sometimes indirect, sometimes
composite.[11]

It is Braun's conviction that the fourth evangelist always
preserves the essential meaning of the Old Testament passages when
he employs them, notwithstanding a certain freedom of citation.
This leads Braun to argue that the fourth evangelist viewed the
Old Testament scriptures as inspired, authoritative literature (a
view which has found confirmation in the work of Anthony Hanson
on John 10:34[12]). If such is the case, it places the fourth evangelist squarely in a Jewish milieu and argues against the claims that
the major influence upon his thought was gnostic, since gnosticism
was not favorably disposed to the Old Testament as authoritative
literature.[13] Such a conclusion, however, assumes that any early
form of gnosticism shared this anti Old Testament view with second
century gnosticism.

A recent study of both the explicit citations and the more
general allusions to Hebrew scripture in the fourth gospel challenges
headlong most of these conclusions held by Freed, Braun, and Schnackenburg. Günter Reim argues that the fourth evangelist had before

---

[8]Edwin D. Freed, *Old Testament Quotations in the Gospel of
John* (Leiden: E.J. Brill, 1965), 6, 95, 130. Cf., Freed, "Some
Old Testament Influences on the Prologue of John," *A Light Unto
My Path: Old Testament Studies in Honor of Jacob M. Myers*, Howard
N. Bream, Ralph D. Heim, and Carey A. Moore, eds. (Philadelphia:
Temple University Press, 1974), 145-161.
[9]Schnackenburg, *Gospel*, vol. I, 123.
[10]Freed, *Old Testament Quotations*, 6; F.-M. Braun, *Jean le
Théologien, Les grandes traditions d'Israël et l'accord des
Ecritures selon le Quatrième Evangile* (Paris: J. Gabalda, 1964),
17. In agreement with Freed is John O'Rourke, "John's Fulfilment
Texts," *Sciences Ecclésiastiques*, 19 (1967), 433-443.
[11]Freed, *Old Testament Quotations*, 37, 129; F.-M. Braun, *Jean,
Les grandes*, 15, 17; Schnackenburg, *Gospel*, vol. I, 123.
[12]F.-M. Braun, *Jean, Les grandes*, 15; Anthony Hanson, "John's
Citation of Psalm LXXXII," *New Testament Studies*, 11 (1964-65), 162.
[13]Erich Fascher, "Christologie und Gnosis im vierten Evangelium,"
Theologische Literaturzeitung, 93 (1968), 725.

him no written texts of the Old Testament whatsoever, except perhaps
the Septuagint Psalm 68. Instead, the evangelist cited and alluded
to the Old Testament only as he was led to do so by his tradition;
the only exceptions to this practice are the allusions to Psalm 69
(in the Septuagint it is number 68)--2:17; 15:25; 19:28. The
citations do not confirm the judgment that the evangelist had wide
and thorough knowledge of the Old Testament. The evidence shows
only that he knew the scripture employed in the traditions he
received and the Septuagint Psalm 68. Nor does the evidence
support the contention that the evangelist alluded to Hebrew scripture from memory. The language used in alluding to Old Testament
material is almost without exception traditional language out of
the sources the evangelist employed. The inaccuracies of the
citations and allusions support the conclusion that the evangelist
did not possess a written Old Testament text and simply perpetuated
the material he found in his traditions.

Furthermore, aside from Psalm 68, it is likely that the evangelist did not know the Septuagint; the Hebrew text of the Old Testament seems to have been the one most heavily influencing the
traditions used by the evangelist. Still, Reim believes the evangelist's traditions indicate that his community was acquainted with
and drew upon a general stock of Old Testament knowledge common to
Jewish and Christian instruction. More specifically, he was probably
related to a community deeply immersed in the wisdom tradition
"whose language and conceptuality is coined from the Old Testament."[14]

Reím's reading of the evidence contradicts Freed's contention
that the evangelist cited the Old Testament from memory; that he was
thoroughly familiar with the Old Testament, as Schnackenburg
believes; and that he was free in his use of Hebrew scripture, as
Freed, Braun, and Schnackenburg would all have it. Still, all the
scholars seem to concur that the evangelist's community was one
rooted in the Old Testament. Reim is probably correct in focusing
attention not upon the evangelist's own use of Old Testament scriptures but upon his traditions; in so doing Reim places the question
of the use of Old Testament in the fourth gospel within the context
of tradition criticism where it properly belongs--something both
Freed and Braun fail to do. The question cannot be simply how did
the evangelist use the Old Testament, but how do his sources/tra-
ditions use it and how then does he in turn use them. Reim perhaps
too helps us to be a bit more honest in assessing the evangelist's
use of scripture by recognizing that he is faithful to his traditions

---

[14]Reim, 93-96, 188-189, 231-232, quote, 282.

and reflects only such knowledge of the Old Testament as is found there. Consequently, Reim's study seems stronger in several ways than either Freed or Braun's. However, Reim uses "tradition" in a slippery manner throughout his investigation, and one is not always sure what constitutes a "tradition." Moreover, he fails to prove that passages had a pre-johannine, "traditional" existence before their employment by the evangelist. Likewise, his contention that the evangelist was indebted to a strong wisdom tradition is not as solidly borne out by the evidence as Reim would seem to assume. These difficulties aside, the clear tendency of the studies of the Old Testament allusions in the fourth gospel is toward demonstrating that the evangelist and his tradition had firm roots in some form of Jewish milieu. Admittedly, however, these studies provide little *unequivocal* evidence toward that conclusion.[15]

2. The Logos Concept.[16]

Of course, no johannine motif has been given greater attention than the alluring conception of the logos in the prologue of the gospel. Not least of all has the argument waged over the background of John's concept. While the purely hellenistic Jewish (i.e., Philonic) parallels have in the past been emphasized, the studies of recent years in this area have looked more and more in the direction of Old Testament and Palestinian Jewish motifs. Raymond Brown's appendix on the logos concept in his commentary investigates the hellenistic background but declares the "basic theme of the Prologue is strange to the Hellenistic parallels that have been offered." On the other hand, "in the Old Testament presentation of

_____

[15]A number of studies of the citation of Psalm 82 (John 10:34) have produced evidence for the Jewish, and more specifically rabbinic, elements in the thought of the evangelist: Hanson, "John's Citation", 160; Hanson, "John's Citation of Psalm LXXXII Reconsidered," *New Testament Studies*, 13 (1966-67), 363-367; James S. Ackerman, "The Rabbinic Interpretation of Psalm 82 and the Gospel of John," *Harvard Theological Review*, 59 (1966), 186-188; J.A. Emerton, "Melchizedek and the Gods: Fresh Evidence for the Jewish Background of John X. 34-36," *Journal of Theological Studies*, 17 (1966), 399-401. Other related studies bearing upon this subject include Dietrich Schirmer, *Rechtsgeschichtliche Untersuchungen zum Johannes-Evangelium* (Berlin: Ragnit, 1964) (see especially, 207) and A. Laurentin, "*we-attah--kai nun*, formule charactéristique des textes juridiques et liturgiques, à propos de Jean 18.5," *Biblica*, 45 (1964), 168-197 and 413-432.

[16]This discussion avoids for the moment the associated question of whether the prologue stems from the evangelist's own work or from the work of another author. On this question see Teeple, *Literary Origin*, 126-135; Brown, *Gospel*, vol. I, 18-23; J.A.T. Robinson, "The Relation of the Prologue to the Gospel of St. John," *New Testament Studies*, 9 (1963), 120-129; Ernst Haenchen, "Probleme des johanneischen 'Prologs'," *Zeitschrift für Theologie und Kirche*, 60 (1963), 305-334.

Wisdom, there are good parallels for almost every detail of the
Prologue's description of the Word."[17] That wisdom is identified
with the word of God is surely implicit in Jewish wisdom literature
(e.g., Sirach 24:3). She is divine (e.g., Wisdom 7:25-26). She
was active in creation (Wisdom 9:9) and came into the world only
to experience rejection (Wisdom 9:10 and Sirach 15:7). These are
clearly parallels to what the evangelist claims of the logos in
his prologue.[18]

Support for Brown is found among such scholars as Henry
Moeller and the French Roman Catholics, André Feuillet and F.-M.
Braun. Moeller, Braun, and Feuillet speak of the convergence of
Jewish wisdom and Old Testament word of God concepts into a single
rabbinic motif which influenced the fourth evangelist. In the
Greek world the logos concept has primarily to do with understanding
and is an intellectual possession. In contrast, the word of God in
the Old Testament is never a human possession, but is the historical
act by which God addresses man. The mutual penetration of the
concepts of the prophetic word and the divine wisdom is increasingly
evident in post-exilic Judaism. It is that combination which lies
behind the johannine logos doctrine.[19]

Braun understands that the merger of these two themes is
further evidenced in the dual christology of John--the logos and
the son of man themes. The former is more fully representative
of the wisdom motif, and the latter of the prophetic, word of God
theme.[20] Moeller's conclusion is perhaps representative of those
who find the wisdom/word milieu most persuasive for the logos concept: "It is hard to resist the conclusion that John consciously
set out to show that Jesus not only fulfilled the messianic
implications of the Torah, Prophets, and Psalms, but also that Jesus
incarnated the Wisdom of God in a unique way."[21]

Others, who in no significant manner are aligned against the
wisdom/word background, find greater evidence of certain explicit
rabbinic patterns of thought betrayed in the johannine logos concept.
James Ackermann, for instance, contends that the wisdom theme in

---

[17]Brown, *Gospel*, vol. I, 520, 523.
[18]*Ibid.*, 522-523.
[19]F.-M. Braun, *Jean, Les grandes*, 137; André Feuillet, *Le
Prologue du quatrième Évangile* (Paris: Brouwer, 1968), 224-225,
239-242; Henry R. Moeller, "Wisdom Motifs and John's Gospel,"
Bulletin of the Evangelical Theological Society, 6 (1963), 93-98.
[20]F.-M. Braun, *Jean, Les grandes*, 137; see further, Basil de
Pinto, "Word and Wisdom in St. John," *Scripture*, 19 (1967), 19-27
and 107-122.
[21]Moeller, 98.

Jewish thought came under the influence of speculation and mythology
centering in the Sinai incident of the giving of the law (see, for
example, Midrash Rabbah, Lev. 11:3). Hence the prologue of John
in general and the logos concept in particular are suggestive of
the "Sinaisms" of later Jewish thought. Both the Sinai myth and
the prologue "describe the coming of God's Word into the world,
and the effect which it had upon those who received it...they became godlike. In both cases God's Word met with rejection." It
is Ackermann's argument, then, that the evangelist was well
acquainted with the Sinai myth and intended to contrast the giving
of the law in Jewish tradition with the appearance of Christ.[22]

Peder Borgen and Martin McNamara have found a somewhat different kind of rabbinic setting presupposed in the prologue of the
gospel. Borgen has argued that these verses are a midrashic interpretation of Genesis 1:1ff in the manner found in the Jersualem
Targum on Genesis 3:21. The words of Genesis 1:1ff are found in
the prologue along with an interpretation by means of "paraphrasing
expansions" in 1:1-5; and in verses 6-18 the same words reappear
and are more elaborately interpreted in reverse order. (In verses
1-2, "word" and "God" are the key words; in verse 3, "all things"
and "came to be"; in verses 4-5, "light." Then in 7-9 "light"is
the theme; in 10, "world" and "came to be"; and in 14-18, "word"
and "God".)[23]

McNamara's extensive studies have tried to lay bare the targumic
background of the New Testament in general, and he has made some
interesting observations regarding the logos concept. In the
Palestinian Targum (Neofiti) on Exodus 15:18 there is an elaborate
interpretative paraphrase of the scripture which stresses the
identification of the word of God with the primordial light. The
parallels between this targumic passage and the prologue are
striking: the prevailing darkness, the word's existence at the
beginning of creation, the identification of word and light, and
the shining of the light in the darkness. McNamara thinks it is
obvious that the fourth evangelist has adapted the hypostatized
light of the targumic exegesis of creation to the new creation in
Christ. Consequently, it may not be in the off-beat Judaism of
the Qumran variety that we find the milieu for John's thought as

---

[22]Ackerman, 188-191, quote 188.
[23]Peder Borgen, "Observations on the Targumic Character of the
Prologue of John," *New Testament Studies*, 16 (1969-70), 288-295.
See also "Logos Was the True Light. Contributions to the Interpretation of the Prologue of John," *Novum Testamentum*, 14 (1972),
115-130; and W.F. Hamby, "Creation and Gospel. A Brief Comparison
of Genesis 1, 1-2, 12," *Studia Evangelica*, vol. V, pt. II, 69-74.

much as in the mainline Jewish traditions, particularly in the
form known to us in the targums.[24]

Against this evidence that the evangelist was most influenced
by Jewish modes of thought in his articulation of the logos concept, there are those who have recently found evidence of more
non-Jewish influence. Rudolf Schnackenburg finds reason to believe
the Jewish wisdom ideas provide meaningful links with the fourth
gospel. But still he contends that the logos concept must be viewed
basically as a Greek idea worked over by the evangelist to encompass
the Jewish notions of the word of God, wisdom, and Torah.[25]
Further, Siegfried Schulz (in an excursus on the history of religions
background for the logos concept) argues that the general concept
of the logos and the whole structure of its presentation in the
prologue root in hellenistic Jewish speculation concerning wisdom
(e.g., Wisdom 9:9-12; Sirach 24:5-31). However, the absolute
personification of the logos in the prologue cannot be accounted
for by such a background; it stems, instead, from a hellenistic
gnosticism where the concept of a fully personalized mediator
was well-known.[26]

---

[24]Martin McNamara, "*Logos* of the Fourth Gospel and *Memra* of
the Palestinian Targum (Ex 12:42)," *The Expository Times*, 79 (1968),
115-117. See also *Targum and Testament* (Grand Rapids, Michigan:
Wm. B. Eerdmanns, 1972), 101-106, and *The New Testament and the
Palestinian Targum to the Pentateuch* (Rome: Biblical Institute
Press, 1966), 255f, 145-149. A valuable and critical review of
Targum and Testament by Daniel J. Harrington raises some funda-
mental questions regarding McNamara's whole thesis: *Catholic
Biblical Quarterly*, 35 (1973), 253-254. On the question of an
Aramaic document behind the gospel and the influence of Aramaic
on its language see S. Brown, "From Burney to Black: The Fourth
Gospel and the Aramaic Question," *Catholic Biblical Quarterly*, 26
(1964), 323-339.
[25]Schnackenburg, *Gospel*, vol. I, 493. In essential agreement
with Schnackenburg is J.C. O'Neil, "The Prologue to St. John's
Gospel," *Journal of Theological Studies*, n.s. 20 (1969), 41-52.
However, Jack Sanders has come to a conclusion of an opposite kind
from Schnackenburg's. Sanders maintains that in Jewish thought
one finds that "there existed an emerging mythical configuration
which could be attached, in the literature and in the religious
consciousness of the Jew of the day, to various and different
redeemer or revealer figures, above all Wisdom, Word, and Man
(Adam)." *The New Testament Christological Hymns* (Cambridge:
University Press, 1971), 96. See also the article by Donald A.
Hagner, who shows the difficulties in describing the milieu as a
Philonic Hellenized Judaism: "The Vision of God in Philo and John:
A Comparative Study," *Journal of the Evangelical Society*, 14
(1971), 81-93.
[26]Siegfried Schulz, *Das Evangelium*, 27-29. Some argue however,
that the personification of the logos is simply the evangelist's
unique addition to or interpretation of the Old Testament-Jewish
themes. See, for instance, P. Hugolinus Langkamer, "Zur Herkunft
des Logostitels im Johannesprolog," *Biblische Zeitschrift*, 9
(1965), 91-94.

Erich Fascher's attack upon the proposed gnostic background for the fourth gospel is directed primarily at Bultmann and was written before the appearance of Schulz's commentary. His arguments against a gnostic milieu for the prologue would, however, seem relevant to Schulz's proposal as well. Fascher argues that for three reasons one cannot postulate a gnostic influence upon the mind of the author of the prologue: First, the conceptions of the world and humanity in the prologue are notably not dualistic but presuppose the work of God. Second, the incarnation of the logos (1:14) defies any effort to root the evangelist's thought in gnostic mentality. Third, there is no concept of the pre-existence of the human soul in the prologue, which surely would not be the case had the prologue emerged under gnostic influence.[27]

The bulk of research published in the recent past has found more reason to locate the author of the prologue in a Jewish-rabbinic setting than any other, and one would have to say that a clear direction of that kind is discernible. The proponents of some sort of non-Jewish setting have not been overwhelmed, but the gnostic hypothesis for the background of the logos concept appears less tenable in the light both of the stronger evidence for an Old Testament-Jewish milieu and the effective refutations of arguments for a gnostic influence. The debate over this difficult question, however, has obviously not been settled.

3. Johannine Christology.

Beyond the specific christological concept of logos employed exclusively in the prologue of the gospel, what can be said about the intellectual milieu which influenced the evangelist's other christological formulations? While the assertion is often made that the christology of the gospel is only a logical extension of the earlier Christian formulations,[28] the uniquely johannine christological features have propelled scholars into the search for an intelligible background for those features.

Naturally, certain critics have claimed that the evidence for the general christology of John, like the logos concept in particular, points clearly in the direction of the complex of Old Testament and Jewish ideas focused about the wisdom and word motifs. Brown finds the general portrait of Christ in the fourth gospel to have been influenced by a number of ways of thinking current in Palestine from the time of Jesus until the completion of

---

[27]Fascher, 726.
[28]E.g., Morris, *Gospel*, 63-64.

the gospel. But more specifically, "the fourth evangelist saw in
Jesus the culmination of a tradition that runs through the Wisdom
literature of the Old Testament." Brown cites a number of parallels
between the wisdom concept and the Christ of the fourth gospel.
For example, just as Jesus provokes a division among those who
encounter him, so the appearance of wisdom upon the earth is said
to divide men (Proverbs 8:17; 1:28; Sirach 6:27; and Wisdom 6:12).[29]
Likewise, Moeller understands that wisdom as an "arbiter of human
destinies" (e.g., Proverbs 1:20-33) parallels the johannine Christ;
so, too, do the patterns found in Ecclesiasticus 24:19-22 and
Wisdom 6:12-16 where wisdom introduces men to God by inviting and
admonishing them to seek her.[30]

F.-M. Braun's second volume in his four-volume study of "John,
the theologian," argues extensively for the prophetic and sapiential
(wisdom) themes interwoven into the christology of the fourth gospel.
The johannine christological concepts of the messiah, the "lamb of
God", the high priest, and the hiddenness of the Christ all root
in prophetic symbolism. Very often Braun finds the fourth evangelist merging Old Testament and wisdom themes of various kinds into
his christological formulations. A case in point is the alleged
interweaving of the royal king messiahship with that of the high
priestly messiah.[31] Studies of the use of the title, *christos*, in
the fourth gospel have tended to confirm the hypothesis that the
evangelist presupposed the Jewish use of the term arising out of
Old Testament interpretation.[32]

Peder Borgen has investigated johannine christology from the
point of view of its similarities with pre-Christian Jewish concepts
of the "agents" of God and is convinced that the evangelist's view
of Christ is shaped around those Jewish concepts. First, one finds
striking parallels between the johannine assertion that Christ is
an agent of the Father and certain rabbinic principles of agency.

---

[29]Brown, *Gospel*, vol. I, cxxiii-cxxiv, quote cxxii.
[30]Moeller, 95-97.
[31]F.-M. Braun, *Jean, Les grandes*, 49-152. See Raymond Brown's
sympathetically critical review of Braun's work, *Catholic Biblical
Quarterly*, 26 (1964), 481-482. Brown is somewhat disappointed in
Braun's volume and dissents from the heavy emphasis Braun places
upon the contrast of Jesus and Moses in the gospel to the exclusion
of Mosaic themes used in a positive way. Still, Brown believes
Braun demonstrates the deep roots which the fourth gospel has in
Israel. A similar view of those roots is advanced by Reim, 247-260.
[32]Marius de Jonge, "The Use of the Word *Christos* in the
Johannine Epistles," *Studies in John*, 71-74. See also, S. Sabugal,
Christos: Investigacion exegetical sobre la cristologia joannea
(Barcelona: Herder, 1972), known to me only through Casimir Bernas'
review, *Catholic Biblical Quarterly*, 36 (1974), 139-140.

In both, the agent is subordinate and obedient to the sender, but is represented as one with the sender. The task of the agent is set within a legal context resembling a lawsuit in both Jewish and johannine thought. Both understand that the agent returns to the sender after having appointed others to continue his function. But this concept of agency is applied to the heavenly world only in the work of Philo where we find a heavenly being fulfilling the function. "The conclusion is that John and Philo have in common the idea of a heavenly figure as one who sees God, associate this figure with Israel, and also have in common several of the other terms and concepts which are crystallized around the same heavenly figure." Hence, Borgen believes and convincingly demonstrates that the evangelist has combined the principle of agency out of rabbinic Judaism with the concept of a heavenly agent in hellenistic (Philonic) Judaism.[33]

Among the more specific themes of johannine christology which have been investigated with an eye toward establishing the intellectual milieu of the evangelist is the descending-ascending son of man theme. Characteristically, we find scholars arguing respectively for Old Testament, later Jewish and rabbinic, and finally gnostic backgrounds for this theme. Bruce Vawter, in a study of the parallels between Ezekiel and the fourth gospel, finds a number of resemblances between the two, but especially the utilization of the myth of a primeval man (*Urmensch*) which provides the backdrop for the johannine concept of the son of man descending and ascending. (Especially compare John 5:24ff and Ezekiel chapters 1-3). The johannine anarthrous expression for the son of man (that is, the absence of the article--"son of man" as opposed to "the son of the man"--in the Greek construction), which is unique among the gospels, may be due to the influence of Ezekiel upon the evangelist's thought.[34]

But Moeller finds the whole idea of the descending-ascending Christ rooted in the wisdom literature in which wisdom comes down to relate to men (Ecclesiasticus 24:8; Apocryphal Baruch 3:37) and ascends once again (Enoch 42). Moreover, wisdom and the son of man concepts are already intimately related in the Similitudes of

[33]Peder Borgen, "God's Agent in the Fourth Gospel," *Religions in Antiquity: Essays in Memory of Erwin Ramsdell Goodenough,* ed. by Jacob Neusner (Leiden: Brill, 1968), 137-147, quote 146-147. Additional evidence for a rabbinic background for johannine christology is offered by J. Massingberd Ford, "'Mingled Blood' From the Side of Christ," *New Testament Studies,* 15 (1969), 337-338.
[34]Bruce Vawter, "Ezekiel and John," *Catholic Biblical Quarterly,* 26 (1964), 451-454.

Enoch 37-71, Moeller points out.[35] However, the exploitation of
the ascension theme in John, argues McNamara, comes most likely out
of a targumic usage. There McNamara claims to have discovered
that an Aramaic word for ascent (*'stlq*) has taken on the meaning
"to die" and "to be exalted"--precisely the double meaning given
to the word "exaltation" in John. So in the Targum of Psalm 68:18
the death of Moses is spoken of in such a way as to suggest his
ascension and exaltation into heaven. John was obviously dependent
upon an Aramaic tradition now embedded in the Palestinian Targums,
McNamara concludes.[36]

     Rudolf Schnackenburg in an article (1964) argues against the
origins of the johannine son of man concept in the gnostic redeemer
myth and finds it much more likely that Jewish-hellenistic wisdom
speculation was the basis of the evangelist's presentation of this
motif. The ingredients for John's son of man christology, in
addition to the Christian tradition itself, are present in Jewish
apocalyptic literature (e.g., Baruch 3:37f) and wisdom literature
(Wisdom 9:16f). There is one element of that christology, however,
which Schnackenburg finds more clearly aligned with gnostic thought,
namely, the concern for the origin and the destiny (the "whence"
and the "whither") of the redeemer (e.g., 7:27f, 34ff; 8:14; 9:29f;
12:35; 14:4ff; and 19:9). But he concludes that the evangelist was
answering a gnostic concern with this theme rather than borrowing
the idea itself.[37]

     In his commentary, Schnackenburg refines his argument a bit
further. He denies that the absolute "son" title is an adaptation
of a messianic designation or that it had reference to the hellenistic concept of the "divine man." He finds some striking parallels
with its use in John and certain gnostic materials (The Odes of
Solomon, The Gospel of Truth, The Epistle of Jacob, and the Apocryphon
of John), e.g., the movement of the son into the realm of the world
and then back to the father, and the conducting to their home with

---

[35]Moeller, 94-95. George MacRae has argued that gnostic concepts of sophia were influenced by and represent a revolt against
Jewish wisdom concepts. By implication his work tends to refute
claims that johannine thought was shaped by gnostic, not Jewish
wisdom motifs. "The Jewish Background of the Gnostic Sophia Myth,"
Novum Testamentum, 12 (1970), 86-101.

[36]Martin McNamara, "The Ascension and the Exaltation of Christ
in the Fourth Gospel," *Scripture*, 19 (1967), 65-73. See also
McNamara, *Targum and Testament*, 143, and *The New Testament and*,
145-149.

[37]Schnackenburg, "Der Menschensohn im Johannesevangelium,"
New Testament Studies, 11 (1964-65), 135-137.

the Father those receptive to the revelation. The differences
lie in the historicity of the redeemer in John's thought and the
absence in the gospel of any concept of the pre-existence of the
human soul.

> However, the formal and structural similarities (above
> all for the gnostic redeemer myth...) make it appear
> possible that the fourth evangelist, in spite of a pri-
> mary dependence on the early Christian tradition, took
> into consideration the gnostic manner of speaking of
> the "Son (of God)" and thereby bound it with his view
> of the Son Christology. He wanted to give the true
> Christian answer to the expression of gnostic questions
> in his environment (cf., 7:28, 33f; 8:14); he opposed
> the mythical form of the gnostic redeemer to the one
> true "Son" who as a true man on the earth revealed the
> Father and led men to Him.[38]

So, while Schnackenburg seems, especially in his later commentary,
to stress the similarities of the johannine son christology to the
gnostic redeemer myth, he still maintains that those similarities
are to be understood less as a borrowing of thought from the gnostic
materials and more as a Christian response to some form of the
gnostic redeemer concept.

But the gnostic proposal finds its strong proponent again in
the person of Schulz. He is convinced that, while the son of man
title stems from late Jewish apocalyptic materials (e.g., Daniel 7
and 4 Ezra 13), it has been "gnosticized" by the time it appears
as the background for the fourth gospel. This is evident particularly in two points: (1) the concept of pre-existence connected
with the son of man idea and (2) the theme of the son's being
sent by the father. A gnostic "speech tradition" has influenced
the johannine meaning of the expression, and a number of passages
suggest that the typical apocalyptic titles in John have been
reshaped by a gnostic conception of Jesus as the son of God and the
one sent by the Father (8:28; 12:23f; 13:31f).[39]

Schulz finds the johannine concept of Jesus' being sent into
the world by his father set within a thoroughly gnostic dualism of
God and the world and expressing a gnosticized understanding of the
divine mediator between the two worlds. But Juan Peter Miranda
contends that the sending or envoy motif is clearly out of the Old
Testament prophetic tradition. His monograph investigates the
johannine formulas employed to express the idea of Jesus' being

---

[38]Schnackenburg, *Gospel*, vol. II, 162-166, quote, 166.
[39]Schulz, *Das Evangelium*, 63-64, 211. See further, Schulz,
Untersuchungen zur Menschensohn-Christologie im Johannesevangelium
(Göttingen: Vandenhoeck und Ruprecht, 1957) and a critical review
of Schulz's work, James Robinson, "Recent Research in the Fourth
Gospel," *Journal of Biblical Literature*, 78 (1959), 242-246.

sent by the Father, and he finds that they are grounded in the call
and sending of the Old Testament prophets (e.g., Exodus 3:12; 4:
12; and Jeremiah 1:8). There is a dualistic element implicit in
these johannine passages, Miranda admits; but it is not the massive
dualism of gnostic thought. In John the "sending" does not bridge
two worlds in the manner it does in the gnostic literature. Arguing in much the same manner as does Fascher, Miranda finds the
historical reality of the redeemer--the "sent one"--so pervasive
in the fourth gospel as to rule out a gnostic background. "This
johannine bond to history is an unbridgeable distinction from the
gnostic conceptions." As a clear expression of this historicity,
the redeemer is *named* in John, while that is never the case in
gnostic literature. So the formulas employed to express the
sending of Jesus come from a prophetic and to some degree a pre-
johannine wisdom christology. Still, Miranda seems to concede that
there are gnosticizing tendencies detectable in the johannine
concepts of the decending-ascending motif and in the questions of
the origin and the destiny of the redeemer (e.g., 3:13 and 7:17f).
Moreover, some of the expressions for the sending of the son seem
rooted in the syncretistic milieu of an oriental hellenism.[40]

Eduard Schweizer's investigation of the general New Testament
concept of Jesus' being sent stresses the implication of pre-
existence in such formulas more than Miranda. Consequently, he
argues that the expressions originate in hellenistic Jewish wisdom
speculations. Apparently he believes that the cosmic aspects of
the motif are too strong to admit a simple Old Testament foundation.[41]

The gnostic debate is waged, too, over the question of the
background for the gospel's incarnational christology. Bultmann
had dared to argue that the allegedly unique Christian theme of
the prologue--the incarnational assertion of 1:14--had gnostic
roots.[42] Schulz continues the Bultmannian tradition by arguing
that the concept of incarnation in the fourth gospel stands in the
tradition of a gnosticizing, oriental primitive Christian thought
which is earlier than either the fourth evangelist or Paul.[43] But
Fascher (in essential harmony with Miranda) continues to argue in
opposition to this idea. He claims that the full historical quality

---

[40]Juan Peter Miranda, *Der Vater, der mich gesandt hat* (Frankfurt: Lang Bern, 1972), 130-307, quote, 305.
[41]Eduard Schweizer, "Zum religionsgeschichtlichen Hintergrund
der 'Sendungsformel,'" *Zeitschrift für die neutestamentliche
Wissenschaft*, 57 (1966), 199-210.
[42]Bultmann, *Gospel*, 64-66.
[43]Schulz, *Das Evangelium*, 211.

of Jesus in the fourth gospel rules out gnostic precedents for its
thought.[44]   The Miranda-Fascher refutation of the Bultmann-Schulz
thesis seems to rely heavily upon the historical character of the
redeemer in the fourth gospel; and the whole gnostic question
seems to be reduced (at least at this point) to two concerns: (1)
how fully historical (fully human) is the Christ of the fourth
gospel, and/or (2) how fully historical (fully human) was the
gnostic redeemer conceived to be in that alleged form of gnosticism
which influenced the fourth evangelist. We know the non-historical,
purely mythological quality of later Christian gnosticism; but does
pre-Christian or pre-johannine Christian gnosticism have that feature as well?[45]

Some efforts have been made to find the roots of johannine
christology in the kind of heterodox Jewish thought typical of the
Qumran community. The presentation of Jesus as "Son" of the Father
and spokesman for God in the fourth gospel has some parallels with
the Qumran view of the teacher in the *Hodayoth* (The Psalms of
Thanksgiving), suggests James Price. Both are attributed a special
knowledge from God and both are commissioned to teach it to a
special group of persons. Both demand a radical change among their
followers, and both view their afflictions as signs of the impend-
ing eschatological event. Both the teacher of the scroll and the
Christ of the fourth gospel seem to be modeled after the suffering
servant of Second Isaiah, although the former is never made to
view his suffering as vicarious. But both do view their salvation
in unity with the salvation of the community (Qumran Hymns of
Thanksgiving 11:10ff; 2:30; 3:19ff; and John 17).[46]

William Brownlee, who has been interested in the relationship
of the New Testament representation of John the Baptist to the
Qumran literature,[47] argues tentatively that the words of the
Baptist in John 1:29 may hint at a concept of the messianic "man"

---

[44]Fascher, 726-730. Franz Mussner appeals to 1:14 as evidence
that the johannine Christ is deliberately pictured as the fulfillment of Jewish cultic practices and expectations. Hence, Jesus is
the temple, the paschal lamb, etc. "'Kultische' Aspekte im
Johanneischen Christusbild," *Praesentia Salutis. Gesammelte Studien
zu Fragen und Themen des Neuen Testament* (Düsseldorf: Patmos, 1967),
133-145.

[45]On the question of the nature of gnosticism prior to the
advent of Christianity, see Edwin Yamauchi, *Pre-Christian Gnosticism*
(Grand Rapids, Michigan: Eerdmans, 1973).

[46]James L. Price, "Light from Qumran upon Some Aspects of
Johannine Theology," *John and Qumran*, ed. by James H. Charlesworth
(London: Geoffrey Chapman, 1972), 30-35.

[47]W.H. Brownlee, "John the Baptist in the Light of Ancient
Scrolls," *The Scrolls and the New Testament*, ed. by Krister Stendahl
(New York: Harper and Brothers, 1957), 33-53.

operative in the fourth evangelist's thinking. In Qumran thought
the messianic man is purged by the spirit of truth and then
communicates the knowledge of God to the community (Qumran
Testimonia 15-17; Qumran Manual of Discipline 4:20f). Brownlee
asserts, "the christology of John...has unmistakable links with
the eschatological language of Qumran."[48]

A study somewhat related to the christology of the gospel has
been done on the argumentation from witness employed by the evangelist. Johannes Beutler has attempted to trace the history of the
tradition of the witness language used in the gospel. In the process he has closely examined the possible roots of this form of
argumentation and its terminology. He concludes that one must seek
those roots in a syncretistic setting in which several intellectual
heritages have flowed together; for the witness terminology of John
seems paralleled by some Greek literature on the one hand and
Jewish literature on the other. For instance, the idea of the
witness of God finds connections with the Jewish-hellenistic
apologetic best known in the writings of Philo and Josephus. On
the other hand, the concept of Jesus' witness to heavenly realities
and to the "Truth" stems without doubt from Jewish apocalyptic
thought and sectarian movements like that at Qumran. So, this
witness language cannot be narrowly assigned to Jewish or hellenistic thought, but must be accounted for out of the inevitable
admixture of these strands of thought, probably in the Jewish
dispersion in the hellenistic world. Beutler wonders if such a
syncretism might not be evident in the interpretations of the Old
Testament (midrashim) of first century hellenistic Judaism.[49]

What may be concluded out of this near morass of views and
counterviews regarding the intellectual milieu of johannine christology? It is evident, I think, that the argument for the gnostic
proposal is stronger with regard to general johannine christology
than it is for the logos thought of the prologue. The wisdom and
agency motifs seem to account for a great deal of John's christological conceptuality, and Brown, Moeller, Braun, and Borgen are
correct in their claims for the influence of these themes on the
evangelist.

---

[48]Brownlee, "Whence the Gospel According to John," *Qumran and
John*, 174-179. See further, Brownlee, "Messianic Motifs of Qumran
and the New Testament," *New Testament Studies*, 3 (1965), 12-30, 195-
210. Similarly, Morris writes, "It is obvious that the sect's
messianism has affinities with John," "The Dead Sea Scrolls and St.
John's Gospel," *Studies in the Fourth Gospel*, 346.

[49]Johannes Beutler, *Martyria* (Frankfurt: Josef Knecht, 1972),
esp. 363-364. See review by Wayne Meeks, *Journal of Biblical
Literature*, **93** (1974), 139-141.

Still, there seems to be a segment of johannine christology which does not reflect a Jewish influence; this includes the descending-ascending motifs and the concern for the origin and destiny of the redeemer. Schnackenburg persuades me that these features betray something like a gnostic milieu, in spite of the efforts of Vawter and others to show otherwise. How shall we account for these features in the evangelist's christology? Is it that he embraced a form of early gnosticism, as Schulz maintains; or that he takes up these features as a part of a polemic against a gnostic movement? Or, is it the case that a syncretistic, helle- nistic Judaism has contributed these otherwise unexplained features of John's thought? Or, shall we attribute them to the creativity of the evangelist? These are difficult questions, especially in the light of our fragmentary knowledge of first century Judaism. It is my judgment that the answer lies in our increasing awareness of the extreme syncretistic and varied character of first century Judaism. It is likely, I believe, that much of what we have called pre-Christian gnosticism will be found to be "heterodox" expressions of Jewish mentality much like the Qumran community. Beutler's contribution is valuable, therefore, because it alerts us to the meshing of notions in the Greco-Roman world of the first century. The envoy concept may be illustrative of the manner in which a variety of modes of thought could employ a simple motif in over- lapping language.

4. The "I Am" Sayings.

One of the unique and complicated characteristics of the fourth gospel is the series of "I am" (*ego eimi*) sayings attributed to Jesus. The rich christological meaning of these sayings will be explored in Part Three, but a part of the research done on these passages in the past decade has involved the inquiry con- cerning the history of religions background for the evangelist's use of this formula. It appears in the fourth gospel in three essential patterns: (1) the absolute use without the predicate ("I am"--8:24, 28, 58; 13:19); (2) the use with an apparently implied predicate ("It is I"--6:20; 18:5); and (3) the use with an expressed predicate (e.g., "I am the bread of life"--6:35, 51; 8: 12; 9:5; 10:7, 9, 11, 14; 11:25; 14:6; 15:1, 5; and possibly 8:18 and 23).

Two prominent studies of the sayings have been most concerned with the more problematic absolute use--Raymond Brown and Philip Harner. Both Brown and Harner argue that the absolute "I am" sayings

find no significant parallels in non-Jewish literature. Both
conclude that the key influence upon the formulations comes from
the Greek translation of passages in Second Isaiah where Yahweh
is made to say literally "I He" (*'ani hu*), and the translators of
the Septuagint have rendered the expression "I am" *ego eimi* (e.g.,
47:8, 10). Brown believes that the only examples of absolute use
can be found in the Old Testament and points to Genesis 28:13 and
Ezekiel 20:5 as well as the Isaiah passages. Harner finds the
Second Isaiah passages alone the viable source of the fourth evangelist's thought. Both agree that in those passages the meaning of
the absolute "I am" is the emphatic assertion of monotheism and
that in effect it came to be used as an abbreviation for the divine
name itself. Hence, Brown can conclude, "Jesus is presented [in
the fourth gospel] as speaking in the same manner in which Yahweh
speaks in Deutero-Isaiah." And Harner concurs,

> Second Isaiah supplied John with a solemn expression that
> was eminently suited for expressing the unity of the son
> and the Father and that had at the same time a strong
> connotation of monotheism which also served to express the
> Christian belief that God continued to be one.[50]

Moreover, both Brown and Harner affirm, in addition to this
influence from the Greek form of Second Isaiah, a knowledge on the
fourth evangelist's part of the rabbinic use of "I am He" (*'ani
wehu*) as a surrogate expression for the divine name, especially in
the liturgy for the feast of Tabernacles (e.g., Mishnah, Sukkah
4:5). Harner favors understanding that the fourth evangelist was
influenced by both the Septuagint form of Second Isaiah and the
rabbinic thought and practice, and Brown seems to agree.[51] Brown
goes on to conclude that the likely milieu for the evangelist's
use of the "I am" formula does not appear there. It is only the
first person singular pattern used by wisdom which suggests some
association with the "I am" sayings of the fourth gospel.[52]

A study of the saying in 14:6 by the French scholar, de la
Potterie, undertakes to establish the literary milieu of the saying
and comes to a conclusion similar to Brown's. De la Potterie
rejects all efforts at finding parallels for the saying in Greek or
gnostic literature and claims instead that it is reflective of "an
ancient style or speech which is derived from Judaism." He finds

---

[50]Brown, *Gospel*, vol. I, 535-537, quote, 537. Philip B. Harner,
The "I Am" of the Fourth Gospel (Philadelphia: Fortress Press,
1970), 15-36, 56-57, quote, 57. In agreement with this is André
Feuillet, "Les *Ego Eimi* christologiques du quatrième Évangile,"
Recherches de science religieuse, 54 (1966), 5-22, 213-240. See
also Reim, 261.

[51]Brown, *Gospel*, vol. I, 537; Harner, 20-22, 61-62.

[52]Brown, *Gospel*, vol. I, 537-538.

literary parallels in Genesis 24:48; Tobit 1:3; Psalms 118; Proverbs 5:5-6; 6:23, and elsewhere. In still later texts the parallels become even stronger, e.g., 4 Ezra 5:1 and the Qumran Manual of Discipline 4:16-20. De la Potterie stresses the form and style of the saying in these texts, not the content.[53]

The evidence cited above is handled in a different manner and combined with new evidence by George MacRae in order to suggest in a tentative fashion the possibility of a gnostic milieu for the "I am" passages. The gnostic use of the *ego* proclamation draws on Second Isaiah, MacRae concedes. But the parallels in the Coptic gnostic library may provide a closer background for the fourth gospel passages than the Jewish literature itself and certainly closer than Bultmann's appeal to the Mandaean texts.[54] One of the Coptic texts, "The Thunder" (Tractate 2 of Codex VI), has a series of "I am" sayings in a paradoxical form, e.g., "I am knowledge and ignorance." MacRae believes that these sayings are intended to stress the transcendence of the redeemer and that a similar meaning is intended for the "I am" sayings in the fourth gospel, e.g., "I am the light of the world." In both cases, the revealer is understood to transcend worldly religious symbolism. The parallel one finds here is "not so much in words or explicit allusions as in religious outlook and religious discourse." We may then conclude that "the evangelist is not merely influenced by a complex and syncretistic religious background, but that he deliberately makes use of such a background for his interpretation of the meaning of Jesus."[55]

MacRae's initial probing of the Coptic gnostic literature suggests that it may well hold a good deal of evidence in the ongoing quest for the intellectual milieu of the fourth gospel, and that with the publication of these texts fourth gospel critics will again be faced with a body of new evidence to be sifted and evaluated.[56] For now the question remains: Did the evangelist draw the source of his ideas and modes of thought from the Old Testament through various Jewish expressions (e.g., the Septuagint and rabbinic materials), or were those modes of thought influential in shaping

---

[53]Ign. de la Potterie, "'Je suis la Voie, la Vérité et la Vie' (Jn 14, 6)," *Nouvelle revue théologique*, 88 (1966), 917-926.

[54]Bultmann, *Gospel*, esp. 225-226.

[55]George W. MacRae, "The Ego-Proclamation in Gnostic Sources," *The Trial of Jesus*, ed. by Ernst Bammel (London: SCM Press, 1970), 123-139, quote, 139.

[56]The publication of the Coptic materials is currently in process: *The Facsimile Edition of the Nag Hammadi Codices: Codices XI, XII, and XIII* (Leiden: Brill, 1973).

a gnosticism which in turn provided the fourth evangelist with his primary ways of thinking and expressing his message?

But Schnackenburg's proposal is of a third kind: The evangelist's fundamental orientation is out of the Old Testament, but his awareness of and dialogue with hellenism have caused him to cast his use of the "I am" sayings in a form similar to that of gnostic thought. Schnackenburg finds impressive Old Testament passages which are precursors of the johannine "I am", but argues that these alone cannot explain the johannine forms. There is evidence of the influence of hellenistic-gnostic thought as well, particularly in the formal structure of the speeches. That structure is similar to the soteriological speech type in oriental hellenism. This confirms, to Schnackenburg's way of thinking, the tendency of the evangelist to be open toward the syncretism of his surroundings.[57]

We are left, therefore, with much the same situation as we face with regard to johannine christology in general: An impressive argument for strong Jewish influences on the evangelist, alongside of some hints at gnostic similarities to be explained either in terms of the evangelist's conscious borrowing with approval or for polemical and apologetic purposes. It does seem, however, that the evidence employed by Harner and Brown is totally convincing. The contacts with gnostic materials are interesting but for the present far less persuasive than those with Old Testament-Jewish backgrounds. Again, it may be that the milieu of the evangelist was of a mixed nature; the gnostic contacts of the evangelist's thought may be indications of gnostic-like language and ideas within the Judaism which influenced our evangelist.

5. The Allegorical Speeches of the Fourth Gospel.

Closely associated with the "I am" sayings are the so-called allegorical speeches. These fascinating passages intrigue critics not least of all in terms of the intellectual milieu for the evangelist which they imply. Within recent research at least four of these passages have been dealt with in works which were at least partially concerned to establish what the source of the allegory was for the author of the passage: the living waters (chapter 4), the bread of life (chapter 6), the shepherd (chapter 10), and the true vine (chapter 15).

---

[57]Schnackenburg, *Gospel*, vol. II, 64-67.

Brown once again finds evidence of wisdom thought in 4:10-14.
Sirach 24:21 has wisdom speaking in a manner which clearly parallels
the words of the johannine Christ, Brown claims. The evidence is
strengthened by the identification of wisdom with the Torah (Sirach
24:23-29), and the law in turn is explicitly described as "living
water" in the Qumran literature (Damascus Document 19:34).[58] He
concurs with Feuillet in finding a similar kind of background for
the lengthy speech on the bread of life in chapter 6.

Feuillet finds three closely related themes interwoven as a
backdrop for the words of the johannine Christ in chapter 6: First,
it is obvious that the whole discourse is intended to call to mind
the Old Testament theme of manna in the Sinai desert. Jesus, the
Mosaic-type messiah, provides the heavenly manna (the bread of life)
for the people who nonetheless murmur against him (Exodus 16:7, 8,
9, etc, and John 6:41, 43, 61). Situated as it is near the Jewish
Passover (6:4), the speech is meant to evoke the suggestion that
Jesus is the new Paschal lamb. Second, the theme of the messianic
banquet (especially, Isaiah 25:6ff; 26:19, etc.) is a source for
the presentation of the discourse. Finally, "It is beyond dispute
that there is a sapiential [wisdom] character to the christology
of John's discourse account." The three "I am" sayings at verses
35, 48-50, and 51 resemble the statements of wisdom in such passages
as Proverbs 8:12, 17, and Sirach 24:16-17. "Thus the text of John
6:35 is, as it were, the synthesis of the complementary themes of
the eschatological banquet and of Wisdom's banquet...it remains
certain, therefore, that the nearest parallel text is Sirach 24:
20."[59]

Like Feuillet, Théo Preiss finds the exodus implications of
the passage evident both in its setting in a Passover period and
in the Mosaic-like function of Jesus. He also agrees that 6:35 is
probably an allusion to Sirach 24:21-22 and that the eschatological
character of the presence of Jesus is involved in the allusion to
the bread of life. Manna is related to Torah in both rabbinic
thought (e.g., Midrash Rabbah Genesis 20:22) and Philonic writings.
Hence the discourse is intended to suggest that the bread of life,
Jesus, is superior to the original manna and hence to the Torah.[60]

---

[58]Brown, *Gospel*, vol. I, 178-179. But Schnackenburg points out
the widespread use of the analogy in the first century, *Gospel*,
vol. I, 429-431.

[59]Brown, *Gospel*, vol. I, 272-274. André Feuillet, *Johannine
Studies* (Staten Island, New York: Alba House, 1965), 58-87, quotes,
81 and 87 respectively.

[60]Théo Preiss, "Étude sur le chapitre 6 de l'Évangile de Jean,"
Études theologiques et religieuses, 46 (1971), 144-156. See also
Josef Blank, "Die johanneische Brotrede" and "'Ich bin das Lebens-
brot'," *Bibel und Leben*, 7 (1966), 193-207 and 255-270.

Another most significant study of chapter 6 has been done by Peder Borgen in his monograph, *Bread from Heaven*. It is Borgen's thesis that the fourth evangelist has employed a rabbinic technique of interpretation of the Old Testament manna theme in this chapter. The chapter itself comprises a homily in which fragments of narratives about manna and Torah are combined in a manner influenced by the gnosticizing tendency of later Merkabah Jewish mysticism. He first demonstrates that, like Philo and a number of Palestinian interpretations, John paraphrases words from the Old Testament about manna by means of certain Jewish narrative (haggadah) traditions on the subject. Second, he argues that the pattern of the paraphrasing in the chapter is that of a homily. A similar homiletic pattern can be discovered in Philo, Paul, and selected Palestinian Jewish interpretations (midrashim). This pattern, Borgen contends, was originally used for preaching in the synagogue. Finally, the evangelist has combined the functions of Torah and wisdom around the manna theme and assigned those life-giving functions to Jesus. But Jesus is himself that manna, and this identification of the agent with the One who has sent the agent is typical, Borgen argues, of a "judicial mysticism" in Judaism.

The evangelist was motivated to produce this homily in this fashion in order to correct tendencies in the church of his day. "The homily in Jn 6:31-58...is a polemic against a gnosticizing tendency to draw a sharp distinction between the spiritual sphere and the external sphere. Jn opposed and was influenced by a docetic Christology and an understanding of the vision of God which was so general that it played down the importance of the external Torah and the unique role of Jesus Christ of history."[61] Borgen

---

[61]Peder Borgen, *Bread from Heaven* (Leiden: Brill, 1965), 148. See also Borgen, "Observations on the Midrashic Character of John 6," *Zeitschrift für die neutestamentliche Wissenschaft*, 54 (1963), 232-240. Schnackenburg concurs with Borgen's major argument and offers a friendly revision of his treatment of 6:52. "Zur Rede vom Brot aus dem Himmel: eine Beobachtung zu Joh 6, 52," *Biblische Zeitschrift*, 12 (1968), 248-252. For a critique of Borgen's thesis, see George Johnson, *The Spirit-Paraclete in the Gospel of John* (Cambridge: University Press, 1970), 134-135, and Lindars, review of Borgen, *Journal of Theological Studies*, 18 (1967), 192-194. The most serious challenge to Borgen's thesis however, comes from Georg Richter who argues that while 6:31-51a may adhere to the proposed homiletic pattern, 51b-58 does not. It is inserted by a later anti-docetic redactor, according to Richter. "Zur Formgeschichte und literarischen Einheit von Joh VI:31-58." *Zeitschrift für die neutestamentliche Wissenschaft*, 60 (1969), 21-55. See also Günter Bornkamm's criticism of Borgen, "Vorjohanneische Tradition oder nachjohanneische Bearbeitung in der eucharistischen Rede Johannes 6?" *Geschichte und Glaube, Zweiter Teil* (München: Kaiser, 1971), 54-59.

attempts then to show how thoroughly Jewish is the milieu out of
which the chapter is written, but furthermore that its Jewish
milieu is of a peculiar kind--in the tradition of the Jewish
exegesis (midrash) but colored by a mysticism which is other than
what is usually conceived to be the "orthodox" Judaism of the
first century. It is impressive that Borgen's argument asserts
even that the fourth evangelist was more Jewish, in some ways,
than was Philo![62]

Borgen's argument for the exegetical-homiletical form of the
passage is a valuable contribution to our understanding of the
intellectual milieu of the evangelist. But more radical is his
suggestion that the Jewish milieu of the evangelist was one influenced by a mysticism--a suggestion which if explored more fully
and demonstrated more persuasively might shed a great deal of light
on the interpretation of the gospel.[63] Furthermore, it may be that
Borgen's proposal gives more precise contours to that syncretistic
form of Judaism which we have suggested may account for the milieu
of the evangelist. The problem with Borgen's theory is to show
that such a gnostic Jewish mysticism existed during the first
century; more evidence to that effect is required if Borgen's
theory is to carry the day.

A major study of the speech in chapter 10 by J.A. Simonis gives
only incidental treatment to the question of the milieu for the
passage. His investigation of 10:1-18 does include, however, a
refutation of the thesis that the Mandaean literature provides the
background for the speech and particularly Bultmann's presentation
of that thesis. Instead, Simonis argues vigorously for the origin
of the passage out of the creativity of the evangelist with some
dependence upon the biblical roots of the image of the shepherd.[64]

In response, Karl Martin Fischer argues that the images of the
shepherd and particularly "the door" correspond closely to gnostic
mythology known to us in earlier forms than the Mandaean literature.
Only against the background of that myth can 10:1-18 be understood,

---

[62]Borgen, *Bread*, 147.
[63]On the question of a Jewish mysticism in first century
Palestine see Gershom Scholem, *Major Trends in Jewish Mysticism*
(New York: Schocken Books, 1946), and *Jewish Gnosticism, Merkabah
Mysticism and Talmudic Tradition* (New York: Jewish Theological
Seminary of America, 1960).
[64]A.J. Simonis, *Die Hirtenrede im Johannes-Evangelium* (Rome:
Papstliches Bibelinstitut, 1967), 320-322. J.D.M. Derrett goes
further to argue that 10:1-8 is actually a midrash on Exodus 22:1-
2, 8-12; Isaiah 56:1-57:19; Numbers 27:15-20; and Micah 2:11-13.
"The Good Shepherd: St. John's Use of Jewish Halakah and Haggadah,"
Studies Theological, 27 (1973), 25-50. But see also John Whittaker,
"A Hellenistic Context for John 10, 29," *Vigiliae christianae*, 24
(1970), 241-260.

for the speech of Jesus and the metaphors there are drawn directly
from the gnostic view of the redeemer. Fischer neutralizes Simonis'
refutation of the proposed gnostic background for this passage by
showing that the gnostic evidence need not be drawn from late
sources. However, Fischer agrees that the evangelist broke out
of gnostic thought patterns at a number of crucial points. The
passage expresses non-gnostic concepts when it suggests (1) that
the redeemer gives his life for the believers(vs. 11, 17), (2)
that the redeemer was truly incarnate, (3) that the redeemer and
redeemed are not fully identified but that a sharp distinction
between them is maintained (v. 14), (4) that the heavenly ascension
of the redeemed is not pictured as a return to their home, and
(5) that Jesus' own ascension is not visualized. Therefore, even
though the background of the passage is clearly gnostic, the evangelist has significantly departed from the gnostic myth to preserve
the uniqueness of his message.[65]

A monograph on the allegorical speech in chapter 15 devotes
a large section to the question of the history of religions background for the speech. Rainer Borig takes some care to examine
the images of the vine in the Old Testament, in other non-biblical
Jewish texts (e.g., the apocalyptic and Qumran literature), and
extensively in the Mandaean texts. While he is willing to concede
that there are parallels between the johannine passage and certain
Mandaean texts, he concludes that it is out of the Old Testament
images and not the Mandaean ones that the evangelist has drawn
for his development of the allegory. The Mandaean texts have
employed the imagery to describe persons, and it is there that we
find the imagery coupled with "I am" sayings. But, first, the
mythical element in the Mandaean use of the image and, second,
the absence from that literature of the key johannine idea of the
life-giving quality of the vine in relation to the branches elimi-
nates its consideration as the background for the evangelist's
thought. More important is that the Old Testament thought and
structure are represented in the johannine passage but in a radicalized fashion, i.e., the *true* vine. Moreover, the vine image
arises out of the Old Testament idea of a "representative individual."
The speech of wisdom in Sirach 24:17, too, might have influenced
the formulation of the johannine passage. In sum, it appears that

---

[65]Karl Martin Fischer, "Der johanneische Christus und der
gnostiche Erlöser," *Gnosis und Neues Testament. Studien aus
Religionswissenschaft und Theologie*, herausgegeben von Karl-
Wolfgang Tröger (Berlin: Gerd Mohn, 1973), 245-267.

the passage was intended to identify Jesus with an image of the people of Israel out of the Jewish tradition.[66]

Feuillet stresses more than Borig the connection of the passage with Sirach 24:17-20 to find more influence of the Jewish wisdom concept on the formation of the speech.[67] Perhaps Raymond Brown proposes a mediating position on both the vine and shepherd speeches when he writes,

> It is clear that John's *mashal* [i.e., a figurative illustration] of the vine and the branches has a unique orientation, consonant with Johannine christology. This orientation is not found in the Old Testament or in Jewish thought, but many of the images and ideas that have been blended together under this orientation are found there. Granting the originality of John's thought, we suggest that the Old Testament and Judaism supplied the raw material from which this *mashal* was composed, even as they supplied the raw material for the *mashal* of the sheepgate and the shepherd.[68]

Brown's moderate position is admirable in that it provides for the creativity of the evangelist. Too often scholars in search of the intellectual milieu of a passage tend to discount the creativity of the mind of the author. Still, the gnostic evidence as it is presented by Fischer and Borgen is too weighty to dismiss without some accounting. I would want to amend Brown's statement above to include the recognition that the Jewish thought which shaped the evangelist's conceptuality in these passages was not in every way a so-called "normative" Judaism, that is a Judaism similar to later rabbinic thought. Rather, there is evidence that it was a Judaism infected by certain gnostic mythologies such as the redeemer concept, and that it was in some ways similar to later Jewish mystical sects. That influence, plus the author's own creative mind, were the ingredients which formed the metaphors and speeches of the allegorical passages.

6.   The Paraclete.

The source of the evangelist's concept of the "Paraclete" (14: 15-17, 26; 15:26-27; 16:7-11, 12-14) has offered critics a problem of formidable proportions for centuries.[69]   Only a handful of studies have recently attempted a solution to this problem, however.   Bruce

---

[66]Rainer Borig, *Der Wahre Weinstock* (München: Kösel, 1967), 135-187, 106-107, 192.

[67]Feuillet, *Johannine Studies*, 87.

[68]Brown, *Gospel*, vol. II, 672.

[69]For a history of the research on this topic see Otto Betz, *Der Paraklete* (Leiden: Brill, 1963), 4-35 and Raymond Brown, "The Paraclete in the Fourth Gospel," *New Testament Studies*, 13 (1966-67), 113-132.

Vawter sees the Paraclete theme along with the son of man christology as two of the strongest indications of the evangelist's
dependence upon the Old Testament book of Ezekiel. The peculiar
combination of the Paraclete's dual roles of a prophetic witness
for Christ which convicts and convinces (15:26-27 and 16:8-11) and
the priestly function of an advocate for the believer before God
(15:26) is strikingly similar to the prophetic-priestly function
of Ezekiel. Influenced by Ezekiel, Vawter argues, the fourth
evangelist conceived of the notion of the Paraclete.[70]

Raymond Brown, too, believes that the "concept of the prophetic
spirit may offer background for the Paraclete." But he does not
find the figure of Ezekiel himself so directly responsible for
influencing the fourth evangelist. Rather, the prophetic spirit of
the Old Testament which moves men to speak God's word may be in
the background of John's concept of the Paraclete. But Brown finds a
more complex pattern of influences converging upon the evangelist.
In addition to the concept of the prophetic spirit of the Old
Testament, Brown argues that the motif of "tandem relationships"
in the Old Testament nourished the evangelist's mind. In this case,
two pairs of figures--Moses-Joshua and Elijah-Elisha--in the Old
Testament offer some parallel to the johannine conception of the
relationship between Jesus and the Paraclete. The relationship
between these pairs of figures is the same: in each case the first
one dies and his spirit is given in some portion to the succeeding
figure who takes up the message of the first (Deuteronomy 34:9 and
2 Kings 2:9, 15).[71]

The third influence upon the evangelist in shaping his concept
of the Paraclete, which Brown finds, is one which has received the
most attention in research on the question in this decade, namely,
Jewish angelology. The developing angelology of late biblical
Judaism was influenced by a dualism which resulted in a division
of the angels and the emergence of superior or leading angels on
both sides. This tendency is detectable even in the book of Job.
But among the sectarians of Qumran the dualistic conception of the
angelic beings is fully worked out, and it is there too that the
expression, "spirit of truth," is used in a manner which Brown finds
compatible with the johannine identification of the Paraclete as
the "spirit of truth" (Qumran Manual of Discipline 4:23-24 and

---

[70]Vawter, 455-458.
  [71]Günter Bornkamm finds evidence of a similar kind of background
to the johannine Paraclete idea. "Der Paraklete im Johannesevangelium,"
Festschrift für R. Bultmann (Stuttgart: Kohlhammer, 1949), 12-35.

John 14:17; 15:26; 16:13). This area of angelology in large part accounts for the forensic nature of the johannine Paraclete, according to Brown.[72]

Pursuing this similarity of the forensic function of the Paraclete and the leading angels in Qumran thought, Otto Betz has done a careful investigation of the parallels between the johannine concept and Qumran thought. He contends that those forensic parallels are the most important, for it is precisely the intercessory role of the Paraclete which is most important in the gospel. In the Qumran literature, Betz says, we find a large number of figures who play intercessory roles, but the angel Michael is given a primary role and is called a "helper", "the angel of truth" and "the prince of lights" (Damascus Document 5:17-19; Qumran War Scroll 13:10; 17:6f). It is here that Betz is able to demonstrate an extensive number of parallels--the theme of a spokesman or helper for the righteous in the cosmic dualism. Betz concludes that Judaism knew and used the expression, Paraclete, and that the fourth evangelist took over this usage from apocalyptic and Qumran literature. The figure of Michael served the evangelist as a model for his Paraclete concept. The reason for John's speaking of the Paraclete both as a person and power is that the evangelist inherited from Qumran the identification of the angel Michael with the spirit of truth. Hence, he has shifted the functions of the angel Michael and the spirit of truth onto Jesus. Betz finds this background convincing; and after examining in the final section of his study the gnostic documents found at Nag Hammadi, he rejects such gnostic thought as relevant to the Paraclete concept in John. It is true that the fourth gospel has some gnosticizing tendencies, but those tendencies are of a different kind than the gnosticism of these newly discovered texts.[73]

George Johnston's monograph, *The Spirit-Paraclete in the Gospel of John*, includes a lengthy summary and critique of Betz's study, even though Johnston does not seem primarily interested in establishing the background for the evangelist's thought. He dissents from Betz's exclusive attention to the forensic function of the Paraclete and his search for parallels dealing only with that function.

---

[72]Brown, *Gospel*, vol. II, 1137-1138, quote, 1138.

[73]Betz, 56-72, 113-166, 206-212, 293-236. The close analogy of Qumran ideas and the johannine Paraclete has also been affirmed by James Price, "Light from Qumran," 24. But A.R.C. Leaney does not agree that the parallel with Qumran ideas is close. See "The Johannine Paraclete and the Qumran Scrolls," *John and Qumran*, 43-53, 57, and "The Historical Background and Theological Meaning of the Paraclete," *Duke Divinity School Review*, 37 (1972), 146-159.

Johnston does not agree that the concept of Michael has so influenced the fourth evangelist and believes that the absence of the name Michael in the gospel suggests a polemic purpose in the evangelist's handling of the Paraclete theme. However, he does agree with Betz that the Qumran literature provides enlightening parallels to the fourth gospel and that the spirit of truth was identified with Michael in pre-Christian Judaism. "The angelic meaning of the spirit of truth had been domesticated in the synagogues and sects of Judaism long before the fourth Gospel was composed." The Greek word, *paraclētos*, was widely used in hellenistic as well as Palestinian Judaism and appears in the Targums as a "loan word" from Greek to translate the Hebrew, *mēlitz*, which designates the angelic mediator of the book of Job. Hence, the Paraclete concept does seem to arise from the Jewish idea of an "angelic intercessor." Johnston sees the concept answering a specific need in the johannine church: The fourth evangelist "combined 'spirit of truth' with 'paraclete' in a deliberate rebuttal of heretical claims for an angel-intercessor as the spiritual guide and guardian of the Christian Church."[74]

So while Brown, Betz, and Johnston all find some roots of the johannine concept in Jewish angelology, Brown adds still one more important background element: the figure of personified wisdom. He contends that there are parallels between the character of wisdom and the johannine Paraclete. Like the Paraclete, wisdom brings understanding from God and "teaching like prophecy" for the people of God (Sirach 24:12, 26-27, 33 and John 16:13) but is rejected by man (Enoch 42:2 and John 14:17). "In summation," Brown writes, "we find scattered in Jewish thought the basic elements that appear in the Johannine picture of the Paraclete."[75]

But we are not surprised to find Schulz in disagreement with this conclusion, since he is convinced that the Paraclete is linked with the son of man tradition. The Paraclete is the bearer of God's spirit and judge of the world and hence is central in the

---

[74]Johnston, *Spirit-Paraclete*, 83, 116-117, 106, 120-121, 99, quotes, 121 and 119 respectively. See also Johnston, "The Spirit-Paraclete in the Gospel of John," *Perspective*, 9 (1968), 29-37.
    [75]Brown, *Gospel*, vol. II, 1139. Brown's contention for a wisdom background for the Paraclete concept is supported by Harald Riesenfeld who summarizes his view in these words: "It is probable that the sapiential texts describing Widsom in her peculiar comforting functions have given rise to the *idea* as well as the *name* of the Paraclete. . ." "A Probable Background to the Johannine Paraclete," *Ex Orbe Religionum: Studia Geo Widengren* (Leiden: Brill, 1972), 266-274, quote, 272-273.

struggle between the world and the community of believers. Therefore, the concept must stem not alone from Jewish apocalypticism
but from the intermingling of that mode of Jewish thought with a
gnosticism in much the same way as is the case with the son of
man theme.[76] Schulz's point of view would seem to contradict both
the findings of Betz's investigation of the gnostic literature of
Qumran and his contention that the Mandaean literature provides
no significant parallels. But Fascher argues against Schulz that
since the Paraclete is in continuity with the earthly Jesus who
was fully human, the Paraclete cannot be conceived of as an idea
in any significant way influenced by gnostic thought.[77]

The preponderance of evidence would seem to point in the
direction of Brown's conclusion, notwithstanding the objections
of Schulz. The Judaism of the first century with its wide variety
of forms seems the richest field of investigation for the milieu
out of which the fourth evangelist conceived the concept of the
Paraclete. But Brown's effort to see the wisdom motif in the
Paraclete notion is the least convincing of the several Jewish roots
he finds for the notion. More impressive is the suggestion of the
influence of Qumran angelology upon the evangelist's thought.
Whether Betz or Johnston's specific understanding of that influence
is judged the more accurate, it appears certain that Qumran sectarian thought provided essential elements for the evangelist's
concept of the Paraclete. Schulz's gnostic hypothesis seems
unnecessary and excessively tenuous as compared with the Qumran
hypothesis. Finally, it is not necessary, I think, to argue for
the Qumran influence exclusively, as Brown has shown. The Old
Testament conceptuality either directly or (more likely) indirectly
through several forms of first century Judaism doubtless contributed
to the evangelist's thought.

7. The Dualism of the Fourth Gospel.

Certainly one of the unique features of the fourth gospel is
its dualistic language--light and darkness, above and below, Christ
and the world, etc. It is in part this dualism that motivated the
strong association of the gospel with gnostic thought, especially
since Bultmann. The central issue in trying to determine the
intellectual milieu of the evangelist's dualism is the clarification
of the nature of that dualistic thought itself. Is it a radical,
cosmic, even physical dualism of the gnostic kind; or is it an

---

[76]Schulz, *Das Evangelium*, 189.
[77]Fascher, 730.

ethical and eschatological type of dualism typical of first century
Jewish thought; or is it a modification of one or both of these?
The problem of locating the evangelist's thought lies not so much
in determining the character of concepts in pre-johannine literature
as in determining the nature of johannine thought itself! We can
generalize the research done in the background for the evangelist's
dualistic thought under two major kinds of investigations: First,
there are those that seek to demonstrate or refute the gnostic
character of johannine dualism, and, second, those that attempt
to define the relationship between johannine and Qumranian dualism.

The early part of Günter Stemberger's study of the symbolism
of good and evil in the fourth gospel is devoted to the symbolism
of ethical dualism. It is Stemberger's continual intent throughout this section of his work to show that gnostic dualism does not
provide as rewarding parallels to the johannine motif as do the
Old Testament and hellenistic philosophy. He rules out the influence of gnostic dualism because it does not imply a moral significance as does the johannine dualism. That moral significance, in
turn, always suggests the necessity of human decision. The light
and darkness images of John, for instance, are best understood as
arising from Isaiah, Jewish wisdom literature, and Jewish apocalyptic and sectarian thought.

On the other hand, the dualism of servitude and freedom in the
fourth gospel shows evidence of influence from the hellenistic
culture, particularly stoicism. This dualistic motif comes to
John out of a Jewish tradition but has been submitted to a hellenistic influence. The polarity of the "above" and "below",
Stemberger contends, already finds expression in the Old Testament
and Jewish thought. Truth and falsehood likewise are employed in
John in a manner comparable to their use in the first century
literature of Judaism. In that literature hellenistic notions have
already been incorporated into the basic Old Testament motifs, e.g.,
the idea of the spirits of truth and falsehood. The contexts of
gnostic passages, on the other hand, are so different that it is
difficult to believe John had them in mind as he formulated his
notions. Stemberger then is convinced that the basic source of
johannine dualistic thought is the Old Testament and early Judaism,
with influences from hellenistic (non-gnostic) thought coming into
that tradition both before and through the evangelist.[78]

---

[78]Günter Stemberger, *La Symbolique du bien et du mal selon
Saint Jean* (Paris: Éditions du Seuil, 1970), 44-144.

A major work on the dualism of the fourth gospel and its relationship with early Judaism has come from Otto Böcher. In brief, Böcher shares Stemberger's contention that johannine dualism is not at all gnostic but takes its roots in Jewish thought. The dualism which emerged out of Jewish thought in the centuries immediately preceding the Christian era was basically the result of Old Testament thought mingled with Jewish piety and reshaped by Iranian religious concepts. There is no serious influence of hellenistic thought, contrary to Bultmann's thesis of a hellenistic, oriental gnosticism. That gnostic dualism which arose later is indebted to Qumranian and johannine thought, not the reverse. Indeed, the dualism evident in late Judaism is primarily an ethical-eschatological type, while the later gnostic brand of dualism takes on the cosmic and physical features. The Jewish dualistic mode of thought continues to be controlled by the Old Testament concepts of creation in which God is responsible for both the realm of good and evil. So, we have the chain: Old Testament (mingled with Iranian thought) to Qumran and other late Jewish literature (especially, The Testament of the Twelve Patriarchs) to the fourth gospel (e.g., Deuteronomy 11:26ff; 28:1ff to Qumran Manual of Discipline 1:1 - 3:12 to 1 John 1:6-7; 2:4-5, etc.). The Böcher monograph undertakes to prove that the ethical-eschatological dualism of John has its roots in the Old Testament and Jewish thought. "In this Jewish world [apocalyptic-sectarian and not pharisaic-rabbinic] the johannine theology is at home.... Where John differs from his apocalyptic Jewish roots, there is visible the new ideas--the specifically Christian ideas."[79]

The research of Stemberger and Böcher stands in direct opposition to the proposals of Schulz who consistently maintains that in the fourth gospel the world stands over against God, and the Old Testament doctrine of creation has been replaced by a dichotomous enmity between God and the world. Hence he would say that the dualism of the gospel is thoroughly cosmic and physical, not just ethical and eschatological.[80]

---

[79]Otto Böcher, *Der johanneische Dualismus im Zusammenhang des nachbiblischen Judentums* (Gütersloh: Gerd Mohn, 1965), 11-16, quote, 16. A defense of the Hebraic background of the johannine light-darkness dualism is found in E.R. Achtemeier, "Jesus Christ, the Light of the World. The Biblical Understanding of Light and Darkness," *Interpretation*, 17 (1963), 439-449.

[80]Schulz, *Das Evangelium*, 70. For a similar view see Schottroff, *Der Glaubende und die feindliche Welt* and "Johannes 4:5-15 und die Konsequenzen des johanneischen Dualismus," *Zeitschrift für die neutestamentliche Wissenschaft*, 60 (1969), 199-214; "Heil als innerweltliche Entweltlichung. Der gnostische Hintergrund der johanneischen Vorstellung vom Zeitpunkt der Erlösung," *Novum Testamentum*, 11 (1969), 294-317. See Part Three of this study for a discussion of Schottroff's thesis.

Schnackenburg treats two of the poles of johannine dualism in two of his excursuses in his commentary, in particular, the johannine concepts of life and truth. In both cases, Schnackenburg recognizes the influence of a form of gnosticism on the evangelist's thought. While he believes that the concept of "truth" in John must be acknowledged as a product of the evangelist's own originality, for the most part, it is also true that gnostic concepts of truth were obviously influential. Some of these gnostic influences were brought to John by means of his knowledge of the Qumran literature. But the johannine concept cannot be dismissed as the simple repro- duction of sapiential, apocalyptic, or even gnostic thought; it is the evangelist's own formulation. Regarding the matter of the notion of "life" in the fourth gospel, Schnackenburg is more willing to grant gnostic influence. "From all of this [evidence from the Apocryphon of John, the Gospel of Thomas, and the Gospel of Philip] it can be seen that a certain relationship between the johannine and gnostic conceptions of life cannot be disputed." Particularly is the formation of the question the same in both John and the gnostic materials--how can one enter the heavenly world of life and light and escape the realm of death? Qumran texts have little to offer at this point, while other Jewish literature of the time, e.g., the Testament of the Twelve Partriarchs, does show parallels. Schnackenburg believes we must conclude that the fourth evangelist was influenced by a Syrian form of gnosticism but that that influ- ence was conditioned by extra-biblical Jewish thought.[81]

The most transparent relationship between the Qumranian and johannine literature is at the point of the dualistic language of both.[82] In the new research on this matter, a general consensus has emerged at least among four critics. Raymond Brown, Leon Morris, James Price, and James Charlesworth have all argued that the similarities between Qumran and the fourth gospel on the matter of dualism necessitate that one establish some association of the two, but that the influence of the former on the latter must be regarded as indirect rather than direct. Brown has maintained that the "parallels are not close enough to suggest a direct literary depend- ence of John upon the Qumran literature, but they do suggest Johannine familiarity with the type of thought in the scrolls." Brown arrives at this conclusion by arguing that the only parallels

---

[81]Schnackenburg, *Gospel*, vol. II, 273-279, 440-443, quote, 441.
[82]For a survey of all the arguments advanced vis-a-vis the dualism of the fourth gospel and Qumran, see Herbert Braun, *Qumran und das Neue Testament*, Bd. II, 119-132.

which are admissible as evidence of a direct relationship between the gospel and Qumran are those in which each is clearly not dependent upon its common background, the Old Testament.[83]

The Australian critic, Leon Morris, agrees; for he stresses the differences between the scrolls and the fourth gospel even amid their common language and thought. For instance, while both John and the Qumran convenanters tend to divide humankind into two groups--the sons of light and the sons of darkness--the evangelist sees that division as a result of the response to Christ. Moreover, the dualistic motif of truth and error is similar in the writings of Qumran and the fourth gospel, but in the former truth is defined by the law and in the latter by Christ. Still, the incidence of agreement is too high to be regarded as accidental or even as the result of a common background. Morris speculates that perhaps knowledge of the Qumranian mode of thought and expression came to the evangelist through followers of the Baptist who had once been members of the Dead Sea sect and were now Christians.[84]

Price opts, on the other hand, to account for the similarities by means of a common background for both John and the sect group: "It is probable that John's two-world dualism was already a common-place conceptual framework in Jewish apocalyptic and wisdom theology which sometimes substituted for, or combined with, the linear division between the present and future ages or worlds."[85]

James Charlesworth has undertaken a detailed comparison of the dualisms of John, The Rule of the Qumran community, and the Odes of Solomon. First, he examines the dualism of the Rule, then the gospel, and finally offers some conclusions. Both characterize the two worlds in a similar fashion, and both employ a "modified dualism"--one that is not cosmically ultimate. Both employ the light-darkness motif in a manner which is unique to them and both have a common view of the final judgment. Furthermore, both use four literary formulas "which show that John was probably directly influenced by the terminology and ideology in 1 QS [Manual of Discipline] 3:13-4:26": the use of "spirit of truth," "holy spirit," "sons of light" for the righteous, and "eternal life" as the reward for the righteous. He demurs however, from claiming a direct copying of the Qumran literature by the fourth evangelist and argues instead that while the evangelist was strongly influenced by the expressions

---

[83]Brown, *Gospel*, vol. I, lxii-lxiii, quote, lxiii.
[84]Morris, *Studies in the Fourth Gospel*, 329-333, 353-354.
[85]Price, 19-25, quote, 19.

and terminology of the scrolls, he did not borrow his dualism from
there. Rather, he used their language to give expression to his
own conception which arose from his Christian convictions.[86]

Charlesworth goes on to argue that the dualism present in
the Odes of Solomon suggests a continuous line of influence from
the scrolls through the gospel to the odist. The most conspicuous
similarities are in the soteriological dualism of the three and the
employment of the light-darkness motif. He concludes that the odist
and the evangelist shared a common milieu and both were influenced
by the Essenes. He believes with such a study he puts to rest the
misguided effort to use the parallels between the odes and the
gospel as an argument for the gnostic character of the fourth gospel
(i.e., Bultmann's thesis).[87] Hence, Charlesworth goes further than
any of the other three critics in finding a dependence of the evangelist upon the Qumran literature for his dualistic thought, but stops
short of ascribing to that dependence a direct literary copying
of any sort. Furthermore, he presents the most cogent case for
turning away from gnostic texts for a source of johannine dualism
and looking instead to the sectarian form of Judaism practiced by
the Essenes of Qumran.[88]

Charlesworth's meticulous study is to be accepted as decisive
proof of the link between johannine and Qumranian dualism and of
the flaw of any effort to root the evangelist's dualism in a form
of gnosticism later expressed in the Odes of Solomon. It is my
conclusion that, given the evidence now available, no resource
for the evangelist's dualism is more likely than that of the Qumran
literature, and the scholarship of late has amply exploited that
resource. Moreover, this similarity of dualistic thought is the
closest link of the gospel and the Dead Sea community we now have.

Still, it is evident as Charlesworth, Brown, and others have
urged that the evangelist did not know Qumran thought directly
through its literature but through some unknown and indirect link.

---

[86]James Charlesworth, "A Critical Comparison of the Dualism in
1 QS 3:13-4:26 and the 'Dualism' Contained in the Gospel of John,"
Qumran and John, 76-106, quote, 101.
[87]Charlesworth, "Qumran, John and the Odes of Solomon," *Qumran
and John*, 107-136. See further, Charlesworth and R.A. Culpepper,
"The Odes of Solomon and the Gospel of John," *Catholic Biblical
Quarterly*, 35 (1973), 298-322. See Charlesworth's new critical
edition, *The Odes of Solomon: Edited with Translation and Notes*
(Oxford: Clarendon Press, 1973).
[88]See also, Roland Bergmeier, "Glaube als Werk? Die 'Werke
Gottes' in Damaskusschrift II,14-15 und Johannes 6, 28-29," *Revue
de Qumran*, 6 (1967-69), 253-260. Bergmeier attempts briefly to
show that the demands of God in the fourth gospel are rooted in
a predestined dualism of men identical with the view one finds in
the Damascus Document.

Such an understanding of the milieu of the evangelist's thought
explains its apparent contacts with gnostic conceptuality; for it
is increasingly evident that the Qumran world-view constitutes a
sort of Jewish proto-gnosticism which contributed significantly to
the later emergence of Christian gnosticism. Moreover, the Qumran
hypothesis for the milieu of johannine dualism also explains the
similarities found by Böcher and Stemberger and others between
first century Jewish apocalypticism and johannine dualism. This is
so, of course, because the Qumranians represent a radicalization
of Jewish apocalypticism. It is this fascinating, eclectic,
sectarian form of heterodox Judaism we discovered at Qumran which
best represents the sort of intellectual environment from which
the evangelist took some of his language and concepts to fashion
the dualistic framework within which he articulates the Christian
message.

　　　8. Passover and Mosaic Motifs.
　　　We have already seen on several occasions how critics have
found Exodus-Passover motifs to be the likely background for certain
aspects of johannine thought and in Part One we have discussed
Wilkens' source analysis which understands that the final redaction
of the gospel involved the superimposition of a paschal structure
upon the gospel. In this section we must take notice of a number
of arguments in the recent period of research which have found a
wide-spread influence of both Passover thought and Mosaic themes
upon the evangelist. While these two themes are obviously interwoven, they have been advanced sometimes in virtual independence
of one another, so we shall treat them separately.
　　　J.K. Howard makes a sweeping, although briefly argued, proposal
for the influence of the Passover themes upon the fourth evangelist.
"It is our contention," he writes, "that the writer [of the fourth
gospel] seems to be concerned with presenting Jesus as the perfect
Paschal Victim, the complete Antitype of the old order..." Howard
sees this influence of paschal thought focused at a number of points
in the gospel: "the Lamb of God" acclamation (1:29-34), the
cleansing of the temple (2:13-25), the feeding of the multitude
(6:1-14 and 22-71), and the farewell discourses and passion narrative
(13:31-17:26 and 19:13-37). The words of the Baptist in 1:29-34
serve as a preparation for the pascal theme throughout the gospel,
Howard asserts. That the title, "lamb of God," is pascal in nature--

a view which is not undebated among interpreters[89]-- is supported
by the Midrash on Exodus 12:6 in which it is contended that the
blood of the paschal victim is atoning blood. Howard argues, too,
that the paschal meaning of these verses does not preclude their
positive relationship with the suffering servant motif of Second
Isaiah.   The cleansing of the temple is still another witness to
the influence of Passover themes upon the evangelist. This
narrative is set within a Passover time (2:13); consequently, the
evangelist wants the reader to understand Jesus' actions in the
narrative as the commencement of events which would constitute the
new Passover.[90]

Leon Morris agrees that the Passover imagery is extensive in
the narrative of the temple cleansing. Morris contends that the
fourth evangelist has not written his gospel under the influence of
the Jewish lectionaries of the first century--the thesis of Aileen
Guilding[91]--but that two Jewish feasts, Passover and Tabernacles,
do play an important part in the gospel. By far, it is the Passover imagery which most clearly influenced the evangelist and "the
most important clue to this aspect of the Gospel is the centrality
of the Passover."[92] In addition, chapter 6, both Morris and Howard
assert, is shaped under the guidance of paschal motifs, particularly
in the implicit reference to the heavenly manna of the exodus event.[93]

The farewell discourses and the passion narrative are also
evidence of the Passover theme in the gospel. That the final meeting of Jesus with his disciples in the fourth gospel is a Passover
meal is argued by Howard. The emphasis of the discourse in chapter
15 is on the fruit of the vine which arose from the Passover thanksgiving, "Blessed art Thou who createst the fruit of the vine."
The vine is a counterpart to the bread motif in chapter 6 which is
related to the Passover blessing, "Blessed art Thou who bringest
forth bread from the earth." In chapter 17 Jesus acts, argues
Howard, as the president of a Passover feast. Howard also advances
the argument that the fourth evangelist has employed a calendar
which allowed him to date the death of Jesus on the eve of Passover
in order to stress the paschal features of the ministry of Christ.[94]

---

[89]J.K. Howard, "Passover and Eucharist in the Fourth Gospel,"
Scottish Journal of Theology, 20 (1967), 330-333, quote, 330.
    [90]*Ibid.*, 331-332.
    [91]Aileen Guilding, *The Fourth Gospel and Jewish Worship*
(Oxford: Clarendon, 1960).
    [92]Leon Morris, *The New Testament and the Jewish Lectionaries*
(London: Tyndale, 1964), 64-68, quote, 72.
    [93]*Ibid.*, 68; Howard, "Passover", 333-334.
    [94]Howard, "Passover", 335-337.

This latter point has been contended by Anne Jaubert for a number of years. Jaubert's case centers around the calendar in use at Qumran, and she maintains that the same calendar was in use elsewhere among Palestinian Jews of the first century. The johannine dating of the last supper and the death of Jesus corresponds with this heterodox Jewish calendar and explains why John has a different dating for the events than the synoptic gospels. That same calendar has influenced the fourth gospel at a number of other points, according to Jaubert, e.g., the accounts of the appearance of the resurrected Christ in the fourth gospel. Jaubert wonders why it is that the fourth gospel places such importance in the fact that Christ appeared eight days after the resurrection Sunday (20:26), for this week after Passover has no special significance in the traditional Jewish calendar. She finds what she believes to be the answer in the so-called Zadokite calendar found at Qumran. In that calendar,

> the day after the Sabbath following the Week of Unleavened Bread...was an essential link, since the fifty days it opened regulated not only the date of the Zadokite Pentecost ...but that of the fifty days following, as the discovery of the Temple Scroll has confirmed. In this calendar alone ...the Sunday of the appearance to Thomas can come from a liturgical source and support the symbolic significance that the author has given to it: the commencement for the time of the church.

Jaubert offers other evidence that the last supper in the fourth gospel is a Passover meal: The four questions posed by the disciples for Jesus in the course of his address (13:36; 14:5, 8, and 22) reflect the Passover custom of addressing questions to the master of the meal at Passover. Second, paschal themes are present in the farewell discourse--Jesus' departure is the exodus, and his coming again reminds one of the paschal attention to the future coming of the Messiah. Finally, the meal has features which mark it as a Passover meal with the participants purifying themselves (the foot-washing) as they would were they at the temple. Jaubert concludes, "the Gospel of John can no longer be considered the great argument against Jesus' last supper being a Passover meal. The sources used by the evangelist favour the paschal and Zadokite character of Jesus' last supper."[95] But Brown, among others, has refused to grant

---

[95]A. Jaubert, "The Calendar of Qumran and the Passion Narrative in John," *Qumran and John*, 62-73, quotes, 64-65 and 72-73, respectively. See further, Jaubert, *The Date of the Last Supper* (Staten Island, New York: Alba, 1965) and *New Testament Studies*, 7 (1960-61), 1-30; E. Ruckstuhl, *Chronology of the Last Supper* (New York: Desclée, 1965); and K.A. Strand, "John as Quartodeciman: A Reappraisal," *Journal of Biblical Literature*, 84 (1965), 251-258.

Jaubert's hypothesis, for it seems to him unnecessarily speculative.
Brown believes that the last meal Jesus had with his disciples in
the fourth gospel is indeed a meal with clear Passover features,
but argues that there is no reason to suppose the acceptance of
an Essene calendar.[96]

But Morris and Howard represent those scholars who see the
passion of Jesus in the fourth gospel as betraying clear paschal
implications. Jesus dies as the priests are preparing the paschal
lambs in the temple (19:14); his blood is poured out like the
paschal victim's (19:34); no bone in his body is broken in accord
with the treatment of the paschal lamb (19:33-36 and Exodus 12:46;
Numbers 9:12); and finally the reference to the hyssop (19:29)
which is unique to the fourth gospel recalls Exodus 12:22.[97]

These efforts toward clarifying the intention of the evangelist
to provoke paschal similarities in the account of Jesus seem on the
one hand most convincing but on the other most excessive.[98] For
while Brown's arguments and those of Morris and Howard commend
themselves, a tendency to exaggerate the evidence presented in the
gospel is betrayed in the efforts of Jaubert. Surely the paschal
motifs shaped the thought of the evangelist to some degree, but
the hypothesis that gospel data is to be explained as a result of
the evangelist's employment of the so-called Zadokite calendar
seems unwarranted. Again, Brown's scholarly caution is wise at this
point.

There is then a good deal of emphasis in contemporary research
upon the Passover themes in the gospel, but there is perhaps even

---

[96]Brown, *Gospel*, vol II, 556, and "The Date of the Last Supper,"
The Bible Today, 11 (1964), 727-733. See further, J. Jeremias,
The Eucharistic Words of Jesus (New York: Scribner's, 1966),
75-79.

[97]Howard, "Passover", 337. Morris, *The New Testament and the
Jewish Lectionaries*, 69-71.

[98]A Passover origin for the johannine concept of "sign" has
also been proposed: Robert Houston Smith, "Exodus Typology in the
Fourth Gospel," *Journal of Biblical Literature*, 81 (1962), 333-
339; Brown, *Gospel*, vol. I, lx, 529; Peter Riga, "Signs of Glory:
The Use of '*Sēmeion*' in St. John's Gospel," *Interpretation*, 17
(1963), 402-424. But others find prophetic symbolism to be the
most likely origin of this concept: Schnackenburg, *Gospel*, vol. I,
526-528 and Reim, 207-209. For other proposals see C.T. Ruddick,
"Feeding and Sacrifice--The Old Testament Background of the Fourth
Gospel," *The Expository Times*, 79 (1968), 340-341. M.-E. Boismard,
Du Baptême à Cana (Jean 1:19-2:11) (Paris: Éditions du Cerf, 1956);
Thomas Barrosee, "The Seven Days of the New Creation in St. John's
Gospel," *Catholic Biblical Quarterly*, 21 (1958), 507-516, and "The
Seven Days of Creation in St. John's Gospel: Some Further Reflec-
tions," *The Evangelical Quarterly*, 44 (1972), 154-158. For a
general survey of research on the background of the Cana sign see
Adolf Smitmans, *Das Weinwunder von Kana* (Tübingen: J.C.B. Mohr,
1966), 31-37.

more research done which defends the thesis that the fourth evangelist was highly influenced by and evoked images of the ancient
figure of Moses.

First, Francis Glasson's investigation of Moses in the fourth
gospel attempts to show how the christology of the gospel is shaped
by the Moses figure, most especially, a popular Jewish belief that
the messiah would be a Mosaic-like figure, a belief which was widely
held (Midrash Ecclesiastes Rabbah on Ecc. 1:9). It is significant
that John begins his gospel with an allusion to the relationship
between Moses and Jesus (1:17). But Moses was also conceived as
the prophet who, with the approach of the messianic age, would
appear to prepare the way for that new advent. The Christ of the
fourth gospel is clearly presented, believes Glasson, in such a
way as to suggest his fulfillment of Deuteronomony 18:16-19 (e.g.,
John 4:25; 8:28; 12:49f). It is obvious, Glasson believes, that
there was a fluidity of messianic thought in first century Judaism
which allowed the identification of Moses with both the messiah
himself and the prophet who was to precede the messiah. The kingship of Jesus, moreover, in the fourth gospel is to be understood
along Mosaic not Davidic lines. Jesus is never called the son of
David in the gospel, yet his royal functions are explicit (especially chapter 19). Moses was sometimes thought of as king (Philo,
Moses I, 158), and it is that model of kingship which the evangelist
has employed in his portrayal of Jesus.[99]

It is precisely this presentation of Jesus as a king and its
associations with his presentation as prophet which is the central
focus of Wayne Meeks' exhaustive study of the traditions concerning
Moses and their influence upon johannine christology. Meeks explores
the thesis that the interrelationship of the motifs of prophet and
king is important in johannine christology, and it is Moses who
provided the fourth evangelist with a model after which to form his
prophet-king christology: "Certain traditions about Moses provided
for the Fourth Gospel not only the figure of this eschatological
prophet, but the figure who combines in one person both royal and
prophetic honor and functions." Meeks proceeds, first, to show the
internal connection of the prophetic and royal motifs in the
johannine portrayal of Jesus. He then attempts to search out a
milieu in which Moses is presented as both a prophet and king. He
concludes this search by the elimination of the Qumran and Mandaean
literature, for one cannot find there this peculiar synthesis of

---

[99]T. Francis Glasson, *Moses in the Fourth Gospel* (Naperville,
Ill.: Allenson, 1963), 20-31.

functions in the figure of Moses. To some degree that synthesis is
present in Philo and Josephus, and it is clearly present in rabbinic
literature; so it is fair to conclude that in both rabbinic and
non-rabbinic sources there existed narratives (haggadah) which
attributed to Moses both prophetic and royal functions. That same
combination of functions is present in Samaritan sources, as well,
which leads Meeks to say:

> The coincidence between the specifically Samaritan ideology
> and some elements in Jewish tradition, both rabbinic and
> especially extra-rabbinic, leads to the probability of
> mutual interaction between Jews and Samaritans in the for-
> mation of the traditions.

Finally, Meeks uses these findings concerning a tradition of
the prophetic-kingly Moses figure to analyze the christology of the
gospel. He finds that it throws considerable light both upon the
direct references to Moses and other themes such as the exaltation
of Jesus, the representation of Jesus as God's emissary, the
forensic language of Jesus' words in John, and the good shepherd
passage in chapter 10. While this brief resume of Meeks' extensive
and scholarly monograph does not do justice to his work, it is
enough to show how Meeks finds the milieu of johannine christology
to include a complex Jewish and Samaritan tradition, probably
centered in Galilee, concerning the figure of Moses.[100]

Glasson's monograph, while not as thorough as Meeks', is concerned with the broader question of Mosaic themes in the fourth
gospel, and he proceeds beyond the christological question itself
to propose other evidence for the nurturing of the evangelist's
thought by traditions concerning Moses. He asks whether or not
"the serpent in the wilderness" (3:14) could not be an allusion to
Numbers 21:8f as it is translated in the Septuagint and whether 19:
18 might refer to Exodus 17:12. "The sixth chapter of John supplies
one of the clearest examples of the importance of the wilderness
imagery..."[101] And here he is joined by Théo Preiss who finds clear
Mosaic typology in chapter 6. Jesus' actions are intended deliberately to recall Moses and the prediction of Deuteronomy 18:15; and
the mountain is designed to evoke Sinai parallels.[102]

Glasson continues his search for Mosaic parallels through other
parts of the gospel and finds, for instance, evidence in the farewell discourses of a Mosaic type since Moses too is represented as

---

[100]Wayne A. Meeks, *The Prophet-King* (Leiden: Brill, 1967),
passim, quote 317. See also, Meeks, "Moses as God and King,"
*Religions in Antiquity: Essays in Memory of Erwin Ramsdell Good-
enough*, 354-371.
[101]Glasson, 37-47, quote 45.
[102]Preiss, 144-145.

giving a final discourse and prayer before his death. Like Meeks, he believes that the shepherd speech of chapter 10 recalls the Jewish treatment of Moses as a shepherd (e.g., Philo, Moses I, 60-62). The parallels between Jesus' relationship with his disciples and Moses' relationship with Joshua are similarly pointed out.[103] Glasson's case is sometimes over-extended and lacks the mass of evidence needed to carry his argument, but still he makes a persuasive thesis for the Mosaic themes in the gospel.

One further kind of Mosaic theme has been argued to pervade the fourth evangelist's thought at least in those passages known as the farewell discourses (13:31-16:33). Aelred Lacomara has recently proposed that it is not the exodus topology that influenced the evangelist but a pattern adopted from the book of Deuteronomy. Lacomara extends the similarity pointed out by Glasson and finds what for him are striking affinities between the farewell discourses of John and the book of Deuteronomy both in their external patterns and in their "internal thematic" considerations. On the first score, both are the final speeches to their followers before the leader's death; both groups of followers are about to come into a new situation--the Israelites into Canaan, the disciples into a covenant community of faith; both speeches are intended to fulfill the need of the followers for consolation and encouragement, instruction and warning.

The "internal thematic" resemblances are more complicated. First, Moses and Jesus serve in both cases as mediators of the divine knowledge. Second, both appeal to the followers' experiences of signs and wonders as evidence of God's presence among them. Third, mutual love is commanded in both the farewell discourses and Deuteronomy. Fourth, the promised rewards to the followers are similar, e.g., answered prayer (Deuteronomy 4:7; John 15:7), God's presence (Deuteronomy 12:11; John 14:15-18). Finally, both are concerned that the words and works of God known among the followers be preserved and handed on to future generations. The conclusion of these similarities is that

> it was principally Deuteronomy and its prophecy of a "new Moses" which the author of John had in mind when he gathered the sayings of Jesus into a final instruction to the disciples. In this sense, the deuteronomic discourses of Moses were the model for the farewell discourses.[104]

Like many a valuable study, Lacomara's search for evidence for his

---

[103]Glasson, 48-105.

[104]Aelred Lacomara, "Deuteronomy and the Farewell Discourse (Jn 13:31-16:33)," *Catholic Biblical Quarterly*, 36 (1974), 65-84, quote 82.

basically sound hypothesis is over-extended, and some of the "internal thematic" similarities are not convincing. Still, his proposal
strengthens the case for the influence of Moses typology on the
evangelist's work.

These explorations of the Passover and Mosaic motifs in the
fourth gospel render strong evidence for some kind of thorough
grounding in the broad Jewish tradition of the first century for
the fourth evangelist; it is hard to dismiss these studies in favor
of a non-Jewish milieu for johannine thought. But, on the other
hand, as Meeks' work shows so convincingly, these studies do not
entirely resolve the complex issue of the kind of Jewish thought
lying as a backdrop to the evangelist's mind. Historical scholarship in the past decades has demonstrated the breadth and variety
of forms of Jewish thought in the first century of the Christian
era, and johannine scholarship has yet to come down clearly on the
specific form or forms of Judaism known to and influential upon the
evangelist. These studies do point persistently, however, in one
direction, namely, toward the probability that the fourth evangelist
had deep roots in that broad intellectual environment which we must
continue to label extra-biblical Judaism. Efforts to locate the
milieu of the fourth evangelist outside of some form of Judaism
would surely flounder within this evidence for the exodus and Mosaic
roots of johannine thought.

B. *Concluding Observations:*

It is clear from this survey that the intellectual milieu of
the evangelist remains a thorny problem for fourth gospel critics.
The alternatives for solving that problem are numerous, as they
have been through the centuries of research on the issue. But the
survey should provide us with some clues as to the direction in
which contemporary research is moving; and if the preceding overview is at all accurate, one clue is crystal clear, namely, that
contemporary research favors a Palestinian, Old Testament, Jewish
setting for the thought of the gospel. We have seen how critics
have elucidated the familiarity of the evangelist with the Old
Testament literature both by his direct and implicit quotations of
that literature and his free and frequent resort to that literature
for his images and analogies.

But the extra-biblical Jewish motifs play as important a role
in the findings of recent research, suggesting that the evangelist
was not only rooted in the Old Testament itself but in the Jewish

traditions since the exile and restoration. Especially prominent
among those traditions in their influence upon the evangelist, if
contemporary scholars are correct, was the wisdom motif. Rabbinic
Judaism and heterodox Judaism are both claimed as the more prominent in the evangelist's thought. There seems to be a growing
scholarly opinion in the favor of the evangelist's familiarity with
extra-biblical Jewish thought. But to what degree his mind worked
out of a thorough acquaintance with rabbinic, orthodox Judaism and
to what degree it was more akin to the forms of Judaism found in
Essene, mystical, and apocalyptic sect groups is not at all clear.
It is surprising, given the trend of johannine scholarship in the
wake of the Qumran discoveries, that we are able to find as little
support for a clear, direct line of contact between sectarian
Judaism of the Essene form as we do. Instead we find scholars for
the most part speaking of a widely diffused kind of non-rabbinic
Judaism, including such features as are present at Qumran, but also
mystical motifs and perhaps even Samaritanism.[105] The suggestion
is clear: The fourth evangelist seems to be at home in a Jewish
tradition which is not unaffected by rabbinic, pharisaic influences
but is similarly well endowed with less orthodox forms of Jewish
thought.

While the strong tendency to relate the fourth gospel to a
pre-Christian gnostic syncretism is not absent from the current
scene, it is obvious that it is no longer the main direction of
scholarship. Critics seem far less interested in crediting some
alleged gnostic pattern of thought with the johannine mode of
thinking. Arguments against the usefulness of Mandaean parallels
for johannine research seem to far outweigh those which continue
to appeal to them for enlightening the milieu of the evangelist.
Appeals to gnostic along with purely hellenistic influences are
on the decline, both in number and perhaps more important in extent
of investigation. One caution must be mentioned: Recent scholarship has seen notice given that the Coptic gnostic materials must
be studied and compared carefully with regard to their bearing on
this issue. Their place in the development of early Christianity
and the relationship of the fourth gospel to their form of Christian
thought must yet be ascertained.

In this connection we must mention, too, that there are a good
number of scholars who seem to accept one feature of the older
gnostic hypothesis for the milieu of the fourth gospel, namely its
syncretistic quality. It may be that no gnostic hypothesis for

---

[105]See Chapter III, Section C., "A Samaritan Mission."

the background of the gospel can be broadly accepted today. But
many will affirm that the milieu of the gospel was extremely
syncretistic. The question of the intellectual milieu of the
gospel is perhaps confused by the fact that the evangelist's background was a mixture of religious motifs and movements characteristic
of his day, and what scholars were once labeling as gnostic are
simply the syncretistic expressions of the evangelist and his
milieu.[106]

---

[106]Bultmann, of course, emphasized this feature of hellenistic
culture and that is in part what allowed him to maintain his gnostic
hypothesis. He could then account for the Qumran findings easily
by calling them evidence for a "pre-Christian gnosticizing Judaism."
Theology of the New Testament (New York: Charles Schribner's, 1955),
vol. I, 13. See further, Wayne A. Meeks, "'Am I a Jew?'--Johannine
Christianity and Judaism," *Christianity, Judaism, and Other Greco-
Roman Cults. Studies for Morton Smith at Sixty*, J. Neusner, ed.
(Leiden: Brill, 1975), vol. I, 163-86.

CHAPTER   III

THE SITUATION AND PURPOSE OF THE EVANGELIST

One factor in the situation of the evangelist is the intellectual milieu in which he conceived his ideas and formulated his
modes of expression. Another factor in that situation is the
more concrete circumstances which influenced the evangelist. Aside
from the intellectual landscape of the evangelist, what were the
historical actualities which existed at the time of his work?
Of course, associated with the description of those concrete
realities which were formative for the gospel comes the question of
the purpose of the gospel. May we not assume that, in addition to
any general motive to articulate the kerygma of the faith, the
evangelist shaped the purpose of his writing out of those prevailing
circumstances in his environment which he deemed important to the
community of faith? Such an assumption arises out of the recognition that the gospels are to some degree circumstantial writings,
that is, works occasioned by certain situations which prevailed in
the author's time and provoked his production. If it is argued that
the epistles of the apostle Paul were occasional writings (for
example, the Corinthian letters are Paul's response to specific,
concrete problems in the Christian community of Corinth), it can be
equally maintained that the gospels were the result of similar
stimulation from concrete, historical conditions in their respective
Christian communities. The prevailing interest in the redaction
history of the gospel materials has greatly enhanced this historical
curiosity regarding the concrete setting for the work of the evangelist. It has come to be acknowledged that the *Sitz im Leben*, the
actual situation in the lived world, of the evangelists is an

indispensable bit of knowledge in the ongoing quest for understanding the New Testament writings.

In the case of the fourth gospel the necessity of such knowledge about the concrete situation and purpose of the evangelist seems even more essential if the formula for solving the problems of that document is to be discovered. The history of johannine scholarship finds the variety of proposals as numerous here as elsewhere on the spectrum of issues concerned with the gospel. The explicit declaration of the purpose of the gospel in 20:30-31 is crippled by a textual variant affecting the tense of the verb *pisteuien* ("to believe"), and further complicated by the evangelist's irregular use of verb tense. (Does the verb mean that the reader might begin to believe or continue in a faith already held?) The result is that critics have been divided over the question of whether this stated purpose of the gospel is to be taken to mean that the evangelist was writing primarily to evoke new faith among those who are not yet Christian believers or to nurture the faith of those who are already identified with the community of belivers.

The question must be settled, it seems, on the basis of the gospel as a whole and its *implicit* purpose. Only by drawing inferences from portions of the gospel concerning the concrete situation of the evangelist and his purpose can the precise meaning of 20:31 be ascertained. As might be expected, those inferences and the consequent meanings assigned to the declared purpose of the gospel vary greatly.[1] Within the mid-twentieth century alone arguments can be found for vastly different reconstructions of the situation and purpose of the gospel, but perhaps most influential in the early 1960s is the work of three scholars who forcefully maintained that the gospel was designed to serve as a missionary document among the Jews living in dispersion. T.C. Smith, W.C. van Unnik, and J.A.T. Robinson all in 1959 advocated this thesis, and for a time it seemed to prevail among critics of the gospel.[2]

More current efforts to infer the purpose of the gospel have become inseparably related to the inferences regarding the peculiar situation of the church out of which and to which the evangelist addresses himself. The range of views is still considerable, but

---

[1]Feine, Behm, Kümmel, *Introduction*, 161-165.

[2]T.C. Smith, *Jesus in the Gospel of John* (Nashville, Tenn: Broadman, 1959); W.C. van Unnik, "The Purpose of St. John's Gospel," *Studia evangelica*, I (1959), 382-411; J.A.T. Robinson, "The Destination and Purpose of St. John's Gospel," *New Testament Studies*, 6 (1959-60), 117-131, also in *Twelve New Testament Studies* (London: SCM, 1962), 107-125. See further A. Wind, "Destination and Purpose of the Gospel of John," *Novum Testamentum*, 14 (1972), 26-69.

some trends are perhaps evident to the discerning observer of
contemporary research.

A. *The Dialogue With the Synagogue*

A proposal which seems steadily to be gaining an increasing
degree of consent among critics of the fourth gospel is that the
evangelist was related to a community of Christian believers engaged
in a serious and perhaps even violent dialogue with a synagogue.
Such a proposed setting has thrown considerable light upon portions
of the gospel. This thesis has its most diligent and clearest proponent in the person of J. Louis Martyn, whose study, *History and
Theology in the Fourth Gospel*, has been met with wide acceptance.[3]
It is Martyn's contention that the evangelist in effect produced
a "two level drama" in his gospel. On the one level, he expresses
bits of Christian tradition concerning the historical life of Jesus
of Nazareth. This level of the gospel drama Martyn calls the
einmalig, meaning "something like 'back there' as opposed to 'now
and here.'" The second level of the drama presents in a slightly
disguised fashion the conflict going on between the church and the
synagogue in the evangelist's own day. The result is a complex
intermingling of two time periods and historical situations. The
johannine Christ is at once the traditional Jesus of the Christian
community's heritage and the contemporary Christian missionary;
the opponents of Christ are the Jewish leaders of Palestine in the
early third of the first century and the Jewish protagonists of
the evangelist's own day. Martyn claims the evangelist was only
partly conscious of his skillful mixture of tradition and the
present.

Martyn proceeds to distinguish between those portions of the
narratives of the gospel which are drawn from tradition and those
which reflect the *Sitz im Leben* of the evangelist. The result is
that Martyn admirably accomplishes his task of demonstrating how
selected chapters (especially 3, 5, 6, 7, and 9) tell us more about
the evangelist's situation than about that of the traditional Jesus.
What he unearths is the likelihood that the Christians of the evangelist's day and of his locale were subjected to open conflict and

---

[3]See reviews: Raymond Brown, *Union Seminary Quarterly*, 23 (1968),
392-394; T.A. Burkill, *Journal of Biblical Literature*, 87 (1968),
439-442; Dwight Moody Smith, *Interpretation*, 23 (1969), 220-223; W.A.
Beardslee, *Religion in Life*, 38 (1969), 150; Rudolf Schnackenburg,
"Zur Herkunft des Johannesevangelium," *Biblische Zeitschrift*, 14 (1970),
7-9; Robert Kysar, *Dialog*, 8 (1969), 70-72; Johannes Beutler,
Martyria, 345.

continuing dialogue with the synagogue and that members of the
synagogue(s) were required to undergo an examination of their faithfulness in the face of growing apostasy in the favor of the Christian
community.   The critic finds reason to believe that these persons
were required to recite the "Benediction Against Heretics" (the
Birkat-ha-minim) which had been revised to encompass (perhaps only
by implication) those who adhered to the Christian faith.   Moreover,
the expression "excluded from the synagogue" (*aposynagōgos*, 9:22;
12:42; 16:2) refers to the experience of Jewish Christians being
expelled from their synagogue home due to their alliance with the
Christians.

The picture is that of a defensive Jewish community attempting
to preserve its identity over against the onslaught of Christian
evangelism, experiencing a growing number of apostates in its
midst, and even harboring "secret Christians" who held a private
Christian faith in the effort to maintain their identification
with the Jewish community. Most illuminating perhaps of Martyn's
skillful treatment of the relevant johannine passages is his exegesis
of the story of the healing of the man born blind (chapter 9) and
the subsequent examination by the Jewish leaders and the expulsion
of the cured person from his synagogue.[4] While Martyn is not the
first to propose that the Christians' exlusion from the synagogue
comprises a vital element in the concrete situation of the evangelist of the fourth gospel,[5] his is certainly the most thorough and
influential presentation in recent years of such a hypothesis.

Confirmation of some proposal comparable to Martyn's has been
developing out of a number of disparate types of works on the
fourth gospel. Wayne Meeks' history of religions study of the
prophet-king motif in the fourth gospel comes to this general conclusion regarding the concrete situation out of which the evangelist
wrote: "   johannine traditions were shaped, at least in part,
by interaction between a Christian community and a hostile Jewish
community whose piety accorded a very great importance to Moses and
the Sinai theophany..."[6] He wrote those words before the appearance
of Martyn's study, and has more recently declared that it seems beyond doubt that the johannine gospel reflects the break of the
synagogue and the church. It betrays the failure of the church's
missionary efforts among the Jews with the result that polemic

---

[4]J. Louis Martyn, *History and Theology in the Fourth Gospel* (New
York: Harper and Row, 1968), *passim*, quote, 9.
[5]E.g., K.L. Carroll, "The Fourth Gospel and the Exclusion of
Christians from the Synagogue," *Bulletin of the John Rylands Library*,
40 (1957), 19-32.
[6]Meeks, *Prophet-King*, 318.

qualities are evident in the symbols (particularly that of "the
Jews") of the gospel.[7]

A form critical study of the use of the enigmatic expression
and misunderstanding in the fourth gospel by Herbert Leroy brings
a startlingly similar kind of conclusion. This analysis demonstrates
a great number of Old Testament and Jewish themes in the gospel
particularly at the points where puzzling statements are made and
misunderstanding results (e.g., 7:33-36; 8:51-53, and 56-58).
Leroy concludes from these that the community with which the fourth
evangelist was aligned understood itself as the true Israel and
suffered from the opposition of the synagogue. By the time of the
final redaction of the gospel the community stood banned from the
synagogue.[8]

Redaction critical studies have likewise led to the general
confirmation of Martyn's hypothesis. Robert Fortna understands
that the evangelist's use of his source evidences that the relationship between the church and the synagogue had significantly changed
since the writing of the "Signs Gospel". Whereas the evangelist's
source (the "Signs Gospel") was written out of a situation in which
the church was still related in a positive way to the synagogue, the
evangelist's redaction of the source took place in a situation of
rupture and hostility between the two.[9] Martyn's own efforts to
relate the findings of Fortna's source criticism of the fourth
gospel and those of the history of religions and development of
Christian theology studies show very convincingly how there is a
convergence of studies on the historical situation of the fourth
evangelist. The hostile dialogue between the johannine church and
the synagogue offers a way of explaining and pulling together the
findings of these three significant trends in fourth gospel criticism.[10] (See the discussion of Martyn's article in Part One.)

The history of traditions study of the witness argumentation
of the fourth gospel done by Johannes Beutler moves further in the
direction of a confirmation of the general hypothesis proposed by
Martyn. Beutler tests the various theories of the concrete setting
in life for the johannine gospel vis-a-vis the witness terminology
and form of argument found in the gospel and concludes that it is
most likely that the setting was one of dialogue with the Jewish
groups in the dispersion. One can easily imagine a setting in which

---

[7]Meeks, "'Am I a Jew?'".
[8]Herbert Leroy, *Rätsel und Missverständnis* (Bonn: Peter Hanstein,
1968), 191-193.
[9]Fortna, "Source and Redaction," 159.
[10]Martyn, "Source Criticism," 247-270.

the kind of argumentation employed by the evangelist would be
effective by supposing a city in which the Christian community
lived in the neighborhood of a synagogue and was engaged in lively
debate with that group, Beutler decides.[11]

In 1972 Meeks published an exploratory article attempting what
might be termed a "sociological analysis" of the function of the
symbol of the descending and ascending son of man in the fourth
gospel. He offers the suggestion that the symbolism of the gospel
is that of a sectarian group which understands itself primarily
in terms of in-group and out-group language. The sectarian nature
of the johannine community reflected in its language is a result,
Meeks ventures, of "the actual trauma of the Johannine community's
separation from the synagogue and its continuing hostile relationship with the synagogue...coming to faith in Jesus is for the
Johannine group a change in social location," that is, of social
isolation from the Jewish community and relocation within a group
attacked by that community.[12]

H. Mulder's efforts to understand the relationship of the
Gentiles and the Jews in the fourth gospel convinces him that the
Gentiles are never central in the gospel and that the gospel is
not concerned with the mission to the non-Jew. The interest of the
evangelist is in the relationship of Christianity to Judaism because
he writes out of a situation of mounting hostility between the
Christians and Jews. The purpose of the fourth gospel is to be seen
as a result of the use of the curse of the Christians intended by
the *Birkat-ha-minim*. The evangelist is trying to strengthen the
faith of the Christians amid this kind of Jewish hostility.[13]

Finally, a study of the polemic quality of the fourth evangelist's treatment of the Jews by Erich Grässer some years before the
publication of Martyn's work anticipates the latter's thesis.
Grässer finds the use of the johannine expression, "the Jews", to
be a stylized type for those who reject the Christian gospel on the
basis of the Torah. The gospel gives a prominent place to the
opposition of Christ and the Torah (e.g., 1:17), but the Torah stands
generally for the synagogue's opposition to the messiahship of Jesus
claimed by the Christians. The discussions of Jesus with the Jews
in the gospel are not over questions of the law--the realm of ethics
and piety--but are used simply as occasions for the articulation of

---

[11]Beutler, *Martyria*, 339-364.
[12]Meeks,"The Man from Heaven in Johannine Sectarianism," *Journal of Biblical Literature*, 91 (1972), 44-72, quote 69.
[13]H. Mulder's article is known to me only through the summary found in Wind, "Destination and Purpose," 40-47.

the identity of Jesus over against Jewish protagonism. "The Jews",
as a matter of fact, represent one pole of the johannine dualism--
that pole which stands counter to the acceptance of the truth in
the revelation of Christ. Hence they are representatives of a
"cosmic type of being". The question with regard to the Jewish
opponents is not a matter of obedience to the Law but decision for
or against the revealed truth, and they are given the role of the
examples of unbelief. The situation which accounts for this kind
of anti-Jewish polemic, Grässer maintains, is the expulsion of the
Christians from the synagogue, and that experience is projected
back into the time of Jesus (a proposal impressively similar to
Martyn's "two-level drama"). The gospel surely reflects the
persecution of the Christians by the Jews and the condemnation of
them as heretics by Rabbi Gamaliel II about A.D. 90. The purpose
of the gospel is not a missionary one, therefore, but is the effort
to strengthen the community in the face of the opposition of the
world, especially the Jews, and articulate the community's claim
that the Christians are the true Israel.[14]

The purpose of the survey of studies concerned with the Jewish-
Christian dialogue thus far has been to show the emergence of a
strong position favorable to the thesis that the johannine community
was suffering severely at the hands of an aggressive and hostile
Jewish group. What is remarkable is that studies of various aspects
of the gospel and studies employing different methods have converged
upon a similar kind of hypothesis for the concrete situation of the
evangelist, one which always involves the prominence of a hostile
Jewish-Christian relationship and very often claims evidence for the
experience of actual expulsion from the synagogue.

Others, too, have found evidence of an anti-Jewish polemic or
apologetic as one of the primary purposes of the fourth gospel.
Both Schnackenburg and Brown give such a polemic high priority in
the various goals of the evangelist. Both have a comparable view
of the meaning of John's stereotypical expression, "the Jews."
These "Jews" are the contemporaries of the evangelist who reject
the kerygma of the church. Brown stresses that the expression is
not ethnic or geographical or even necessarily religious in content,
but symbolizes those who reject the Christian faith. This, he

---

[14]Erich Grässer, "Die Antijudische Polemik im Johannesevangelium,"
New Testament Studies, 10 (1964-65), 74-90. One might add to this
list C.K. Barrett's contention for the dialectical character of
johannine theology which he acknowledges might have been a result
of circumstances like the ones described by Martyn. "The Dialectical
Theology of St. John," *New Testament Essays* (London: SPCK, 1972),
49-69.

maintains, is evident from a comparison with the synoptic gospels.
"It is this situation in which the Gospel was written that explains
the use of the term 'the Jew'"--a situation in which "the disciples
of Moses and the disciples of Jesus (9:38) are locked in struggle."
The time of the missionary effort in relationship to the Jews had
passed and hostility prevailed. The gospel declares that the
Christians are the real successors to the Old Testament heritage;
they are the true "Israel."

Other evidence for this conclusion is cited by Schnackenburg:
(1) The synagogue ban has affected Christians in the evangelist's
community. Schnackenburg believes that such bans may date back as
early as 70 and were only made official in the declaration of
Gamaliel II in the *Birkat-ha-minim* of about A.D. 90. (2) The evangelist treats Jewish feasts and customs in an aloof manner (e.g.,
2:6; 19:40). (3) Debates over the messiahship of Jesus are found
throughout the gospel (e.g., 7:27, 41f; 12:34). (4) The scriptures
are cited in a polemic fashion (e.g., 5:45).

> In all this, there must have been a polemic intention against
> the Pharisee rabbinate of the time of the evangelist....Thus
> the presence of an anti-Jewish tendency in John, occasioned
> by the contemporary situation, can hardly be doubted.

Brown believes that the justification of Christian claims
over against the charges of the Jews is the primary goal of the
gospel, but it is to be seen alongside of an equally important
intent of the evangelist, namely, an appeal to the Christians who
have maintained their place in the synagogues of the dispersion.
The evangelist wants to counter Jewish propaganda, and he has little
missionary intent. Still, it may be that a kind of evangelistic
purpose is present in his concern for Jewish Christians still in the
synagogue. They stand on the brink of decision; they must surrender
either their Christian or their Jewish allegiance. The evangelist
intends to persuade these Jewish Christians to hold to their Christian faith and leave the synagogue for a place in the community of
the true Israel. The struggle evident in the gospel was probably
taking place outside of Palestine, as the interpretation of 8:35
would indicate, if one understands the tone of that verse as
ironic. But the language used in relation to the Jews remains
apologetical and polemical rather than primarily evangelical.
Schnackenburg consents that there may have been a missionary purpose
of the gospel with relationship to the hellenistic Jews, but claims
that that intent is not primary nor does it distract from the

fundamentally hostile attitude of the evangelist toward the Jews.[15]

Still another avenue into the discovery of the concrete situation of the fourth evangelist has been the investigation of Jewish ideas appearing throughout the gospel. Meeks has summarized these efforts most clearly. He finds that the way in which the evangelist has employed Jewish concepts is to force those ideas to their extreme. "His use of Jewish tradition in this respect is a kind of *reductio ad absurdum*; the result in Jewish ears was blasphemy." Hence, "the Fourth Gospel is most anti-Jewish at the points it is most Jewish." This is to say that the gospel written in the midst of the Jewish-Christian dialogue freely invokes Jewish notions only to radicalize them so thoroughly by placing them in a Christian (worse, a johannine Christian) context as to render them offensive to the Jew.[16]

The primary investigations of this matter (to which Meeks refers his readers) have been done by Marinus de Jonge and have to do with messianic-christological ideas. In three related articles de Jonge consistently maintains that even the most Jewish sounding notions of the fourth gospel are radically "johanninized." The investigation of the statements attributed to Jesus' Jewish opponents in the fourth gospel leads to the conclusion that these statements have a johannine flavor and tell us little or nothing about Jewish belief itself.[17] The messianic categories, "prophet" and "king", are thoroughly transformed in the johannine gospel by being interpreted in the light of that gospel's view of Jesus as the son sent from the Father (e.g., 1:19-34; 7:40-44; 18:28-19:16, 19-22).[18] Even the title "Christ" itself is used in the fourth gospel in a way which at once presupposes but corrects the Jewish use.[19] The inevitable

---

[15]Schnackenburg, *Gospel*, vol. I, 165-167, quote, 167; Brown, *Gospel*, vol. I, lxx-lxxv, quote, lxxii. Other studies which propose a Jewish polemic as the primary purpose of the gospel include the following: Harald Riesenfeld, "Zu den johanneischen *ina*-Sätzen," *Studia Theologica*, 19 (1965), 213-220; Fritz Neugebauer, *Die Entstehung des Johannesevangelium* (Stuttgart: Calwer, 1968), 14; and Georg Richter, "Die Gefangennahme Jesu nach dem Johannesevangelium (18, 1-12)," *Bibel und Leben*, 10 (1969), 26-39. But J.W. Bowker understands the occasion of the gospel more in terms of an intra-Jewish debate over the meaning of messiahship: "The Origin and Purpose of St. John's Gospel," *New Testament Studies*, 11 (1964-65), 398-408.

[16]Meeks, "'Am I a Jew?'".

[17]Marinus de Jonge, "Jewish Expectations About the 'Messiah' According to the Fourth Gospel," *New Testament Studies*, 19 (1973), 262-263.

[18]de Jonge, "Jesus as Prophet and King in the Fourth Gospel," *Ephemerides theologicae lovanienses*, 49 (1973), 262-263.

[19]de Jonge, "The Use of the Word, *Christos*, in the Johannine Epistles," *Studies in John*, 71-73.

conclusion of this is that the johannine christology is developed
out of a contrast with Jewish thinking concerning messiahship and
that the purpose of the gospel is an intra-church effort to show
that Christians could indeed reply to the objections of Jewish
protagonists.[20]

In a related study on Nicodemus, de Jonge claims that that
figure is representative in the gospel of all those Jewish Christians
who are trying to maintain their Jewish affiliations (like the
other "secret disciples" of the gospel, 12:42-43; 9:16; 2:23-25).
The evangelist says to such Jewish Christians of his own time that
they must make a full declaration of faith in Christ, be fully
reborn, or else their faith is worthless. It is here that de Jonge
explicitly endorses Martyn's thesis for the concrete situation of
the gospel as the best explanation for the features he has found in
his research.[21]

No one could doubt that the present day has seen the publication
of an impressive number of studies which focus on the same task or
result in the same conclusion: The actual situation in which the
gospel was written and for which it was designed was one of strained
and even hostile relationships of dialogue and controversy between
the johannine church and the Jewish synagogue. When this research
is viewed in the light of the growing tendency to see the Jewish/
Old Testament intellectual milieu as most influential for the gospel,
one has a convincing picture of the setting--intellectual and
concrete--for the gospel. The evidence seems--at least to me--
decisive. One could only wish that our understanding of Jewish-
Christian relations in the first century were better than it is,
so that we could speak with more authority about the gradual exclusion of Christian believers from the synagogues. Our meager knowledge of this matter is only illustrative of our general need for
better information regarding first century Judaism. It is to the
credit of Martyn and his allies that the thesis of John's origin
amid a Christian dialogue with the synagogue is founded upon the
best available information regarding Judaism of that time. But not
all would admit that this dialogue was the only purpose or occasion
of the gospel, or in some cases that it was the primary purpose.

---

[20]de Jonge, "Jewish Expectations," 262-263.
[21]de Jonge, "Nicodemus and Jesus: Some Observations on
Misunderstanding and Understanding," *Bulletin of the John Rylands
Library*, 53 (1971), 338-358.

B. *An Anti-docetic Polemic*

It was Irenaeus' contention that the fourth gospel was addressed
to that heretic and gnostic villain, Cerinthus (*Against Heresies*,
III, 11, 7); hence one cannot say by any means that the possibility
of the fourth evangelist proposing to undermine a gnostic, or more
specifically a docetic, view of the faith is an invention of the
modern critical mind! Still, in spite of its prestigious supporter
of the second century, the anti-docetic hypothesis has not received
strong corroboration in recent years. Although many seem willing
to grant that in passages like 1:14 and 19:34 there are assertions
which sound as if they were intended to put aside any doubt of the
fleshly reality of the johannine revealer, few are willing to claim
for that purpose a prominent place in the design of the gospel.
The last significant effort to compose a commentary around such an
assertion is the work of Edwyn Hoskyns.[22] Perhaps it is the
accomplishment of Bultmann in pointing up the actually sympathetic
attitude of the gospel toward gnosticism which has discouraged
efforts to support the hypothesis that it is anti-gnostic; or
perhaps it is the conviction that docetism did not become such
a threat to the faith until the years following the composition of
the gospel that has dampened the anti-gnostic hypothesis. At any
rate, we find few who are concerned to sketch the concrete situation
and the consequent purpose of the gospel around the motif of a
prominent anti-docetism.

James Dunn, however, has undertaken to argue that an anti-
docetic motif is combined with an anti-sacramentalism in chapter
6. It is his contention that in the johannine church the docetic
threat had loomed so large that Christians had responded by a
literalistic emphasis upon the eucharist--the bread and wine are
indeed the flesh and blood of the Savior. The evangelist's carefully constructed response to both the threat of docetism and
the response of his fellow Christians is found in the discourse
following the feeding. Dunn is concerned, first, to argue that
the passage is not eucharistic in nature.

> If eucharistic language is used in vv. 53ff, therefore, it
> is not that John wishes thereby to stress the necessity of
> the Lord's Supper and its celebration, but rather that he
> uses eucharistic terminology with a metaphorical sense,
> namely to describe not the effect of the sacrament as such,
> but the union of the ascended Jesus with his believing
> followers through the Spirit.

---

[22]Hoskyns, *The Fourth Gospel*.

But verses 51c-58 surely do stress that Jesus had really become
flesh and really died. Hence, the evangelist has struck in the
direction of both the docetists and the sacramentarians. The
"eucharistic overtones" of the passage are negative in significance. But his attack upon the docetic claims is cautious too,
for he stresses the incarnation as meaningful only in the light of
the belief that it is the incarnate one who dies and gives the
life-bestowing Spirit to the believer.[23]

Dunn's view is not widely held, yet many would recognize a
sub-stratum of anti-docetic polemic in the gospel. Schnackenburg
itemizes the evidence for a possible anti-gnostic polemic, but
concludes that only the evidence for the refutation of a gnostic
christology (the incarnational language of 1:14 and the assertion
of the physical reality of the resurrection, 19:34f) is secure.[24]
Brown agrees but lists 8:38-39 and 6:51-58 as further evidence.
He concludes, "an anti-docetic motif is possible and even probably
in the Gospel, but it has no great prominence."[25] Other commen-
tators who follow suit are Sanders and Lindars; although the latter
is cautious, for he believes that the strongest evidence for the
anti-docetic polemic emerges from the first epistle of John.[26]
Consequently, both Lindars and Brown are inclined to understand
that the anti-docetic assertions of the gospel come from the later
stages of the composition of the gospel and were not in the earlier
form of the document.[27] We have seen earlier that Wilhelm Wilkens
also found the anti-docetic theme worked into the gospel by the
redactor of the earliest form of the writing.[28]

Georg Richter has taken a somewhat different stance while
still maintaining that the anti-docetic polemic is not early in the
developing composition of the gospel. He argues that 5:15b-58 and
1:14 are not from the hand of the original evangelist but are
redactional additions to the gospel. To these passages he adds
others which are in his judgment both anti-docetic and redactional
in their tone: 19:34b-35, 39-40; 20:2-10, 24-29. Consequently, it
is his contention that the incarnational passages of the gospel are
the work of an anti-docetic interpolator of the gospel who was
concerned with the christological and the sacramental assertions of

---

[23]James D.G. Dunn, "John VI--A Eucharistic Discourse?", *New
Testament Studies*, 17 (1971), 328-338.
   [24]Schnackenburg, *Gospel*, vol. I, 169-172.
   [25]Brown, *Gospel*, vol. I, lxxvi-lxxvii. See also, Borgen,
Bread, 148.
   [26]Sanders, *Gospel*, 52; Lindars, *Gospel*, 61-63.
   [27]Brown, *Gospel*, vol. I, lxxvii; Lindars, *Gospel*, 63.
   [28]Wilkens, *Zeichen und Werke*, 167-168.

the document.[29]

Two general conclusions of this brief survey of treatments of the anti-docetic theme in the gospel are possible: First, it is clear that there is no effort to argue for a major anti-docetic purpose in the gospel, and that critics are inclined to see this motif as a secondary one. Second, it is noteworthy that a number of critics assign the anti-docetic motif to some kind of later stage in the composition of the gospel. This is done in a number of different ways: in the developmental composition theories of the origin of the gospel, the anti-docetic theme is assigned to later stages (Lindars and Brown); in a source theory hypothesis, it is attributed to the redactor of the source, not the source itself (Wilkens); and in the context of the view of the gospel as the result of a composition and then redactional interpolation, it is credited to the interpolator (Richter).

It may be fair to conclude that the tendency is to see the presence of this polemic in the gospel as the result of later developments in the situation of the johannine community rather than a feature early in its life and in the origin of the gospel itself. Such a view of the anti-docetic polemic as a secondary theme imposed upon the gospel in its final stages of composition is surely correct. Dunn's efforts are to be faulted for his not taking into account the process of the gospel's composition and working instead as if it were the produce of a single author at one time. Understanding the anti-docetic polemic as a later addition to the gospel has the further virtue of illuminating the relationship of the gospel and the first epistle of John. It would appear that the epistle was written amid the same situation which resulted in the addition of the anti-docetic motif to the gospel.[30]

---

[29]Georg Richter, "Die Fleischwerdung des Logos im Johannes-evangelium," *Novum Testamentum*, 13 (1971), 81-126 and 14 (1972), 257-276. For a similar view see J.C. Meagher, "John 1:14 and the New Temple," *Journal of Biblical Literature*, 88 (1969), 57-68.

[30]Two other proposed polemics are sometimes found in the gospel: A polemic against an alleged John the Baptist movement and an anti-petrine polemic. The former was first promulgated by Wilhelm Baldensperger, *Der Prolog des vierten Evangeliums, sein polemisch-apologetischer Zweck* (Tübingen: J.C.B. Mohr, 1898). It is recog-nized as a secondary purpose of the evangelist by Brown, *Gospel*, vol. I, lxxviii-lxx, and Schnackenburg, *Gospel*, vol. I, 167-169. Schnackenburg earlier assigned more significance to the anti-baptist tone of the gospel; see "Das Evangelium und die Johannesjünger," *Historisches Jahrbuch*, 77 (1958), 21-38. The only recent effort to promote the anti-petrine thesis is Graydon F. Snyder, "John 13:16 and the Anti-Petrinism of the Johannine Tradition," *Biblical Research*, 16 (1971), 5-15. Neither of these proposals seems to articulate a major motif of the gospel, but only minor and isolated tones.

C. A Samaritan Mission

In 1967 Wayne Meeks concluded his careful study of the history
of religions setting for the prophet-king motifs of the gospel of
John with two general conclusions, the second of which is: "it is
clear that the Johannine church had drawn members from that Jewish
group [which gave great importance to Moses and the Sinai theophany]
as well as from the Samaritan circles which held very similar
beliefs..." Meeks shows in the course of his monograph that Samaritan
beliefs were probably influential in shaping the prophet-king motif
in the gospel, and furthermore that the geographical symbolism of
the gospel emphasizes Galilee and Samaria as the regions of acceptance of Jesus as opposed to Judea, where Jesus is typically met
with constant hostility. Meeks' proposal is cautious and tentative,
but it is clear that he understands the fourth gospel to have been
associated in some way with a Samaritan milieu and to have been
related to a community which had drawn its members, at least in
part, from among the Samaritans.[31]

This provocative thesis is not entirely without some precedent
in scholarship, although certainly Meeks' evidence for his conclusions is fresh. Odeberg as early as 1929 suggested that chapter
4 of the gospel was intended as a missionary appeal to the Samaritans,[32] and more recently John Bowman argued that the attitude of
the gospel toward the Samaritans might be inferred as an indication
of the peculiar missionary task of the gospel among the Samaritans.[33]
For the most part, however, the interest in finding a strong Samaritan setting for the gospel and a missionary purpose for the gospel
among those people is a relatively recent undertaking. Since 1960
we have seen a considerable acceleration of that interest begun,
perhaps, with the profound work of Meeks.[34]

In 1968, independent of the findings of Meeks, George Wesley
Buchanan undertook to develop the thesis of "The Samaritan Origin
of the Gospel of John." His contention is that the fourth evangelist
came from an anti-Judean, Samaritan Christian church. While we

---

[31]Meeks, *Prophet-King*, especially 216-257, 313-319, quote, 318.
See also, "Galilee and Judea in the Fourth Gospel," *Journal of
Biblical Literature*, 85 (1966), 159-169.
    [32]Hugo Odeberg, *The Fourth Gospel* (Uppsala, Stockholm: Almquist
and Wiksells Boktryckeri, 1929).
    [33]John Bowman, "The Fourth Gospel and the Samaritans," *Bulletin
of the John Rylands Library*, 40 (1958), 298-308.
    [34]For a survey of proposals relevant to the place of Samaritanism
in early Christianity see Charles H.H. Scobie, "The Origins and
Development of Samaritan Christianity," *New Testament Studies*, 19
(1973), 390-414.

cannot summarize all of the arguments he advances in support of his
thesis, his primary reliance seems to be upon three kinds of data:
First, the distinction between the use of the terms "the Jews"
and "Israel" in the gospel leads Buchanan to the conclusion that
these are geographical expressions--the "Jews" refers to the
inhabitants of the southern kingdom and "Israel" to the old northern
kingdom. Second, the Samaritans are treated well in the gospel,
Buchanan observes (e.g., 4:7-28). Jesus pointedly does not deny
that he is a Samaritan when that charge is made against him (8:48-
49). Other such favorable hints are found in 1:47-51 and in the
avoidance of the title "son of David," on the one hand, and the
employment of the title "son of Joseph," on the other--Joseph,
Buchanan claims, was highly favored among the Samaritans. Finally
and most extensively, Buchanan points out that there is a distinct
favoring in the fourth gospel of the old northern prophets of Israel's
past, particularly Elijah and Elisha. He then attempts to argue
that clear parallels between the Elijah-Elisha legends and the signs
of Jesus are intended by the evangelist (e.g., John 2:1-11 parallels
1 Kings 17:1-6 and 2 Kings 4:1-7). He conjectures that the signs
of Jesus were originally part of a source which presented Jesus as
the "new Elisha." "It is clear," he concludes, "the Gospel attributed
to John came from the Samaritan Christian Church."[35]

Edwin Freed published articles in 1968 and 1970 which similarly
contend that the gospel grew out of an environment at least strongly
influenced by Samaritanism. His case begins with a number of place
names which appear in the fourth gospel and have strong Samaritan
associations (e.g., Ephraim, 11:54, and Mount Gerizim, 4:20).
Second, the strong emphasis upon Moses and demonstration of the
superiority of Jesus to Moses suggests Samaritan interests, especially in the light of the fact that Abraham does not play a large
role in the gospel. The detachment from the Jewish law and tradition
--"*your* father" and "*your* law" (6:49; 8:38, for instance)--can be
explained by the Samaritan hypothesis. The other evidence Freed
advances builds upon these primary reasons for claiming a Samaritan
environment for the gospel, and produces a cumulative effect which
he trusts makes his case. For example, he suggests that the johannine dual eschatology--both present and futuristic--may be due to

----

[35]George Wesley Buchanan, "The Samaritan Origin of the Gospel
of John," *Religions in Antiquity*, 149-175, quote, 175. See a study
which supports the thesis that the fourth evangelist tried to
represent Jesus as an Elijah-Elisha figure: B.P. Robinson, "Christ
as a Northern Prophet in St. John,"*Scripture*, 17 (1965), 104-108.
See also Reim, 207-209.

the fact that Samaritan eschatology was just beginning to take
shape in the first century A.D., and the johannine eschatology may
have been especially conceived to appeal to both the Jews and the
Samaritans. Freed concludes:

> The evidence seems to me to lead to a reasonable conclusion
> that the writer of John was influenced by Samaritanism,
> and...he was attempting to make Christianity as he was
> presenting it appeal to Samaritans as well as to Jews in
> hope of winning converts from both.[36]

But we return to where we began our survey of the possible
Samaritan concern of the fourth gospel, namely, to the work of Wayne
Meeks; for Meeks has recently declared himself doubtful of the
efforts to account for too much in the fourth gospel by means of the
Samaritan hypothesis. "The Fourth Gospel itself does not give the
impression that the Samaritans were a dominant factor in the composition of the Johannine group.... Further, the author of the gospel
shows no sensitivity to specifically Samaritan concerns and terminology." While 4:31-38 does suggest that a mission among the Samaritans was involved in the birth of the johannine community, Meeks
contends that Buchanan and Freed are attempting to carry the evidence
much too far.[37]

Meeks seems to be suggesting a moderate employment of the thesis
that an appeal to the Samaritans was part of the motivation of the
gospel, and would relegate it to a secondary role. Such a moder-
ation would seem to be a preferable position in the light of the
rather tenuous evidence presented in the Freed and Buchanan articles
and in the face of the much stronger evidence that the Jewish-Christian dialogue stands so prominent in the gospel.[38] Moreover, our
knowledge of first century Samaritanism is only beginning to reach

---

[36]Edwin D. Freed, "Samaritan Influence in the Gospel of John,"
Catholic Biblical Quarterly, 30 (1968), 580-587, and "Did John Write
His Gospel Partly to Win Samaritan Converts?," *Novum Testamentum*,
12 (1970), 241-256, quote, 256.

[37]Meeks, "'Am I a Jew?'".

[38]The further study of the Samaritan religion may provide a
better base of information upon which to assess the possible influ-
ence of that movement on the fourth gospel. Among the recent
studies of the Samaritans see: John Macdonald, *The Theology of the
Samaritans* (London: SCM, 1964); John Bowman, *Samaritanische Probleme*
(Stuttgart: Kohlhammer, 1967); A. Ben-Hayyim, *The Literary and
Oral Tradition of Hebrew and Aramaic Amongst the Samaritans* (Jerusalem:
Academy of the Hebrew Language,1967); H.G. Kippenberg, *Garizim und
Synagoge* (Berlin: W. de Gruyter, 1971); James D. Purvis, *The Samar-
itan Pentateuch and the Origin of the Samaritan Sect* (Cambridge, Mass.:
Harvard Press, 1968); and M. Collins, "The Hidden Vessels in Samar-
itan Traditions," *Journal for the Study of Judaism*,3 (1973), 97-116.
On the relation of the early church to Samaritanism see Abram Spiro,
"Stephen's Samaritan Background" in Johannes Munck, *The Acts of the
Apostles* (New York: Doubleday, 1967), 285-300.

that point at which clear contacts between the gospel and the
Samaritans could be established. The work of Buchanan and Freed
does not reflect that knowledge. It seems, too, that these two
have pressed the evidence too far; they have taken evidence which
is sufficient only to show that there was some contact between
Samaritanism and the johannine tradition, and they have tried to
make that evidence support a Samaritan origin of the gospel. One
wonders how much of their purported evidence might not be used
with equal force to support the more viable thesis that the evangelist wrote out of a heterodox Jewish milieu (e.g., Buchanan's use
of the Elijah-Elisha parallels).

D. A Universal Appeal to Christians

The purpose of the gospel, finally, may reside in its attempt
to appeal not exclusively to the Jews--either hellenistic or
Palestinian--Samaritans, or Gentiles, nor to Christians of a peculiar
kind or in this or that situation, but to the whole body of Christians
of the time. The perplexing question of the delineation of the
intellectual milieu of the evangelist may just be the clue that
the evangelist does not want to present his message exclusively in
the thought modes and expressions of one heritage alone, but indeed
to demonstrate dramatically the encompassing appeal of the Christian
kerygma. Such a proposed purpose for the writing of the gospel is
found in several forms on the scene of contemporary johannine
research.

First, at the end of his discussion of the fourth gospel and
the Jews, C.K. Barrett proposes that the evangelist did not write
primarily out of a missionary motivation. The evangelist's motivation is above all to be found in his theological not evangelical
interests. He held a dialectical view of truth ("dem johanneischen
Verständnis der Dialektik der christlichen Wahrheit") which allowed
him to hold together in paradoxical tension diametrically opposed
points of view and thus present a universal type articulation of the
Christian gospel. It is no surprise then that in this gospel we
find Jewish and anti-Jewish elements, gnostic and anti-gnostic ideas,
apocalyptic and non-apocalyptic materials, institutional and anti-
establishment themes. To try to explain the whole of the gospel
on the basis of any one of these pairs of opposites is to do the
evangelist an injustice. It is only when we view him as a profound
theologian employing a sophisticated dialectic that we understand

his purpose and his goal.[39]

In a similar fashion, if considerably more brief, George
MacRae ponders the variety of christological titles and various
forms of religious understanding in the gospel, and suggests that
the evangelist was deliberately trying to assimilate a wide assortment of religious backgrounds. All this was in order to say that
Jesus transcends them all! MacRae finds a similar kind of characteristic in the evangelist's redaction of his proposed sources;
that is, his redaction was intentionally done with the purpose of
propagating the universality of Jesus. That the evangelist undertook such a task is evidence of the influence of the process of
hellenization on his way of thinking, MacRae asserts. That process
included the use of forms of various milieus to exhibit how a
primary religious idea sufficed in all sorts of settings. Witness,
MacRae points out, the manner in which Philo dealt with Judaism
under the influence of hellenization.[40]

Barrett's and MacRae's theses might find support in a specific
study of the prologue of the gospel by Lamarche, who argues that
those eighteen verses systematically develop the idea of the universal
relevance of the Logos-Christ. Verses 1-9 are addressed to the
Gentile nations, and 14-18 to the Jewish people.[41] Brown likewise
gives support to such a thesis when he refutes Robinson and Van
Unnik's claim that the gospel is addressed to hellenistic Jews in
the hope of winning converts from among them. The universal appeal
of the gospel is expressed in passages such as 1:9, 29; 3:17; and
12:35--an appeal which includes Gentiles as well as Jews, as other
passages show (e.g., 10:16; 11:52; 4:35). "Much of the Gospel,"
Brown concludes, "is addressed to the Christian believer without
distinction of whether his derivation is Jewish or Gentile."[42]

Such a thesis which proposes that the fourth gospel must be
understood as the presentation of a universal appeal to a widely
dispersed and heterogeneous audience of Christian believers is a

---

[39]Charles Kingsley Barrett, *Das Johannesevangelium und das
Judentum* (Stuttgart: W. Kohlhammer, 1970), 70-75, quote, 72.

[40]George W. MacRae, "The Fourth Gospel and *Religionsgeschichte*,"
Catholic Biblical Quarterly, 32 (1970), 17-24.

[41]P. Lamarche, "Le Prologue de Jean," *Recherches de science
religieuse*, 52 (1964), 497-537. Richard Longenecker has been the
most recent to propose that the evangelist employed the Logos
concept intentionally in order to provide a "terminological bridge"
between hellenistic and Jewish thought. *The Christology of Early
Jewish Christianity* (London: SCM, 1970), 147.

[42]Brown, *Gospel*, vol. I, lxxvii-lxxviii.

truly attractive one, for it allows the scholar to account for the
diversity of the gospel material in a rather easy manner. Still,
to propose such a thesis to the exclusion of some of the other
proposals we have surveyed in the section (which incidentally is
not the intention of Brown's endorsement of the broad purpose of
the gospel) is to credit the evangelist with a remarkably broad
range of knowledge and a truly elaborate theological system. However that may be, it is fair to note that the evangelist doubtless
had some wider audience in mind and some more universal purpose
than the one immediately confronting him. But it is that specific
purpose and that concrete situation which dominate his gospel, and
I believe recent scholarly research has shown that purpose to be
the Christian-Jewish dialogue. But while embracing that dominant
concern it may be that the evangelist, secondarily, hoped to
demonstrate the universality of the Christian message.

CHAPTER IV

THE DATE OF THE EVANGELIST'S WORK

It may be generally said that there has been a decreased
interest in the dating of the fourth gospel since the earlier years
of the historical critical method when it was deemed one of the
vital questions. Currently it has been enough to describe as
exactly as possible the other pressing concerns surrounding the
fourth gospel--the traditional materials contained in it, the
intellectual and concrete settings of the evangelist, etc.--and
allow the date of the gospel to emerge as a general implication of
the findings on these questions. It is interesting, for instance,
that Rudolf Schnackenburg's exhaustive commentary on the fourth
gospel (already in two volumes, totaling about 1200 pages and
completed only through chapter 12) nowhere undertakes a discussion
of the date of the document--surely not because Schnackenburg wishes
to avoid the question, but because it is deemed less important than
other matters which imply the date.

Still, having observed this trend away from a vital concern
for the dating of the gospel, one must acknowledge another movement
quite to the contrary, namely, the efforts expended toward dating
the gospel earlier than has traditionally been the case. These
efforts have been greatly enhanced by a number of movements in
contemporary johannine scholarship, such as the increased recognition
of the affinities of the gospel with certain forms of Palestinian
Judaism (largely but not exclusively a result of Qumran). But
additionally these efforts have been spurred on by the discovery in
1935 of the Roberts Fragment (P^{52}) of the gospel which is generally
dated 135-150 and the subsequent consensus that the gospel of John
was circulating in Egypt by this date. While there has not been

extensive research lately undertaken in an effort to date the
gospel, we must briefly mention these two trends discernible in
the critical world today.

"Thus today it is almost common opinion that John was written
in the last decade of the first century," concludes the recent
edition of Feine, Behm, and Kümmel.[1] Indeed, the majority of the
scholars working on the gospel in the past decade have taken a
position that the document reached something like its final form
toward the end of the first century A.D. Among those who could
be listed in this category are de Boor, Brown, Schnackenburg (by
implication), Lindars, and Hunter.[2] A later date is proposed by
Howard Teeple, namely, 100-110. Teeple holds this position for
a number of reasons: First, he is convinced that the evangelist
wrote after the formal expulsion of the Christians from the synagogue in A.D. 90. Second, one of the sources the evangelist
employed (Teeple's proposed "G") must be dated no earlier than 90
because of its semi-gnostic ideas, its tendency to blame the Jews
exclusively for the death of Jesus, and the evidence that it
knows the break of gentile Christianity from Judaism.[3] Teeple's
is the latest date for the gospel I could find asserted in recent
scholarly works.

But a surprisingly strong movement toward pushing the date of
the gospel back before 70 is detected. The arguments for such
are varied and the proposed datings likewise are not entirely
consistent. Among the arguments advanced in defense of the earlier
dating of the gospel are these:

(1) The evangelist had no knowledge of the synoptic gospels
which must mean he wrote before they did.[4]

(2) He used the present tense in referring to geographical sites
(e.g., 5:2), and there has been archaeological confirmation of
certain of those place names.[5]

(3) The evangelist has affinities with the Qumran movement
whose existence was terminated in A.D. 70.[6]

---

[1]Feine, Behm, Kümmel, *Introduction*, 175.
[2]de Boor, *Das Evangelium*, Bd. I, 30; Brown, *Gospel*, vol. I,
lxxx-lxxxvi; Schnackenburg, *Gospel*, vol. I, 101-104; Lindars,
Gospel, 42-43; Hunter, *Gospel*, 2; *According*, 101.
[3]Teeple, *Literary Origin*, 150, 152.
[4]Leon Morris, *Studies*, 288; *Gospel*, 33. F. Lamar Cribbs, "A
Reassessment of the Date of Origin and the Destination of the Gospel
of John," *Journal of Biblical Literature*, 89 (1970), 39-41.
[5]Morris, *Studies*, 288, *Gospel*, 33. George Allen Turner, "The
Date and Purpose of the Gospel of John," *Bulletin of the Evangelical
Theological Society*, 6 (1963), 83.
[6]Morris, *Studies*, 289, *Gospel*, 33-34; Turner, 83.

(4) The powerful Jewish offensive against Christianity witnessed in the gospel is probably pre-70 when Christianity was still part of the Jewish faith.[7]

(5) The fourth gospel has general Palestinian characteristics, such as the concern for the coming of the "prophet like Moses."

(6) It possesses primitive traits in the portrayal of Jesus, e.g., the use of *Christos* as a name is absent.

(7) It contains emphases which are similar to concerns of the church during the period 40-70 but not during a later period (70-100), e.g., the appeal for church unity, and the polemic against John the Baptist.[8]

Certain of these arguments have convinced Leon Morris and George Allen Turner of a date prior to 70; and Lamar Cribbs has declared himself to favor a date in the late 50s or early 60s.[9]

Arguments quite different have been advanced by Wolfgang Gericke in order to maintain a similar conclusion, specifically a dating of the gospel at 68. Gericke finds an allusion to Caesar Nero. in the reference to "a stranger" in 21:18. He maintains this has to do with Nero's persecution of the Christians, 61-64. In 5:43 the mention of "another" refers to the visit of Nero to the provinces of his empire about 66. Therefore, Gericke concludes, we must date the gospel A.D. 68.[10] Gericke's highly speculative and tenuous argument is hardly to be commended!

While these arguments for an early dating of the gospel have not won wide acceptance and they continue to represent a minority movement in johannine scholarship, it must be acknowledged that current research in several areas has converged upon the possibility that a later date for the gospel is no longer as necessary as it once was thought to be. Indeed, while the evidence may not yet necessitate an earlier dating, one can argue that it does open the possibility that such may have been the case. What does appear certain is that the date of the gospel is inseparably allied with other broader issues and will not be resolved until those issues have themselves been dealt with more thoroughly. For example, the concrete situation of the evangelist must be described. Then once it has been sketched in some detail, we may ask when is it most likely that such a situation existed.

---

[7]Morris, *Gospel*, 33; Turner, 84.
[8]Cribbs, "A Reassessment," 41-53.
[9]Morris, *Studies*, 291, *Gospel*, 34; Turner, 82; Cribbs, "A Reassessment," 55.
[10]Wolfgang Gericke, "Zur Entstehung des Johannes-Evangelium," *Theologische Literaturzeitung*, 90 (1965), 807-820.

CONCLUSION OF PART TWO

Käsemann's charge that scholars are but groping in darkness
when asked about the historical origin of the gospel is in part
still a valid one. Many of the old problems surrounding this issue
are still haunting the critic of the gospel, and solutions would
seem to be almost as numerous as the students who undertake the
questions. It must be admitted that current scholarship has not
laid to rest the historical enigma of the fourth gospel; to conclude otherwise would amount to gross dishonesty. But, on the
other hand, it is less than accurate to deny that configurations
of solutions have begun to emerge from the scholarly efforts of
the past few years. That certain trends toward scholarly harmony
on some of the vital questions are evident in what we have pre-
viewed is discernible. One can detect a demonstrative portrait
of the evangelist and his situation appearing.

The identity of the evangelist seems least agreed upon of the
four questions with which we have dealt, but it would seem that
the bulk of evidence points in the direction of the theory that
he was an anonymous figure who at best was privy to a tradition
which might have had some historical roots among the earliest
disciples. Although Part One has demonstrated that there is a
strong likelihood that the evangelist was able to avail himself
of a tradition which pre-dated his work, we must not conclude that
the tradition roots necessarily among the earliest disciples. It
is tempting to suggest that the evangelist's tradition originated
with an eye-witness, perhaps even John, son of Zebedee. But such
a theory cannot be supported with evidence, only desirability.
Although the possibility of such rootage in a historical eyewitness
must never be eliminated a priori from consideration, it is far
safer and more consonant with the direction of contemporary
research to hold that the evangelist is an anonymous figure who
availed himself of a tradition, the origin of which is equally
anonymous.

Likewise, the results of redaction critical analysis of the
gospel make it more and more probable that the person of the beloved
disciple in the gospel is a symbolic figure, probably invented by
the evangelist or his community to contemporize the ancient traditions of Jesus of Nazareth. The function of the beloved disciple
is that of a paradigm of some sort. Whether he is a purely ficti-
tious figure used paradigmatically, or a figure out of the history
of the johannine community given a symbolic function by the evange-

list is not certain and matters little. It does seem to me that
the evidence of contemporary scholarship has moved understandably
away from any sort of effort to link the evangelist with an eyewitness figure in the ministry of Jesus, who in the gospel is
described as the beloved disciple.

The anonymous evangelist was surely at home in the Jewish world
of the first century. Efforts toward solving the question of the
intellectual milieu and those aimed at revealing the concrete
historical situation have tended toward one conclusion, namely,
the importance of Jewish thought, modes of expression, arguments,
etc. The evangelist's thought and modes of expression are shaped
most by the Old Testament and Jewish literature. But that Jewish
literature which influenced him was of a varied and syncretistic
sort. The fourth gospel should have taught us one clear lesson
in recent years: The Judaism of the first century of the Christian
era was polymorphic. We must put to one side any effort to read
the gospel in the light of any one form of early Judaism and most
certainly in the light of a Judaism without any contacts with
hellenism. The Judaism which fashioned the evangelist's thought
knew a strong wisdom tradition as well as a mixed and flexible
tradition regarding Moses. The evangelist's Judaism was tutored
in rabbinic   and Philonic exegetical method (midrash), but knew
a dualistic world view not unlike that common among apocalyptic
sectarians of the time.

Amid this syncretistic blending of many of the various directions of Jewish thought, a kind of pre-gnosticism emerged which
was later to provide the ingredients for a Christian gnosticism
in full maturity. In its pre-johannine form this syncretistic
Jewish phenomenon, which we will call pre-gnosis, harbored a
mythology regarding the messiah which was shaped out of wisdom-
Torah-word speculations, but was not clearly docetic. Docetism
became a recognizable entity only after the fourth gospel, or at
least only in the very last stages of its composition. Within
that pre-gnosis may have resided those mystical motifs which some
(e.g., Borgen) have detected in the fourth gospel. In sum, the
fourth evangelist was a child of a multiformed, syncretistic
Judaism!

The evangelist took up the task of preparing his document
motivated by the conviction that the tradition available to his
church was not adequate to meet the new challenges resulting from
the increased hostility of a Jewish body in his locale. That
synagogue had lost members to the Christian community and still

harbored within itself secret believers. In all likelihood the
hostility was enhanced because the Christian movement had been
allied with the synagogue since its inception and the struggle
had the character of an intra-family conflict with all of the
bitterness and anger which only brothers and sisters can know.
For its part, the synagogue had expelled all its members who confessed Christ and was aggressive in its propaganda against the
church. For its part, the church was reacting defensively, with-
drawing into itself, and responding with arguments as best it
could. The church for which the evangelist wrote was a body
aborted from its womb within the circle of Jewish believers and
desperately seeking symbols and defenses of its own. The evangelist proposed by writing his two-level drama to show how the
Jewish attacks could be handled. He wrote not to evangelize--
hopes of winning the Jewish brothers and sisters to belief had
been crushed for the most part--but to strengthen the weakening
faith of the church and arm it for the dialogue with the synagogue.
The fourth gospel is a highly occasional writing, whose purpose
was to respond to an experience of crisis proportions in the
evangelist's church.

All of this requires a date late in the century, perhaps at
least as late as 80. The relationship of the johannine community
to a defensive Judaism dictates a post-70 date. It would seem
most likely that before that fateful date Judaism remained strong
and certain of itself and could entertain variegated forms of
the faith, e.g., the Qumran Essenes. After 70, however, the trend
was toward the forging of a "normative Judaism," a trend accel-
erated by the council at Jamnia. We need not assume that the
expulsion from the synagogue which the evangelist apparently knew
was the formalization of that movement by Rabbi Gamaliel II, but
only the localized expression which at a later time culminated in
the formalization. This evidence plus the other standard arguments for a later date dictate the decision in favor of 80 to 90.
The proponents of the earlier dating must still convince us that
the concrete setting of the gospel is more conceivably pre-70 than
post-70.

The historical enigma remains; there is no denying that. But
the fourth evangelist is not so much a man without definite contours,
as Käsemann would have us believe, as he is a man only now gradually
emerging from within the shadows of history. We can begin by
deduction to define his features and to reconstruct with the

historian's complementary materials of evidence and imagination
a picture of the man and his setting. As with all historical
inquiries, this one will never result in certainty. But the
trend is clearly toward a highly probable reconstruction.

PART THREE:

THE EVANGELIST

AND

HIS THOUGHT

The richness of the religious thought of the fourth gospel has
long been recognized. From the first sentence with its seemingly
cosmic orientation to the concluding chapter with its puzzling
dialogue between the resurrected (?) Christ and his disciples, the
book utterly teems with subtleties and apparent paradoxes. Its
symbolism seems endlessly rich and titillating. It is for good
reason that the book is often taken to be the most "theological"
document of the four canonical gospels, for it presents itself
immediately to its reader as a provocative essay in early Christian
thought, whatever else it may be. The fully initiated student of
the book might well conclude that the thinker responsible for this
gospel was one of the most sophisticated early Christian theologians.
Perhaps the richness of the thought of the evangelist is best
immortalized in the vast range of interpretations to which it has
been subjected. One need only glance through the theologies of the
fourth gospel written since the middle of this century to experience
the variety of modes of understanding johannine thought: a statement of Barthian orthodoxy,[1] a continuation of the heritage of
ancient Greek philosophy,[2] a "liberation" gospel understood in terms
of contemporary social and political theologies,[3] a pronouncement
of Christian Buddhism![4]

If the interpretation of johannine thought has been endlessly
difficult, it is for good reason. The gospel presents in their most

---

[1]Hoskyns, *The Fourth Gospel*.
[2]A. Ehrhardt, *The Beginning* (New York: Barnes and Noble, 1968).
[3]Frederick Herzog, *Liberation Theology* (New York: Seabury,
1972).
[4]J.E. Bruns, *The Christian Buddhism of St. John* (Paramus, N.J.:
Paulist, 1971).

serious form some of the fundamental hurdles for biblical hermeneu-
tics. The interpretation of the gospel has been plagued with two
general types of difficulties which we may hastily and simply
summarize as those connected with the interpreter and his method,
on the one hand, and the nature of the content of the document, on
the other.

In the first case, the theological interpretation of the
fourth gospel demands the most meticulous methodology. This point
may be illustrated by reference to the manner in which the theological interpretation of the critic continuously depends upon the
historical and literary judgments he or she has reached on the
issues we have discussed in Parts One and Two. Bultmann's understanding of the position of the evangelist on the sacraments
exemplifies this inter-relatedness of critical methodologies.
Bultmann maintains that the evangelist was "critical or at least
reserved" in his attitude toward the sacraments because the explicit
mentions of them in the gospel (3:5; 19:34b-35; 6:51b-58) are the
result of the interpolations of a redactor and not the words of the
evangelist himself.[5] This understanding of the evangelist's thought
clearly leans upon the source and redaction analyses done by Bultmann, and of course those analyses in turn utilize a content (or
ideological) criterion for the separation of the various strata of
the gospel--sources, evangelist, and "ecclesiastical redactor."
Bultmann's position is but illustrative of the sense in which the
understanding of the thought of the gospel presupposes positions on
such thorny issues as the evangelist's use of traditions, the intellectual milieu of the gospel, its purpose, and so on.[6]

The methodology of the theological interpreter of the fourth
gospel is still further most acutely vulnerable at the point of the
dogmatic and philosophical presuppositions brought to the task.
Nowhere else does the dogmatic pre-understanding of the interpreter
seem more evident than in the interpretation of the thought of this
gospel. The careful observer of the criticism of the fourth gospel
will note in dismay, for instance, the degree to which the lines of
difference on the theological meaning of the gospel coincide with
the differences among the theological persuasions of the critics.
A case in point, again, is the interpretation of the sacraments in
the gospel. Too often it seems that those interpreters, who are

---

[5]Bultmann, *Theology of the New Testament*, vol. II, 59.
[6]This point is clearly made by Schnackenburg, "Das Johannesevangelium als Hermeneutische Frage," *New Testament Studies*, 13
(1966-67), 206-209.

themselves wedded to a sacramental heritage, find the evidence in the
gospel overwhelmingly in favor of the view that the evangelist was
a profound sacramentarian. On the other hand, those who argue for
the position that the evangelist was anti-sacramental, or at best
a sacramental revisionist, are more often than not adherents to a
non-sacramentarian Christian tradition. Let this generalization
not be too widely applied! There are critics who have achieved an
admirable suspension of their own commitments in order to allow the
gospel to speak for itself. But the incidence of dogmatic interpretation seems, in the case of this gospel, to suggest the painfully
difficult task involved in theological interpretation.

But the difficulties in interpreting the thought of the gospel
do not lie only in the method of the critics. The nature of the
evangelist's thought and language poses unusual perplexities. Without minimizing the similar difficulties involved in other New
Testament writings, one may say that the peculiar structure of the
johannine categories of thought and symbolism are unequaled in their
opaqueness. It is the uniqueness of the evangelist's thought and
language that has kept his students diligently at their task. Moreover, in addition to the nature of his language and intellectual
categories, it is the method of his "reasoning" which stumps the
interpreter. Far from a straightforward linear argument, the
evangelist's thought seems to move in circles (more optimistically,
spirals), doubling back upon itself. It is replete with contradictions, repetitions, and simple gaps. Not least among the tasks of
contemporary interpretation is the general task of attempting to
understand the nature of johannine thought itself.

One could further enumerate the difficulties confronted by
the interpreter of johannine thought, but these will suffice to
suggest the dimensions of the assignment. When we turn to the more
immediate undertaking--the survey of the recent significant contributions to our understanding of johannine thought--other kinds of
obstacles are encountered. Unlike the various topics covered in
the Parts One and Two, the survey of johannine scholarship on the
evangelist's thought is imbued with hazards of a new and different
kind. For one thing, whereas the critical nature of the works in
historical and literary matters was quite evident, in the area of
theological interpretation such is not the case. The student may
take up a volume or article which at first appears to be a critical
articulation of the thought of the evangelist only to find that it
is a meditative exposition intended for consumption by those more
interested in the rewards of the study of the gospel for their

religious faith rather than for historical understanding. On the
other hand, a professed meditative enterprise may render rich
insights for the historical understanding of the gospel. Hence,
the well of material pertaining to our subject in this chapter
is vastly richer but more difficult to assess. The selectivity
and qualified objectivity of this survey to which the reader was
altered in the introduction are to be recalled in preparation for
the following discussion.

Our survey will attempt to embrace the major contributions of
recent years under some of the traditional topics: christology
eschatology, dualism, witness, signs, faith, the Paraclete, the
sacraments, and ecclesiology.

CHAPTER ONE

THE CHRISTOLOGY OF THE GOSPEL

Raymond Brown has shown that amid all of the disputes pertaining to the understanding of johannine thought there can be no doubt
as to the centrality of the person and work of Jesus in the gospel;
indeed, those divided over the issues of the sacraments and the
place of the institutional church in the fourth gospel converge in
their understanding of the importance of christology in the thought
of the evangelist.[1] There is little doubt that for the fourth
evangelist the person and work of Christ is the heart of the gospel
from which all other concepts are sustained. But beyond this consensus over the centrality of christology the convergence of critical
opinions ends. A massive and variegated literature on the interpretation of the johannine Christ exists, and current scholarship
has contributed more than its share to that body of literature. The
question is, how shall one understand the johannine view of Christ;
what is the key to its interpretation? If the heart of the evangelist's theology resides in his view of Christ, the penetration of
the mystery of his christology promises to open the whole of his
theology to understanding. Again, it is Bultmann who provides us
with an example of how the critic must take hold of a hermeneutical
key to johannine christology and then illuminate the whole of the
gospel's thought from that understanding of its view of Jesus. Bultmann found to his satisfaction that a gnostic-like concept of the
descending-ascending revealer was the underlying foundation of the
johannine view of Christ. With that "revealer christology" as his

---

[1]Raymond Brown, "The Kerygma of the Gospel According to John,"
Interpretation, 21 (1967), 387-392.

reference point, Bultmann interpreted the johannine christological
passages and the whole of the thought of the gospel.

Today the issues involved in the quest for the key to understanding the christology of John seem to be three in number: First,
there is the issue of the relationship between history and faith.
The synthesis of the historical tradition regarding Jesus of
Nazareth and the Christian community's experience of the living
Christ may be taken as the primary content of johannine christology.
The evangelist was undertaking to articulate both the historical
and experiential realities of Christ in his gospel. The unique
manner in which he went about this, the distinctive synthesis of
history and faith which he achieved, say some scholars, accounts
for his view of Christ.

The second issue which is articulated in the contemporary
literature on this subject is the relationship of flesh (*sarx*) and
glory (*doxa*) in the johannine Christ. The peculiar relationship
between these two found in the fourth gospel alone can yield the
treasures of its christology, according to the view of some contemporary students. In other terms, the issue in interpreting
johannine christology is the discernment of the character of the
incarnation articulated by the evangelist; or in still other (and,
from the point of view of the gospel, anachronistic) terms, the
understanding of the humanity and divinity of Christ and their
relationship is the constitutive element of johannine christology.

Finally, still another relationship has been posed as the key
in grasping the evangelist's thought, namely, that between the
person and the function of Christ. To what degree shall the
christological assertions of the gospel be taken as "functional"
as opposed to "personal" or "essential"? To determine that issue--
to discern just what the evangelist had in mind--is to make
intelligible the whole scope of the evangelist's views. Around each
of these three approaches to the understanding of the gospel is
clustered a number of contemporary views.

A. *History and Faith*

There are few scholars who pose the christological problem of
the gospel of John in the terms of history and faith, but their
contribution to contemporary scholarship is significant. In a
sense it might be argued that their putting of the question is the
most insightful of the three categories we have devised for our
analysis; this is so because the posing of the question of history

and faith goes directly to the heart of the search for an understanding of the evangelist's theological method as a whole. It is
Franz Mussner whose study best articulates the issue residing at
the base of this inquiry. Mussner, informed by the existentialist
view of history and most especially by the works of Martin Heidegger,
Wilhelm Dilthey, and Hans-Georg Gadamer,[2] wants to examine the
question of how the fourth evangelist "sees" his subject, Christ.
How does John grasp and understand Christ? In other words, what is
the hermeneutic method at work in the mind of the evangelist as
he constructs his gospel?[3]

With the question posed in this manner, Mussner proposes that
the evangelist's "historical understanding" may be analyzed best
by a study of the verbs which he employs to denote access to knowledge of the person of Christ--"to see," "to hear," "to come to
know," "to testify," and "to remember" ("gnoseological terms" is
the expression Mussner uses to refer to these words). The result
of this analysis Mussner calls the "johannine vision"--the peculiar
manner in which the evangelist bridges the historical gap between
himself and his subject (the historical Jesus) and articulates his
view.

> The Johannine mode of vision is that of a believing and
> informed witness who, in remembrance, "sees" his subject,
> Jesus of Nazareth, in such a way that the latter's hidden
> mystery becomes "visible" and expressible for the Church
> in the kerygma. This act of vision is, therefore, a creative
> process. It renders possible the transposition of the
> knowledge obtained by it into the testimony of the kerygma
> ...the Johannine kerygma, we may say, is the product of the
> Johannine mode of vision.

The components of this "vision" are for Mussner, first of all, the
evangelist's own eyewitness experience of the career of Jesus, the
inspiration of the paraclete, the tradition of the church (which
Mussner suggests supplied the presuppositions of the evangelist's
method of hermeneutic), and finally, the evangelist's way of supply-
ing his subject, Jesus, with the evangelist's own language.[4] It is
this latter point that is one of the major contributions of Mussner's
study, namely, the demonstration of the manner in which the evange-

---

[2]Martin Heidegger, *Being and Time* (New York: Harper and Row,
1962);Hans-Georg Gadamer, *Wahrheit und Methode* (Tübingen: Mohr,
1960); Wilhelm Dilthey, *Meaning in History* (London: Allen and Unwin,
1961) and *Pattern and Meaning in History* (New York: Harper, 1961).
[3]Franz Mussner, *The Historical Jesus in the Gospel of St.
John* (London: Burns and Oates, 1967), 7-9.
[4]For a similar view see C. Traets, *Voir Jesus et le Père en
Lui selon l'Évangile de Saint Jean* (Rome: Pontificiae Universitatis
Gregorianae, 1967), 194-197.

list transferred his own symbolical system back onto the lips of
the historical Jesus.[5]

We find an informative parallel with Mussner's provocative
proposal in a small article by Heinrich Schlier, whose presuppositions would seem to betray a philosophical stance not dissimilar
to the existentialist orientation of Mussner. Schlier too speaks
of the evangelist's historical understanding and asks why the
Christ of the fourth gospel appears in some ways as a historical
figure (the features of historical time and place comprise part of
the context of the Jesus in the gospel) while the evangelist's
report lacks a full historical character (there is no concern for
Jesus' inner motives, for example). The evangelist was interested,
Schlier concludes, not in history itself but in the *essence* of his
subject which lies "under" its empirical reality. He was interested
to articulate the essential *nature* of the person Jesus, and this
subject transcends the historical realm.[6] This "essentialist"
concern would seem to constitute for Schlier the "johannine vision,"
to import Mussner's terminology, and is similar to what Mussner
means when he suggests (in the quotation above) that the vision of
the evangelist unlocks and makes visible and expressible the "hidden
mystery" of Jesus. Schlier likewise understands that the evangelist's insight was achieved by virtue of the revelation of the
Paraclete who removes the puzzle of the identity of Jesus for faith.
The evangelist's own view is represented in his portrayal of faith
in the gospel, particularly characterized by a "seeing in seeing."[7]

Oscar Cullmann's vigorous defense of a salvation history method
employed by the fourth evangelist comes out of a markedly different
orientation. Moreover, Cullmann does not pose the issue explicitly
in terms of the relationship of history and faith; but it is surely
the case that the salvation history theme is a way of understanding
the dialectic between those two principles. For Cullmann we might
say the evangelist's historical understanding was that of a scheme
of the stages in the saving acts of God. The evangelist perceived
the Christ figure as the center of the three saving epochs, the
history of Israel preceding and the history of the church following

---

[5]Mussner, *The Historical Jesus*, 17-90, quote, 45. An argument
for the influence of the early church's kerygma upon the fourth
gospel and the adherence of that gospel to the ancient kerygma is
undertaken (without success in my opinion) by David R. Carnegie,
"The Kerygma in the Fourth Gospel," *Vox Evangelia* 7 (1971), 39-
74. Carnegie's parallels between the kerygma and the elements of
the thought of the fourth gospel are strained and unconvincing.
[6]Heinrich Schlier, "Zur Christologie des Johannesevangelium,"
Das Ende der Zeit (Freiburg: Herder, 1971), 85-88.
[7]*Ibid.*, 98-100.

him. While the salvation history scheme in the New Testament,
Cullmann claims, is characterized by the three sequential epochs,
"all are bound together among themselves by their orientation towards Christ, the midpoint of salvation history, who supplies this
history with its meaning and sums up the epochs of salvation history in himself."[8] This means that for the evangelist the incarnate Christ is the center of all history. The evangelist writes
in the genre of the gospel in order to emphasize just this point,
namely, that it is history with which he is dealing, but more
importantly the meaning of history, its salvific sense. The events
in the life of Jesus constitute for the evangelist the links between
the past history of God in Israel and the activity of God in the
evangelist's own church. From the point of view of Cullmann's
salvation history, then, the evangelist understood himself linked
with the historical past of Jesus on a continuum of God's saving
events, the heart of which was the subject of his gospel.[9]

Both Mussner and Cullmann can say then that the past career
of Jesus of Nazareth and the evangelist's and his community's
experience of the exalted Christ are merged. Cullmann writes,

> The line now leads from this brief space of time [the
> life of Jesus] to the time of the Church, so that in
> each event and in each saying during the historical
> life of Jesus its effect in the activity of the exalted
> Lord in the early Church is announced...[10]

Mussner speaks of "the essential identity of the Jesus of history
with the glorified Christ" and argues that there is a continuous
and unbroken line between the pre-existence of Christ and his
glorification in the church.[11] While it is commonplace to find
interpreters claiming that in the fourth gospel the historical Jesus
and the exalted Lord are identified, Mussner and Cullmann give a
structure of understanding by which the evangelist was able to do
this.

While J.C. Fenton has not unfolded that structure of understanding as completely as Cullmann and Mussner, his suggestions
for comprehending the evangelist propose an implicit historical
understanding which results in this identity of the historical Jesus
and the Christ of faith. His thesis is simply that the evangelist's

---

[8]Oscar Cullmann, *Salvation in History* (New York: Harper and
Row, 1965), 285. See also, "L'Evangile johannique et l'histoire
du salut," *New Testament Studies*, 11 (1965), 11-122.
    [9]*Ibid.*, 270-278.
    [10]*Ibid.*, 278.
    [11]Mussner, *The Historical Jesus*, 82-88, 109. See also Joachim
Gnilka, "Der historische Jesu als der gegenwärtige Christus im
Johannesevangelium," *Bibel und Leben*, 7 (1966), 270-278.

mind worked "backwards" from what *is* to what its *origin* is, from
effect to cause. The evangelist's understanding of Christian
existence in his own time, for instance, is the framework out of
which he develops his view of Christ (as the Christian is born
from above, 3:3, so Christ is from above, 3:16; as the Christian
obeys God, 3:36, so Christ does, 8:29, 55). The fourth evangelist's
"account of Jesus is understandable only if we consider...that his
life of Christ is a projection backwards of the Christian life;
in short, that his understanding of Christian existence is our
starting point for understanding his gospel."[12] In this remarkable
fashion, then, the evangelist projected his own experience into the
past and onto Jesus to produce the christology of his gospel and
link the reality of the living Christ with the historical Jesus.

The enterprise exemplified in the work of Mussner, Schlier,
Cullmann, and Fenton represents the most basic kind of approach
to johannine christology. Without posing the question of the
relationship between faith and history all christological analyses
of the gospel remain partial. The basic question of johannine
christology is, then, the way in which the fourth evangelist understood the relationship between his own and his community's faith,
on the one hand, and the historical origins of the Christian movement, on the other. To probe this matter is to seek the mode of
understanding utilized in the evangelist's grasp of Christ.

Yet the enterprise is seriously infected with difficulties.
It seems to result in some form (mild or extreme) of bisection.
The very category which we employ to summarize these views--faith
and history--already embodies a dichotomy which obtains in each of
the analyses in one form or another. Faith and history perhaps
should not be understood as separable poles in experience or understanding. This partition is most evident in Schlier's attempt to
speak of the empirical realities of history on the one hand and
the "essence" or sense of history on the other.[13] Cullmann's
thesis performs a more radical partitioning by separating out one
history as "salvation history", as if all other history were

---

[12]J.C. Fenton "Towards an Understanding of John," *Studia
Evangelica*, vol. IV, 28-37.

[13]The same sort of bifurcation in its more popular form is
the proposal of Leon Morris that the fourth evangelist's thought
is to be understood in part, at least, in terms of the distinction
between fact (objective history) and interpretation. "History
and Theology in the Fourth Gospel,"*Studies in the Fourth Gospel*,
65-138.

"profane" or "damning".[14] Fenton's surprisingly simple proposal
offers enticing opportunities to develop such a "backward" reasoning as the key to fourth gospel thought, but care must be exercised
here too to prevent an implicit separation of past and present in
the collective mind of the johannine community.

Clearly Mussner's study suggests the most helpful lines along
which the probing of the evangelist's historical understanding
might be pursued. His efforts are solidly founded on an understanding of history and the understanding of understanding itself.
What cripples the analysis he proposes is his essaying to hold
together a number of not entirely harmonious theses. First, he
contends for a "historical understanding" which utilizes his
fundamentally existentialist grasp of history; then, he argues for
the "inspiration" of the Holy Spirit in the evangelist's work and
the founding of that work on the church's tradition; and finally
he maintains unwaveringly that the evangelist was an eyewitness of
the historical Jesus. These theses seem to move on different
levels. It would seem that the first two are not supplementary but
somehow derivative of one another. That is, the "historical understanding" of the evangelist would seem to be another way of speaking
of that insight which is his *because* of the ingredients of inspiration
and tradition rather than standing alongside of inspiration and
tradition. The argument for the eyewitness testimony of the evangelist, while possibly a sound thesis in and of itself, seems at best
just another ingredient and not a necessary one. Mussner has chosen
the wrong context within which to argue for the eyewitness character
of the fourth gospel.

Moreover, one wonders if with the combination of Mussner's
claims that the evangelist was informed by both his own eyewitness
experience with Jesus and the church's tradition about Jesus does not
have the force of minimizing the effectiveness of his suggestion
that the evangelist's historical understanding accounts for the
uniqueness of his gospel. That indeed would seem to be the case.
If the theses of the evangelist's use of his own eyewitness and the

---

[14]Raymond Brown's suggestion that Cullman transports the lukan
theology of history into the interpretation of John is surely
correct. "The Kerygma of the Gospel According to John," 395-396.
Bultmann's insistence against Cullmann to the effect that the
fourth gospel is totally lacking in the elements of the salvation
history scheme may be an overstatement but is near the truth.
Theology of the New Testament, vol. II, 8. This is so in spite
of the widespread use of that scheme in the interpretation of the
gospel. See, for example, Anne Jaubert, "L'image de la Vigne (Jean
15)," *Oikonomia. Heilsgeschichte als Thema der Theologie*, Felix
Christ, Herausgeber (Hamburg: Herbert Reich, 1967), 93-99.

church's tradition are true, the peculiarity of his historical
understanding would be compromised and brought more closely into
line with that of the other gospels. The uniqueness of johannine
christology is thereby left unexplained. In sum, however, Mussner's
proposal offers the most promising of the ones we have examined thus
far, and one would wish for the development of his major thesis
without the unnecessary baggage of his extraneous contentions.[15]

B. Flesh (*sarx*) and Glory (*doxa*)

The second issue taken as the clue to the meaning of the
evangelist's view of Christ is the relationship between Christ's
humanity and his divine glory.[16] The importance of 1:14 for
johannine christology is commonplace knowledge, but what relationship between flesh and glory is intended by the assertion, "the
Word became *flesh*...and we saw his *glory*"? If the divine Logos
becomes fully human, how is it that his character as divine being
is still visible? How is one to read 1:14? Should it be understood in terms of the domination of the fleshly form of the Logos
over his divine nature, with the result of veiling his glory? Or
is the evidence of the visible glory to be taken as the qualification
of the extent of the humanity of the Logos?

Bultmann resolves this dilemma by claiming that the fourth
evangelist formulates the nature of Christ in the form of a radical
paradox--flesh and glory coincide in the person of Jesus.[17] But
Bultmann also understands that the glory present in the person of
Christ is understood to have been hidden by his fleshly existence.
The flesh functions almost as a disguise which faith must overcome
if it is to perceive the revelation of the glory of Christ. "If
man wishes to see the *doxa*, then it is on the *sarx* that he must
concentrate his attention, without allowing himself to fall a victim
to appearances. The revelation is present in a peculiar *hiddenness*."[18] As influential as Bultmann's interpretation continues to
be,[19] the debate over this issue goes on, much of it centering on
Bultmann's view.

---

[15]Robert Kysar, review of Mussner, *Journal of the American
Academy of Religion*, 36 (1968), 142-144.
[16]See the earlier and very influential work of W. Thüssing,
Erhöhung und Verherrlichung Jesu im Johannesevangelium (Münster:
Aschendorff, 1960).
[17]Bultmann, *Theology of the New Testament*, vol. II, 50.
[18]Bultmann, *Gospel*, 63.
[19]For example, C.K. Barrett, "The Prologue of St. John's
Gospel," *New Testament Essays* (London: SPCK, 1972), 27-48.

Our categories for analysis run dangerously close to over-
simplification, but we will venture to suggest that the debate has
spun off in three directions: On the one side, some have emphasized the dominance of the glory of Christ in the fourth gospel and
understood that his humanity is but a disguise of varying effectiveness. On the other extreme, some have insisted that the evangelist
fully accepted the flesh of Christ and that his divine glory was
made subservient in the incarnation to his earthly existence. Between these two extremes are those interpreters who have found the
evangelist to make sense only if one understands him to be saying
that the flesh and glory are indivisibly one in the person of Jesus.

1. *The Dominance of Glory*

One of Bultmann's own students, Ernst Käsemann, has radicalized
his teacher's position and proposed the most extreme emphasis upon
the dominance of divinity in the johannine Christ. It is fair to
say that Käsemann's work, *The Testament of Jesus*, is the most
important and most controversial study of johannine christology in
the past decade. His work has been the center of the scholarly
storm on johannine christology much as Bultmann's work was the
center of all johannine interpretation until more recently.
Käsemann's deceptively short study (78 pages) contains a meticulously
argued and daring thesis.

Käsemann undertakes the examination of John 17 as the heart of
johannine thought. He believes that Cullman's salvation history
hermeneutic for the gospel is misguided, for the evangelist is
uninterested in history. Bultmann's effort to demythologize the
gospel is likewise wide of the mark, and the evangelist's symbols
are to be taken literally. Read in that manner, the evangelist
presents what Käsemann labels a "naive docetism." The johannine
Jesus is throughout the gospel the glorified one. Far from being
the humbled divine being of Philippians 2, the johannine Christ
experiences no humiliation except that he is the Son exiled into the
world. He in no sense has laid aside his divine glory while in
exile, but carries it with him. Hence, while the Philippian hymn
seems to conceive of glorification as the *result* of Christ's obedience, Käsemann understands the fourth evangelist to see obedience
as a *form* of glorification which characterizes the whole of Christ's
earthly existence.

Correspondingly, there is no real worldly history in the gospel
of John; history is made into the world's reaction to the Christ.

"Incarnation in John does not mean complete, total entry into the
earth, into human existence, but rather the encounter between the
heavenly and the earthly." The concentration of johannine narratives and discourses on the person of Christ indicates to the
interpreter that the evangelist has a dogmatic interest in Christ.
There is a *proper* understanding of the nature of Christ, and faith
means simply knowing who Jesus really is. Therefore, the evangelist
has one dogma, namely, the unity of the Father and the Son. The
evangelist betrays the fact that he was a part of a conventicle in
the early Christian movement, perhaps rooted in the Corinthian
enthusiasts group (1 Corinthians 12-14). John's community contributed its dogmatic interpretation of faith to the development of
early Christianity, on the one hand, and its docetic christology to
the nurturing of Christian gnosticism, on the other.[20]

Käsemann's claim that one must see in John the total concentration upon this dogmatic docetic view of Christ and the extreme
disinterest in the historical, worldly realm into which the Christ
is exiled presents us with the most radical formulation of the
dominance of glory in the johannine Christ. But it has been asserted
that Siegfried Schulz's christology is closely akin to that of
Käsemann's.[21] In a sense this is certainly the case, for like
Käsemann, Schulz understands the evangelist to have no interest in
the humanity of Jesus. Jesus is supremely the divine revealer in
the fourth gospel, "God striding upon the earth." "In Jesus a
divine being tarries on earth among men." The Old Testament sense
of the son of man as the corporate representative of Israel is
entirely swallowed up, claims Schulz, in the conception of Christ
as the pre-existent, heavenly God who has descended to earth. All
of this emphasis upon the divine character of the revealer roots
in the strong influence an oriental, gnosticized form of early
Christianity had on the evangelist.[22]

To this point Schulz sounds as if he is in essential harmony
with Käsemann, and indeed one even finds Schulz arguing that the
fourth evangelist has a dogmatic interest in the person of Jesus
and the faith recognition of him. But the dominance of glory in
the conception of johannine christology proposed by Schulz stops

---

[20]Käsemann, *The Testament of Jesus*, 7-13, 21-26, 34-35, quote,
65. See also "Aufbau und Anliegen des johanneischen Prologs,"
Exegetische Versuche und Besinnungen (Göttingen: Vandenhoeck und
Ruprecht, 1964), Bd. II, 155-180.
[21]J. Edgar Bruns, review of Schulz, *Das Evangelium*, *Catholic
Biblical Quarterly*, 35 (1973), 115.
[22]Schulz, *Das Evangelium*, 64, 211, quote, 209. See also *Die
Stunde der Botschaft*, 352.

just short of the radical position of Käsemann. Schulz will admit
that neither 1:14 nor the whole of the johannine view is docetic
in nature, even though it obviously stands under the sway of gnostic
conceptions. "Jesus is a common man; for the eyes of faith, however, he is at the same time the heavenly Son and revealer." Jesus'
worldly existence is real, Schulz asserts. He prefers to reject
the label "naive, gnosticizing docetism" in favor of "christology
of exaltation." "God becomes man without doubt, according to John,
but his heavenly being is not confounded by his manner of existence
in the world. John 1:14 is, therefore, in no way to be interpreted
in the sense of a Christology of humiliation."[23] The humanity of
the revealer is actually a transparent "disguise and veil" of his
divinity; and it is in the form and appearance of the flesh that
the revealer's divinity is held. What the fourth evangelist has
done, then, according to Schulz is bind together a pre-existent,
incarnational christology with the traditional materials regarding
the life and career of Jesus. This accomplishment marks one of the
evangelist's most valuable contributions to early Christian thought.[24]

Käsemann and Schulz agree that in the fourth gospel the dominance of glory prevails in the person of Christ. Both would deny
that there is a genuine theme of humiliation in the johannine conception of the incarnation. But against Käsemann, Schulz finds a
recognition of the humanity of Jesus in the fourth gospel, although
it in no sense constricts the divine glory of the revealer. Moreover, there is for Schulz a genuine historical interest expressed
in the gospel, and the gospel genre is employed by the evangelist
without emptying it of its historical orientation. Schulz seems
closer to Bultmann than to Käsemann when he suggests that the
humanity of the revealer is a disguise or veil which becomes transparent to the eyes of the believer. There is no doubt that Schulz's
reading of johannine christology highlights the gnostic emphasis
upon the glory of the revealer, but it lacks the radical docetic
claim of the work of Käsemann.

Schulz's assertion that the fourth evangelist had no real interest in the human quality of the revealer recalls the conclusions
of Luise Schottroff's study of johannine dualism. (See Part Two.)
Like Schulz, Schottroff finds the christology of the fourth evangelist best understood in the context of the dualistic thought of
the writer, and also like Schulz, she finds the fourth gospel to be
a creative synthesis of gnostic and Christian thought. At the

---

[23]Schulz, *Das Evangelium*, 211.
[24]*Ibid.*, 211-212; *Die Stunde*, 323, 331.

conclusion of her investigation of johannine dualism, Schottroff
discusses the johannine view of Christ. She contends that the
fourth evangelist inherited the concept of the fleshly existence
of the revealer from earlier forms of Christian thought and placed
it within the gnostic dualism. 1:14, then, is part of the baggage
the evangelist carries from the Christian tradition. He understands
"flesh" to designate the inner-worldly reality, and "glory" the
other-worldly, heavenly reality. That the revealer was a fleshly
creature for a time is the "irrelevant given" with which the
evangelist deals. Jesus was temporarily an ordinary man, but for
the believer that fact is totally insignificant. Faith concentrates
upon the glory of the revealer and in effect ignores his flesh. In
a statement which sounds remarkably like Schulz, Schottroff insists
that Jesus' heavenly reality is not confounded by his earthly being.
Jesus is not simply a divine-like man, but the other-worldly
revealer who stands over against this world, the realm of the flesh.

Neither Bultmann nor Käsemann, Schottroff says, correctly
understands the two-reality scheme of the fourth gospel. Against
Bultmann, she argues that these two realities are not related as
paradox; the flesh is never the object of faith even as it is
linked with the glory in the person of the revealer. The two
realities are parallel and separate "tracks" which have no contact
with one another. Käsemann too is wrong, then, in seeing the
evangelist's thought as docetic. 1:14 is neither anti-docetic nor
docetic, Schottroff asserts. It is not that the fourth evangelist
thought the fleshly being of Jesus was unreal (docetism) nor that
he seemed unconsciously to imply that view (naive docetism); but
he simply thought it irrelevant for faith.[25]

We must return to Schottroff's provocative study still again
in connection with the subject of johannine dualism, but for now
suffice it to say that hers is still another contribution to the
interpretation of johannine christology which understands the
dominance of glory. Her perception of the meaning of the incarnation for the evangelist would seem to differ from Käsemann's in
a manner distinct from Schulz, although the contacts with Schulz's
thought are obvious. Where Schulz would want to say, seemingly,
that the historical, fleshly being of Jesus was real to the evangelist and perhaps even indispensable, Schottroff labels it "irrelevant."
From Schulz's works it is inferred that the evangelist by choice and
preference believed in the human character of the revealer. Might
one not infer from what Schottroff writes that she thinks the

---

[25]Luise Schottroff, *Der Glaubende und die feindliche Welt*, 268-
279, 289-290.

evangelist declared the fleshly reality of the revealer almost
exclusively because it was a part of the tradition with which he
was working? The peculiar position of Schottroff on this matter
must not be subsumed under either that of Käsemann or Schulz but
stands as a distinct articulation of johannine christology, associated with those of Käsemann and Schulz by its emphasis upon the
other-worldly character of the Christ figure, but differing from
them in the subtle way in which the evangelist is understood to
regard the fleshly reality of Jesus.[26]

Those who understand the christology of the fourth gospel
under the aspect of the dominance of glory in the earthly career
of Jesus have doubtless picked up one of the unique features of
this gospel. There is no doubt that, compared with every other
christological formulation of the New Testament, the fourth gospel
witnesses to a "higher" view of Christ. Still, the studies we have
examined in this subsection are highly assailable at a number of
points. First, it may be charged that they are each guilty of
selecting their evidence from only a portion of the data of the
gospel. That is, they have disregarded some assertions of the
document in favor of others which support their thesis. 1:14a
cannot be easily shoved under the dominion of 1:14b. Presumably
the presence of 1:14a in the text is deliberate and must be taken
seriously. Käsemann especially has too easily dismissed the evidence

[26]A number of shorter studies have made contributions related
to the exaltation christology of the fourth gospel. On the question of the exaltation motif itself, see, Ignace de la Potterie,
"L'exaltation du Fils de l'homme," *Gregorianum*, 49 (1968), 460-
478; G.B. Caird, "The Glory of God in the Fourth Gospel: An Exercise in Biblical Semantics," *New Testament Studies*, 15 (1968-69),
265-277; Th. C. De Kruijf, "The Glory of the Only Son (John 1, 14),"
Studies in John, 97-110; P. Van Boxel, "Die Präexistente Doxa Jesu
im Johannesevangelium," *Bijdragen*, 34 (1973), 268-281. On the
son of man motif in the gospel, see Eugen Ruckstuhl, "Die johanneische Menschensohnforschung, 1957-1969," *Theologische Berichte I*,
Josef Pfammatter und Franz Furger, Herausgeberen (Zürich: Bensiger,
1972), 171-284; Hyacinthe -M. Dion, "Quelque traits originaux de
la conception johannique du Fils de l'Homme," *Science Ecclesiastiques*,
19 (1967), 49-65; Edwin D. Freed, "The Son of Man in the Fourth
Gospel," *Journal of Biblical Literature*, 86 (1967), 402-409; Barnabas
Lindars, "The Son of Man in the Johannine Christology," *Christ and
Spirit in the New Testament*, Barnabas Lindars and Stephen S.
Smalley, eds (Cambridge: University Press, 1973), 43-60; M. de
Jonge, "Jesus as Prophet and King in the Fourth Gospel," *Ephemerides
Theologicae Lovanienses*, 49 (1973), 160-177; Robert Beauvery, "'Mon
Père et votre Père,'" *Lumière et Vie*, 20 (1971), 75-87; C.-J. Pinto
de Oliveira, "Le verbe *Didonai* comme expression des rapports du
Père et du Fils dans le IVe evangile," *Revue des sciences
philosophiques et théologiques*, 49 (1965), 81-104. On the chris-
tological meaning of the "I Am" sayings, see André Feuillet,
"Les *Ego Eimi* christologiques du quatrième Évangile," *Recherches
de science religieuse*, 54 (1966), 213-240.

which tends to contradict his proposal of naive docetism.   None
of these critics seems to have come to grips with the evidence
for the subordination of the revealer to God (e.g., 14:28; 17:3;
5:19).[27]

Nor can Schottroff be allowed to dismiss 1:14 as the baggage
of tradition borne by the evangelist as the "irrelevant given."
Such a theory demands, first, a convincing tradition analysis of
the passage which shows the place of that tradition in pre-johannine thought, and, second, a reasonable suggestion for why the
evangelist chose to preserve a traditional statement which generally is dissonant with his own view. On the whole, these critics
have not accounted for the entire thought of the gospel with their
exaltation christology proposals.

The second major weakness of the studies we have just surveyed
is the failure to deal adequately with the theological implications
of the gospel genre. Unless we have vastly misunderstood the
gospel form (and there is no doubt that more work must be done on
this subject), the simple fact that the evangelist has chosen to
express himself through the means of a gospel indicates that there
is a real historical human life at the root of the central character
of his witness. If flesh is irrelevant to the evangelist or if
the revealer in no sense really took upon himself fleshly existence,
why did the evangelist write a *gospel*?[28] Schulz is to be commended
among this group of scholars for attempting to take seriously the
gospel form. Schottroff and Käsemann, it seems, never face this
fact head on.

A third point of vulnerability is that these scholars have
not adequately considered the relation of faith and history in the
evangelist's hermeneutic. The Jesus of the fourth gospel, as Mussner
and others have taught us, is surely the synthesis of the community's
experience of faith with their risen Lord and the historical traditions regarding Jesus of Nazareth. Surely the fourth evangelist
does not pretend to describe the latter to the exclusion of the
former, but neither does he intend that his exaltation christology
lose its relation to the historical Jesus. Those who would stress
the dominance of glory in the johannine picture of Christ must then
move to a consideration of the relationship of the historical figure
of Jesus as an ingredient of that picture and the Christ of the

---

[27]Werner Georg Kümmel, *The Theology of the New Testament* (New
York: Abingdon, 1973), 269.
[28]George W. MacRae, review of Käsemann, *Testament, Journal
of the American Academy of Religion,* 38 (1970), 328-332.

church's faith as the other.[29] It seems to me that neither Käsemann nor Schottroff does that with sufficient clarity or precision.
On the other hand, Schulz's insight that the fourth evangelist
has bound together a pre-existent and incarnational christology
with the traditional Jesus materials is a helpful contribution and
places the exaltation christology of the gospel in a more satis-
factory context.

The opposite side of the coin is that these studies have made
a number of invaluable contributions to our understanding of
johannine christology. First, it is surely the case that in the
gospel of John something radical has happened to the traditional
humiliation theme. It has been reworked and paradoxically stood
on its head with the result that humiliation is made to serve
exaltation. The son of man motif is widely employed but with a
decisive reversal of its implications. Second, these studies have
faced and articulated the obvious fact that a dogmatic feature
emerges (perhaps for the first time in the Christian movement) in
the gospel of John. That the view of the relationship of the Father
and Son is treated as a necessity for faith seems an inescapable
conclusion from a careful reading of the gospel; but for too long
that fact has not been admissible (perhaps because of the dogmatic
presuppositions of some of the interpreters). Finally, the emphasis
upon the dominance of glory in the johannine christology yields
salutary results for efforts to seek out the historical accuracy of
the fourth gospel. A clearer understanding of the prevalent christology of exaltation tempers those ambitious efforts to discern the
historical Jesus in the johannine Christ. These efforts are not
necessarily excluded by what is discovered in the christological
studies, but they are shown the boundaries, as it were, of the quest
of the historical Jesus in the fourth gospel.[30]

2. *The Dominance of the Flesh*

It is not surprising to find there is little scholarly effort
<u>to argue that</u> the divine nature of the johannine Christ is over-

[29]Eduard Schweizer, "Jesus der Zeuge Gottes," *Studies in John*,
186.

[30]Other discussions of Käsemann's contribution are found in the
following: Reviews of *Testament* by G. Delling, *Theologische
Literaturzeitung*, 93 (1968), 38-40; Edwin Freed, *Interpretation*, 23
(1969), 349-351; Wayne A. Meeks, *Union Seminary Quarterly Review*, 24
(1969), 414-420; J. Giblet, *Louvain Studies*, 2 (1968-69), 398-399;
Robert Kysar, *Perspective*, 10 (1969), 180-181. Günther Bornkamm,
"Zur Interpretation des Johannes-Evangelium," *Geschichte und Glaube*,
Erster Teil (München: Chr. Kaiser, 1968), 104-121; Brown, "The
Kerygma of the Gospel According to John," 396-400.

shadowed by his thorough involvement in fleshly existence. In
spite of frequent arguments that the humanity of the Christ figure
is strongly maintained by the fourth evangelist (e.g., 4:7, 31;
11:35),[31] most students of the thought of the gospel recognize that
the humanity of the johannine Christ is at least well balanced off
by the divine glory. In a little noticed book published post-
humously, W.H. Cadman pursues an exposition of the fourth gospel
which seems to be the closest thing to an argument for the dominance
of the flesh in the johannine Jesus to be found in recent literature. The thesis of Cadman's study is

> that what Jesus in the Fourth Gospel reveals is not the
> eternal nature or truth of God, not even the eternal
> purpose of God, but rather the fact that this eternal
> purpose is being enacted in His own life and ministry and
> will reach its full accomplishment in His impending passion
> and its aftermath, the sending of the Spirit; that, when
> John speaks of Jesus as the only Son in the bosom of the
> Father, and when Jesus speaks of Himself as the Son of Man
> who is in heaven, these are to be understood as metaphorical
> descriptions of the close union with God enjoyed by Jesus
> during His earthly life; and that, when Jesus speaks of his
> having ascended to heaven, or having heard and seen heavenly
> things in the presence of His Father, He is referring to the
> process by which he came to know and identify Himself with
> the will of God for Himself and incidentally for mankind.[32]

The ways in which Cadman's fragmentary explication of the
theology of the fourth gospel betrays the sort of orientation we
have ascribed to it are several. First, he proposes that all the
christological symbolism of John be understood metaphorically rather
than literally. For instance, the descending and ascending of the
Son of Man refers to Jesus' origin (descent) and to his eventual
awareness of that origin (ascent). What Cadman in effect does with
the symbolism is to demythologize it but in quite different categories than the existentialism of Bultmann. Second, Cadman gives
a pervasive human quality to the johannine Christ when he concludes
that the "Son" titles refer to the humanity of Jesus. "Son of Man"
refers to the perfect manhood of Jesus, Cadman stresses. If the
favorite title of the fourth evangelist for Jesus suggests the
fleshly existence of the revealer, that gives the entire gospel a
much more strongly historical, human orientation than others have
proposed.[33]

Furthermore, Cadman argues that the evangelist intended to
present Jesus as the ideal example of humanity. Christ is presented

---

[31]Kümmel, *The Theology of the New Testament*, 271.
[32]W.H. Cadman, *The Open Heaven. The Revelation of God in the
Johannine Sayings of Jesus* (Oxford: Blackwell, 1969), 59.
[33]*Ibid.*, 13, 29-30.

as "the Proper Man, man living as God intended him to live, in continuous communion with Himself, totally dependent on God's authority and totally obedient to His will..." That perfect humanity exemplified in the johannine Christ, moreover, is extended to all persons. All are capable of the kind of humanity presented in Jesus. This is Cadman's understanding of the meaning of 17:24. Fourth, Cadman indicates his preference for the dominance of the flesh in the incarnation when he speaks again and again of the manhood of Jesus being taken into unity with the Logos.[34] This suggests that the manhood of Jesus has some sort of identity independent of the Logos, and the two are brought into unity.

The contrasts between the position of Cadman and those of Käsemann, Schulz, and Schottroff are obvious, but a few examples might be mentioned. Käsemann contends that the evangelist intended his symbolism to be read literally, but Cadman builds his entire interpretation on the presumption that it should be taken metaphorically. While Schulz maintains that the evangelist has no interest in the earthly life of Jesus as such, this is the focus of johannine christology for Cadman--Jesus' emerging self-awareness of his divine origin. Schulz insists that the origins of the son of man title are irrelevant to the johannine meaning, for the evangelist takes that title to describe the God among men in Christ. Cadman would have it just the reverse: The son of man title epitomizes the real humanity of the johannine Christ.[35] Rather than irrelevant (as Schottroff would have it), the flesh of Christ is a necessary link in the scheme of salvation in the fourth gospel if believers are to find in Christ the type of manhood to which they are invited to strive.[36]

---

[34]*Ibid.*, 74, 40-42, quote, 41.

[35]Some support for the thesis that the Son christology of the fourth gospel refers to the historical, human Christ is found in recent scholarship: Elizabeth Kinniburgh, "The Johannine 'Son of Man'," *Studia Evangelica*, IV, 64-71; John Howton, "'The Son of God' in the Fourth Gospel," *New Testament Studies*, 10 (1963-64), 227-237 (Howton's thesis that the Old Testament corporate sense of "Son of Man" controls its meaning in the fourth gospel sounds at least remotely similar to Cadman's contention that Christ becomes a corporate, inclusive manhood--42.); Stephen S. Smalley, "The Johannine Son of Man Sayings," *New Testament Studies*, 15 (1968-69), 278-301; Rudolf Schnackenburg, *Johannesevangelium*, Bd. II, 166-167.

[36]Recent studies which argue for a genuine suffering of Christ in the fourth gospel on the model of the suffering servant of Isaiah may be relevant to the demonstration of an authentic fleshly existence of the johannine Christ: Feliks Gryglewicz, "Das Lamm Gottes," *New Testament Studies*, 13 (1966-67), 133-146; David Hill, "The Request of Zebedee's Sons and the Johannine *Doxa*-Theme," *New Testament Studies*, 13 (1966-67), 281-285; Manfred Weise, "Passionswoche und Epiphaniewoche im Johannesevangelium. Ihre

Cadman's book is difficult to read and summarize, for it is loosely organized and structured. (The book is the result of G.B. Caird's efforts to bring together into one volume the unfinished manuscripts and scattered notes of his former teacher.) It would appear in many ways to border upon a meditation for faith rather than a scholarly study, for one is sometimes led to think that Cadman is really more concerned to ask how the gospel can be understood in a meaningful way for the believer today than with the question of the original meaning and intent of the evangelist. His proposals lack the strength of roots in a study of the intellectual milieu in which it can be claimed johannine thought is to be understood; and, for the most part, his argument is done in isolation from contemporary scholarship. On the positive side, it might be said that Cadman's study is a bold attempt to make sense out of the puzzle of johannine symbolism. As different as their proposals are from each other, Cadman and Käsemann are similar in their endeavor to interpret the christology of the gospel in a rather bold, new way. Cadman's findings are faintly reminiscent, however, of an older liberal biblical interpretation which might have been popular in the United States in the early part of this century, and in fact his handling of johannine symbolism has all the earmarks of a pre-Bultmannian day!

3. *The Indivisibility of Flesh and Glory*

To no one's surprise the survey of current studies in johannine christology discovers that the largest number of scholars proposes something like what might be called a mediating position on the question of the relationship of flesh and glory in the johannine Christ. The reality of the flesh and the presence of the divine glory are both maintained by the evangelist, they argue, without one eclipsing the other. How they articulate this common position is what separates these scholars from one another; it is the conceptual framework in which they understand the evangelist to have arrived at his balanced christology that marks the distinctions in scholarly contributions here.

The frequency of the occurrence of the Greek verbs "to send"

Bedeutung für Komposition und Konzeption des vierten Evangeliums," *Kerygma und Dogma*, 12 (1966), 48-62. More distantly related are the studies of Athanase Negoitsa and Constantin Daniel, "L'Agneau de Dieu est le Verbe de Dieu," *Novum Testamentum*, 13 (1971), 24-37, and Georg Richter, "Die Deutung des Kreuzestodes Jesu in der Leidengeschichte des Johannesevangeliums (Jo 13-19)," *Bibel und Leben*, 9 (1968), 21-36.

(*apostellein, pempein*) in reference to Jesus and his mission in the
fourth gospel (e.g., 5:38; 6:29; 7:29; 8:42) have prompted a number
of scholars to think of the nature and mission of Jesus in terms
of the "envoy," "the one sent," etc. We have seen in the Part Two
how there has been an investigation of the intellectual milieu for
this idea;[37] but we must now examine two scholars who have attempted
to use this category as the basic christological expression of the
gospel. The "envoy" concept allows one to formulate the johannine
insistence upon both the reality of the flesh and the reality of the
glory in the person of Jesus. Ernst Haenchen's article on the
subject has been widely read and discussed; Josef Kuhl's full book-
length study of the mission theology in the fourth gospel which
includes a comprehensive development of the theme of Jesus as God's
envoy has, on the other hand, been given limited notice. The latter
certainly has not been discussed as widely as it should be as a
contribution to johannine scholarship.

Haenchen understands that the envoy motif presupposes a dualism
of knowledge in the fourth gospel; that is to say, the world cannot know God since the two are separated as two poles of the dualistic scheme. The only way for humans to have information of God
is if God "sends" such information into the world. The fourth
evangelist conceives of that communication in the formula of God's
sending his Son. Both Haenchen and Kuhl describe characterizations
of the johannine envoy which prove to be strikingly similar.
Enumerating the "roots and characteristics of the mission of Jesus,"
Kuhl lists (1) the obedience of Jesus to the will of the one who
sent him, the Father; (2) Jesus' perfect unity of action (8:28) and
being (14:9-11) with the Father; and (3) the love of the envoy
which is the basic motive and character of the mission. Haenchen
describes what is meant by the envoy and mentions the obedient
speaking and doing of the Father's will (3:34; 5:17) by which he
perfectly fulfills the will of the one who has sent him (5:30). He
is "the voice and the hand of the Father: and as such can demand
honor from men (5:23, 44). Haenchen also speaks of love as the
primary characteristic of the mission of Jesus. "John has seen the
entire earthly life of Jesus as the revelation and realization of
this divine love."[38]

Both these scholars, however, are careful to say that Jesus is

---

[37]Juan Peter Miranda, *Der Vater, der mich gesandt hat.*
[38]Ernst Haenchen, "'Der Vater, der mich gesandt hat,'" *New
Testament Studies*, 9 (1963), 210-212, quotes, 211 and 212 respec-
tively. (Also in *Gott und Mensch*, 68-77.) Josef Kuhl, *Die Sendung
Jesu und der Kirche nach dem Johannes-Evangelium* (St. Augustin:
Steyler, 1967), 94-106.

more than a human representative (prophet) of God. Haenchen understands that the evangelist wants to say that in the envoy the Father
himself becomes *word* in Jesus' words. One hears the Father in the
words of Jesus when one hears him correctly; this is especially
the case in the "I Am" sayings. Kuhl formulates the matter somewhat differently. Jesus is the "absolute envoy of God." The envoy
concept sheds light upon the sonship theology of the gospel, and
suggests that the envoy enjoys a unique relationship with the
Father. But Jesus is also the revealer in the fourth gospel. To
be the revealer of God roots in the concept of sonship which
corresponds to "being sent." Jesus' whole existence is the revelation of the Father, as the "I Am" sayings best articulate.[39]

Kuhl goes on to discuss the crucifixion as the completion of
the mission of Jesus and ties the earthly life of Jesus with his
pre-existence and post-resurrection existence as a limited journey
in the world. The earthly being of Jesus is like an "intermezzo"
or a station along the whole journey of the divine envoy. Hence,
the sending of the divine envoy is bracketed with the sending of
the disciples, and the earthly envoy is followed by the gift of
the pneumatic envoy, the Paraclete. Haenchen, too, links the
preaching of the earthly envoy, Jesus, with the preaching of the
disciples in the post-easter church and claims that John can describe
them as one.[40]

It is unfair to press the comparison of the work of Haenchen
and Kuhl any further, since the former is an exploratory article
on johannine christology, and the latter a full-length study not
of johannine christology but of the mission motif in the gospel.
Still, they are representative of the attempt to utilize this
category of the "sending of the Son" as a comprehensive christological
formulation. There is much about this category that rings true to
the gospel and places the christology of that document in continuity
with the prophetic theme of the Old Testament. What is inadequate
about it as a christological expression of the thought of the evangelist is that it leaves the relationship of flesh and glory largely
unexplored, although it affirms the reality of both. That is, the
sense in which Jesus' humanity conditions his divine origin is not
articulated by the categories employed by Haenchen and Kuhl, and the
basic issues of the humiliation-exaltation motif are, for the most
part, not explored. Kuhl's work may be designed only to show the
sense in which the envoy christology is associated with the mission

---

[39]Haenchen, "'Der Vater'", 211; Kuhl, 65-88.
[40]Haenchen, "'Der Vater'", 216; Kuhl, 106-128, 130-138.

theology of the gospel as a whole, and it is therefore unfair to
expect his christological section to articulate all the issues we
are interested in here.[41]

Two other studies of the johannine christology may be mentioned
in conjunction with those who endeavor to argue for the insepara-
bility of flesh and glory in the evangelist's view. They are F.-M.
Braun and André Feuillet. In the third and fourth volumes of Braun's
study of the theology of the fourth evangelist, he expounds the
christology of the gospel. He speaks of "the indivisible Christ"
of the fourth gospel who is both human and divine at once, and this
might be taken as the prominent theme of his view of the subject.
It is his contention that the Jesus of history and the Christ of
faith are continuous; Jesus is identical with the Holy Spirit, and
the earthly life flows into the time of the church without inter-
ruption. So, the work of Christ is divided into two stages: The
first is the stage of the earthly ministry and the second the
ministry of the Spirit. The first is marked by the *visible* presence of the unique Son of the Father, "who being God assumed a
humanity like ours." During this period, he is bound to time and
space; and the second stage is distinguished by the freeing of Christ
from those constraints. The eternal glory is fully present in the
earthly life of Jesus, Braun argues, but it is veiled and constrained,
limited by its fleshly form. But after the passion and resurrection,
the divine glory is unleashed from these limitations. The distinction between the two stages is that of visible and invisible, constrained and free, and preparatory and fulfilling. The incarnation
made Christ visible in order that persons could be drawn near to
him; his exaltation extends his presence to all humanity in and by
means of the Spirit.[42]

André Feuillet leaves no doubt in his reader's mind that he
understands the christology of the fourth gospel from the standpoint
of an orthodox view of the trinity. He speaks again and again of
the trinitarian quality of the johannine presentation. The johannine Jesus is, for Feuillet, fully equal with God. The dependence
upon the Father which the gospel attributes to Jesus is a "dependence
within the equality of the Son through relationship with the Father."
The whole incarnational concept of the gospel is filled with a mystery

---

[41]Karl Wennemer, review of Kuhl, *Theologie und Philosophie*,
44 (1969), 573-376. For Kuhl's contribution to johannine ecclesiology,
see Chapter VI of this Part.
[42]F.-M. Braun, *Jean le Théologien. Sa Théologie. Le Mystère
de Jésus-Christ* (Paris: Gabalda, 1966), 224, 243-246, quote 243.
Jean le Théologien. Sa Théologie. Le Christ, Notre Seigneur (Paris:
Gabalda, 1972), 288-289.

that transcends human comprehension, Feuillet seems to suggest.
But the incarnation is a real taking on of fleshly existence. It
is no simple superfluous vestment which covered the divine glory
in the incarnation. It involved a debasement and a "humble passage"
for the divine Logos. But it was a provisional debasement and
not a permanent state of being. Therefore, the johannine Jesus is
genuinely but temporarily human while retaining his equality with
God in the mystery of the divine trinity.[43]

Neither of these studies succeeds in overcoming the deficiency
of those which undertake the question from the perspective of the
envoy christology. Both Braun and Feuillet articulate an understanding of the relationship of flesh and glory which maintains the
indivisibility and actuality of both in the incarnate Christ; but
neither is able to present a model for comprehending the way in
which the two are interrelated in the fourth gospel. Feuillet's
continual reference to the "mystery of the incarnation" poses,
however, an honest and viable position, namely, that the relationship
of flesh and glory in the johannine Christ is not subject to the
categories of human rationality. However that may be, the critical
study of johannine thought must beware of appealing to the category
of the inexplicable, lest the hard work of analysis be left undone.

Both of these works are commendable for the manner in which
they synthesize johannine ideas: Braun succeeds in doing this for
the whole of johannine theology; Feuillet, here at least, for the
phenomenon of divine love in the johannine literature. Still,
neither of them is able to present an attractive and compelling
understanding of johannine christology. Feuillet seems to take far
too much for granted and fails to argue any kind of cogent case,
while Braun too easily harmonizes johannine concepts with other
New Testament ideas without taking seriously the uniqueness of the
fourth gospel.[44] It may very well be that no position on this
question of the relationship of flesh and glory will do justice to
the fourth gospel except one which maintains the indivisible
balance of the two. We must, however, await in the future a convincing articulation of a position which proposes an understanding
of the interrelationship of flesh and glory in the johannine
Christ.[45]

---

[43]Andre Feuillet, *Le Mystère de l'amour divin dans la théologie
johannique* (Paris: Gabalda, 1972), 69-77, 239-240.
[44]Floyd V. Filson, review of Braun, *Jean. Le Mystère*, *Journal
of Biblical Literature* 86 (1967), 345-346. James M. Reese, review
of Feuillet, *Le Mystère de l'amour divin*, *Catholic Biblical Quarterly*
35 (1973), 83-85.
[45]Evidence for an equal or balanced dialectic between flesh and

C. *Function and Person*

     Some claim that the categories of flesh and glory are rendered
anachronistic at least in the way they are handled by the scholars
we have just examined. This might be the response of many who
find either the relationship of faith and history or of flesh and
glory inadequate to articulate the johannine point of view. Instead,
the language and thought of the evangelist himself are more nearly
brought under control with the categories of function and person.
It is what Jesus *does* in the fourth gospel and how that relates
either explicitly or implicitly to his person, say some, that is
the model by the means of which johannine christology can best be
understood. The active language of the fourth gospel with its
preference for verbs as opposed to substantives should guide us,
propose some scholars, to the relationship of person and work which
is really essential to the johannine view of Christ. For our
analysis we have grouped under the rubic "function and person"
four critics who all in some way or the other seem to want to
understand the contribution of the fourth evangelist to early christology in terms of what Jesus is said to have done and what he is
made to say about his work.
     First, there are three who at least imply that in johannine
christology function is prior to person. That is, these three
understand that what the johannine Christ does is more important
than any statement we may find about who he was. John A.T. Robinson
states this proposition in its most radical form. He claims that
the christological language of the fourth gospel is parabolic in
nature and that the functional relationship between Christ and God,
and not absolute status, is the concern of the evangelist. In
10:34-38, for instance, Jesus is given a metaphysical status no
different from any human but is assigned a unique function. Still,
Robinson does not go so far as to say that it is function alone with
which the johannine view of Christ is concerned. Metaphysical
uniqueness is also claimed for Jesus (e.g., 10:30), which demonstrates that the evangelist did not regard metaphysical unity and
functional affinity strict alternatives. Robinson understands that
the evangelist held these polarities together (just as the evangelist

---

glory in the johannine concept of the incarnation is found in the
studies of the "I Am" sayings by Harner, *The "I Am" of the Fourth
Gospel*, 53-65 and Schnackenburg, *Johannesevangelium*, Bd. II, 69-70.
Less important but related to this position are Yves-Bernard Trémel,
"Le Fils l'Homme selon Saint Jean," *Lumière et Vie* 12 (1963),
65-92 and Leon Morris, *The Gospel*, e.g., 115-126 and 172-173.

did not polarize human and divine in the Christ figure, thinks Robinson). Still, the primary goal of the johannine christology, Robinson seems to be arguing, was to present a picture of *how* Jesus was rather than *what* he was. John was trying to depict the "feel" of one "who is utterly human and yet whose entire life is lived from God as its centre and source...a man whose life was lived in *absolutely intimate dependence*...upon God as his Father."[46]

If Robinson wants to emphasize the function of Christ almost exclusively, while still maintaining that function does not exclude metaphysical status, Johannes Riedl has produced a careful study which may generally be said to claim that the function of Jesus in the fourth gospel *reveals* his person. Riedl's study of the "work theology" of the fourth gospel is really a contribution to both johannine christology and eschatology and we will return to it below with regard to the latter subject. For now it is enough to show how Riedl argues that the works of the johannine Christ are an integral part of the total christology of the gospel. His thesis with regard to christology is that the expressions used in the gospel for the works of salvation (*erga, ergon, ergazesthai*) describe the function of Christ and hence imply the nature of his person and what is accomplished in his works. He qualifies his study by asserting that the evangelist clearly held a metaphysical and not merely a functional view of Christ's sonship; but function and person are not to be strictly separated. The evangelist seems to presuppose, however, that in the functions one performs, his or her person can be discerned.

It is understandable, then, that Riedl should believe that in the terminology regarding the saving *work* of God in Christ the christology of the fourth gospel is epitomized. The analysis of this terminology suggests that the Father and Son in the fourth gospel are two free and independent actors doing their work. The unity of wills and work, as well as unity of nature (5:19), does not minimize the individuality of each. Johannine christology is binitarian. Still, Jesus performs the saving works in the fullest dependence upon his Father. Therefore, the analysis of the function of Christ in the fourth gospel leads us to the understanding of his person--a free individual united with his God in will and nature and fully dependent upon him.[47]

---

[46]John A.T. Robinson, "The Use of the Fourth Gospel for Christology Today," *Christ and Spirit in the New Testament*, 68-76, quotes from 76 and 68 respectively.

[47]Johannes Riedl, *Das Heilswerk Jesu nach Johannes* (Freiburg: Herder, 1973), 24-26, 40, 414, 420-423.

For Robinson it is function alone which is the message of johannine christology; for Riedl it is the person revealed through the explication of his function. Heinrich Schlier's position, as it is expressed in a short article on the revealer and his work in the fourth gospel, might be summarized with the assertion that for the fourth evangelist *function is person*. Schlier argues that the description of Jesus as the Word of God is not mere analogy; it is not parabolic, as Robinson would have it. Rather, Jesus actually does what the Word is and does. The obedient doing of the Father's will is the performance of Jesus' being, that is, of his being the eternal Word in history. This involves the gift of his life and his self-witness in both word and sign. The consequence is that Jesus reveals the Father when he reveals himself; his revelation is singular--"Jesus himself and God in him."[48] So, in Robinson, Riedl, and Schlier we have three outlooks on johannine christology which all claim that the function of Christ is prior to his person, and which all claim that function is the clue to the identity of the johannine Christ.

A far different kind of approach to the subject of the function of Jesus according to the fourth gospel is found in the recent study by Klaus Haacker. Haacker's work is one of the most creative approaches to the christology of the fourth gospel in recent years because it is comprised of a unique approach to the puzzlement of the johannine Christ. His contention is that the theology of the fourth gospel is centered around the conception of the man Jesus as the historical founder of and original authority for a religion which claims to be the source of salvation. 1:17 provides the key to this central concept, for there it is claimed that Jesus is the founder of Christianity as Moses was the founder of Judaism. The comparison of the role of Jesus and the role assigned to Moses in Judaism and Samaritanism, plus the roles assigned historical founders of other religious traditions (especially Islam), demonstrates the dominant concern for this view in the gospel. But particularly the Moses-Jesus comparison is the clue to the structure of John's theology.

The results of Haacker's rather unique approach to johannine theology include the following: First, Jesus is presented in the

---

[48]Heinrich Schlier, "Der Offenbarer und sein Werk nach dem Johannesevangelium," *Besinnung auf das Neue Testament. Exegetische Aufsätze und Vorträge* (Freiburg: Herder, 1964), Bd. II, 254-260. See a somewhat comparable proposal by Karl Wennemer, "Theologie des 'Wortes' im Johannesevangelium. Das innere Verhältnis des verkündigten *Logos theou* zum persönlichen *Logos*." *Scholastik* 38 (1963), 1-17.

gospel as the turning point in time. Second, the christological
formulations in the gospel are presented as continuations of Jesus'
own self-proclamation during his ministry. Third, the johannine
understanding of the Christian community grows out of the sense
that the community is grounded in and has its origin in the historical works of Jesus. Fourth,

> The historical representation of Jesus' word and way is
> the formative power in the life of the Christian. The
> existence of believers in the world stems neither from
> institution...nor intuition...but from the representation
> of the earthly Jesus. The theology of John is therefore
> neither "early Catholic" nor enthusiastic. [It is bound]
> ...to the historical Jesus who is the Word become flesh.

Fifth, christological motifs are employed in the gospel in order to
establish the divine origin of the founder, e.g., the spatial symbol
of descending and ascending and the temporal symbol of pre-existence.
Sixth, the attention to the farewell address of Jesus in the gospel
is the evangelist's attempt to respond to the problem posed by the
departure of the founder of the faith, hence the emphasis there is
upon promise. Seventh, the soteriological themes in John are
concentrated in the concept of Jesus as the founder; hence, he is
the revealer in the sense that he is the historical founder, and he
is one who takes away sins by virtue of his historical acts. The
result of Haacker's position is a view of the christology of the
gospel which emphasizes the earthly, human, and historical function
of Jesus and the continuing dependence of the believers upon that
historical reality.[49]

These four critics add immeasurably to our store of studies
of the johannine christology, and their utilization of the categories of function and person open up new avenues of creative interpretative insight. One may argue, too, that the functional approach
to johannine christology is the most nearly indigenous of the types
we have found on the contemporary scene; that is to say, that of
the three sets of relationships used to understand johannine christology (faith and history, flesh and glory, and function and person),
the functional category tends the least to impose contemporary modes
of thought upon the gospel. While flesh and glory are categories
drawn directly from the gospel itself, they tend to become translated
into the non-johannine categories of human and divine; and faith
and history are clearly terms formulated out of the problems of the
contemporary mind and not necessarily out of the problems of the
evangelist. On the other hand, the category of function and person

---

[49]Klaus Haacker, *Die Stiftung des Heils. Untersuchungen zur
Strucktur der johanneischen Theologie* (Stuttgart: Calwer, 1972),
25-173, quote, 90.

seems to be akin to the kind of Old Testament/Jewish milieu out of
which we believe the fourth gospel emerged, and this category moves
least perhaps into anachronistic language.

It is, at least in my opinion, more likely that the early
Christian movement first rooted itself in an existential sense of
what this man Jesus had done in the lives of those who contacted
him than it is to imagine the early emergence of a set of assertions
about the identity and origin of this figure. The function of the
Christ figure could conceivably give rise to the assertions about
his person; but the function-person approach to the christology of
the fourth gospel holds constantly before the interpreter the proper
priority of function.[50]

Having said all of this in a positive way about the general
approach we have just examined, some serious reservations about
the specific accomplishments of these four critics must be voiced.
It is clear, to begin with, that Robinson's approach to the christology of the fourth gospel in the article we have examined is
prejudiced by his concern that the evangelist's christology yield
a believable position for the modern person. Robinson's emphasis
upon function in the evangelist's thought, then, moves toward
accomodation to modern thought rather than faithful exposition.

On the other hand, Robinson reminds us forcefully of the
symbolic nature of johannine christological language in his suggestion that it is parabolic; this is a point which Schlier's position
lacks, much to the loss of his formulation. He tries to ignore the
symbolic character of the evangelist's thought with his assertion
that function is person. Nowhere else does the symbolic character
of religious language seem to be more deliberately used than in
the fourth gospel, and yet Schlier tries to ground his position in
a basic denial of that fact. All God language is symbolic, modern
theological and philosophical work has taught us, and it seems
that the fourth evangelist is most aware of that and most free
among the New Testament writers to exploit it.

Riedl's position is the most successful of the three who are
concerned with what we have called the priority of function to
person in the fourth gospel. Function does reveal person, Riedl
insists, and that premise has obvious affinities with both the
formulations of the fourth gospel and what we know of the relationship between actions and personality in modern psychology. Riedl,
it seems to me, has proposed an approach to the christology of the
fourth gospel which at once does justice to the priority of function

---

[50]Schnackenburg, *Gospel*, vol. I, 154-156.

which appears in the gospel and at the same time the undeniable
fact that function and person are not separable in the thought of
the evangelist. The prominent place of the terminology of work in
the gospel should cue us, as it did Riedl, to this avenue to johannine christology. Still, it seems the statements which Riedl
eventually makes about the person of Christ in the fourth gospel
are not simple extensions of the function of Christ. He seems to
have a propensity to find a binitarianism in the gospel which does
not follow as logically from his analysis as it should. The
recurring thorn in the flesh of interpreters of the christology of
the fourth gospel is not successfully extracted by Riedl despite
his careful surgical efforts, namely, the pronounced dependence of
the Son upon the Father. In my judgment, Riedl's method is sound
and promising, but his application of that method and its results
are less than totally satisfying.

   With Haacker we have an illustration, perhaps, of one of the
new kinds of biblical interpretation to be done in the future.
The effort to apply the "religious typology" developed in the study
of the phenomenology of religion to the christology of the fourth
gospel is, in my estimate, ingenious and exciting. For too long
biblical interpretation has been done in the confines of its own
discipline, and Haacker is asking us to overcome those confines.
It is hard not to concur with the judgment of I. Howard Marshall
about Haacker's work: "He may perhaps seem to have a glimpse of
the obvious, but the point is that nobody else has seen it quite
so clearly before, and used it to present a thoroughly viable
alternative to radical scholarship [e.g., Käsemann]."[51]

   But the initial excitement over Haacker's enterprise wears off
with reflection. The first sort of alert to be sounded apropos of
Haacker's work is the simple question, "Is this founder christology
really the view of the evangelist?" Does 1:17 justify imposing on
the fourth gospel as a whole a modern history of religions category
like that of the "founder"? One should be nervous about allowing
one verse (1:17) or even one motif (the Jesus-Moses comparison) to
bear such enormous weight. It is doubtful that the category of the
historical founder of a religion was operative in the mind of the
evangelist in such a major way as Haacker proposes. Second, the
reader should be alerted to the results of the kind of functional
approach Haacker uses. One may ask after reading the thesis of
Haacker's study, "so what?" The evangelist certainly means to say

---

[51]I. Howard Marshall, review of Haacker, *The Evangelical
Quarterly* 44 (1972), 173.

more than that Jesus was the historical founder of Christianity.
Certainly to say that the evangelist visualized Christ as the
founder of a new era of existence is to articulate only part of
what he meant to say with the whole of his christological formulations. Haacker's method does not reveal the *kind* of founder
Jesus is claimed to be by the fourth gospel, and one must develop
additional methodology to deal with that question once Haacker's
thesis has been established.

In conclusion of the section on johannine christology, the
points of view taken by scholars seem ever-widening and the range
of categories utilized for the analysis of the subject endlessly
expanding (e.g., envoy, works, founder). But our short-range
historical survey must be corrected by the assurance that the
subject of johannine christology has always been one over which
there was a wide range of differing opinions. The crucial issues
do appear to be coming into sharper focus in the recent years,
however. Those issues which seem to be sharpening are the ones
we have employed for our survey: How are the historical facts of
Jesus related to the faith experience of the evangelist and his
community? In that context of history and faith in the gospel, how
did the evangelist understand the relationship and the interaction
of flesh and glory in the incarnate Christ? And how is the function
of the incarnate Christ related to his person in the fourth gospel?
The methodology of christological analysis must focus upon these
three questions with none excluded, but it must also overcome a
number of other continual problems we have witnessed in the works
of the scholars we have surveyed. First, the method must deal with
all of the data of the gospel without denying the presence of the
"harder texts." Second, it must develop categories for analysis
which grow up out of the gospel itself and are not impositions of
modern thought upon the gospel. The construction of such a methodology will not be easy, but its prospects for realization are bright
if the quality of current christological analysis is carried into
the future.

CHAPTER II

THE ESCHATOLOGY OF THE GOSPEL

From the christology of the gospel to its eschatology is but
a short step; for, as we shall see, there is universal agreement
that the eschatological teachings of the evangelist are rooted in
and constitute little more than extensions of his view of the person and work of Christ. Short step although that may be, it is a
creative one, for the eschatology of the fourth gospel, without
doubt, comprises one of its most creative contributions to early
Christian thought. As one scholar has put it, not without some
playfulness, perhaps: "The Gospel of John contains the *last* word
of the New Testament on eschatology (not so much in the chronological
as the theological sense)."[1]

Still, johannine eschatology has been a storm center of scholarship, especially in recent years. This is in part due once again
to a provocative thesis advanced by Bultmann to the effect that
the evangelist himself entirely denies the older apocalyptic,
futuristic eschatology and has demythologized it. The results are,
according to Bultmann, that the evangelist proposes that all of
the realities associated with the final days (the eschaton) were
present in Christ and experienced by the believer. The gospel
evidence for this view is abundant (e.g., 3:18; 5:24, 25, etc.); but
there is also ample evidence that the evangelist holds to the view
that the eschatological realities are yet in the believer's future
(e.g., 5:28; 6:39-40, 54; and 12:48). Bultmann accounts for these
latter·passages by means of his theory that the present gospel is
the result of the work of the evangelist and the additions of a later

[1]Paola Ricca, *Die Eschatologie des vierten Evangeliums* (Zürich:
Gotthelf, 1966), 180. Italics mine.

ecclesiastical redactor. The futuristic apocalyptic eschatology in
the fourth gospel is found only among the additions effected by
the redactor, who wants to adjust the teachings of the gospel so as
to make them more compatible with the orthodox teachings of the
church of his time. Consequently, the futuristic passages are
an intrusion into the thought of the evangelist, Bultmann claims.

The debate over the question of how to account for the
futuristic teaching in the context of a rather obvious emphasis
upon the actualization of the eschaton in the believer's life has
been a lively and continuous one.[3] At the heart of the debate is
the very nature of the evangelist's view of the "last things,"
which is hardly separable from his view of the person and work of
Christ.

Recent years have seen at least five major works on, or related
to, the eschatology of the fourth gospel. They all agree in their
emphasis upon the christocentricity of johannine eschatology. All
argue in some way or another that the eschatology of the fourth
gospel is grounded in the christology of that gospel. Josef Blank's
study, *Krisis*, takes as its major thesis that eschatology is part
of johannine christology and must be understood and explicated that
way and not as if christology were subordinate in the evangelist's
thought to eschatology.[4]

Similarily, Paolo Ricca's essential point is, "The johannine
eschatology is a 'personalized' eschatology in the sense that the
time of the incarnation to the end of Christ is dominant; Christ
embodies the eschaton and encompasses it; he introduces it into
history." By "personalized eschatology," of course, Ricca means
that it is an eschatology centered in the person of Christ.[5] Riedl,
whose work we have already noted in conjunction with christology,
also claims that the eschatology of the fourth gospel is correctly
understood only as a function of christology, and that the evangelist has "christologized" the eschatology, centering it in the
person and work of Christ.[6] Schnackenburg's point is much the same,[7]

---

[2]Bultmann, *Theology*, vol. II, 39-40; *Gospel,ad loc.*
[3]Robert Kysar, "The Eschatology of the Fourth Gospel. A
Correction of Bultmann's Redactional Hypothesis," *Perspective*, 13
(1972), 23-33, especially n. 3, 31-32.
[4]Josef Blank, *Krisis. Untersuchungen zur johanneischen
Christologie und Eschatologie* (Freiburg: Lambertus, 1964), 65,
109.
[5]Ricca, 179, 90.
[6]Riedl, 34, 39.
[7]Schnackenburg, *Gospel*, vol. I, 159-60; *Johannesevangelium*,
Bd. II, 543.

and even Käsemann agrees that the eschatology of the gospel is
controlled by its christology, although his resultant understanding
of the eschatology, as might well be imagined, is far different.[8]

Still more startling, perhaps, is the fact that all five of
these explications of johannine eschatology affirm the genuine
presence of a futuristic eschatology of some kind in the gospel.
The way they each understand the relationship of the present and
future eschatologies of the gospel and hence the nature of the
eschatological realities themselves varies, however. Ricca affirms
that in the gospel one can find all three "acts" of the eschatological drama for the Christian, namely, the fact that the eschaton
has come in Christ's appearance, that it is present in the believer's
life now, and that it is yet to come in the future. That the
eschaton appeared with the coming of the historical Jesus is one of
the central affirmations of the gospel, according to Ricca. The
evangelist intended to say that with the appearance of Jesus the
messianic expectations were fulfilled and the eschaton realized.

The eschatological realities of judgment and eternal life
are present realities henceforth. The content of the future is
already present regarding these two matters. The unbeliever is
already judged in the sense that his or her future is without hope,
has no positive content, and is identical with the past. The
believer has, on the other hand, a future hope and therefore has
passed beyond judgment. The believer participates in the saving
history and therefore in eternal life, Ricca understands. The
questions about the future are made superfluous by the faith in
Christ. But eternal life is not identical with resurrection, and
it is that resurrection which the believer has to hope for in the
future. The believers' every "now" is the eschatological "now"
(*nun*), for the Spirit continues to make the eschaton actual in the
believers' lives. The Spirit is the continuous presence of the
eschaton in the time between the appearance of the eschaton in
Christ and its final fulfillment in the resurrection.[9]

Blank's focus is more narrowly upon the matter of judgment in
the fourth gospel and its relationship to the view of Christ, but
his articulation of the present and future dimensions of johannine
eschatology is similar to that of Ricca. The evangelist has consciously utilized the two meanings of the word *krisis*, Blank claims--
judgment and decision. Judgment is realized or eliminated by virtue
of the nature of the individual's decision. The saving purpose of

---

[8]Käsemann, *Testament*, 16.
[9]Ricca, 63-180.

God achieves its goal in the believer, and judgment is thereby eliminated. The unbeliever has, on the other hand, already experienced judgment. Therefore, judgment is the result of the human response to the saving event--a personal decision regarding a concrete, historical person. Salvation is transformed into judgment at the hands of human rejection.

The eschatology of the fourth gospel is realized in the sense that the eschatological realities (life and judgment) are present in Christ. It is an eschatological moment because it is a christological one. Similarly, Jesus' "hour" is the eschaton. But the future dimension of the eschatological teaching of the gospel is not to be denied. In a manner somewhat like Ricca, Blank affirms the future hope for the resurrection for the believer. 5:28-29 does not speak of the resurrection of those who are "dead" but of *those who are in their tombs*. The future hope is the resurrection of those who embrace life in Christ but are "entombed" until the last day. The transition from death to life, which the believer makes, anticipates the future, eschatological quality of life. But the fourth gospel never explains how the realization of the future is achieved in the present life of the believer; it only asserts it to be the case.[10]

For Riedl, the fourth evangelist holds the present and the future dimensions of eschatology together by assuming that the present eschatological realities are veiled, are only partially discernible. The future hope of the Christian is, according to Riedl's interpretation of the fourth gospel, the revelation of the true facts of the situation of the believer, namely, that the believer is already free from death and embraces life. The future in the evangelist's thought will remove the concealment and reveal what now is only known in faith. Like Ricca, Riedl understands that the believer's now (*nun*) is the present of the believer in the post-easter church. It is the time of the experience of the "continued presence" of the exalted Lord.[11] The present becomes the basis for the future, making it possible in a new way.[12]

Schnackenburg's contention that the eschatology of the fourth gospel is both present and future is more concisely stated and hence more difficult to decipher. He asserts that the johannine emphasis

---

[10]Blank, 42, 94-99, 124-139, 179.

[11]James P. Martin argues that history and eschatological experience are bound together in chapter 11. "History and Eschatology in the Lazarus Narrative. John 11:1-44," *Scottish Journal of Theology*, 17 (1964), 332-343.

[12]Riedl, 18-23, 35-36, 39.

upon the actualized eschatological realities "does not do away
with the whole of the old ('dramatic') eschatology in favour of
each present moment of decision." It is true that judgment is
the "self-caused" result of unbelief (3:18-21) and the expression,
"the last day," is used by the evangelist as a mere image for
Jewish apocalyptic beliefs (11:23) or is imitated by a later redactor (6:39, 40, 44, 54; 12:48). However, the evangelist has not
rejected the future expectations of the Christian kerygma, but has
rethought them entirely and interpreted them in new categories which
are not horizontal-temporal but vertical, ontological ones.[13]

Käsemann's interpretation is expectedly quite different. While
he contends that there is a futuristic eschatology in the fourth
gospel, it is not the older apocalyptic future expectation. That
eschatology is entirely rejected by the fourth evangelist, Käsemann
insists. The resurrection passages of the gospel can only mean
that the believer is resurrected *now* in his response to Christ.
Just as the understanding of Christ has been shifted from what he
was to become in the resurrection to what he was in his pre-existent
home ("protology," as Käsemann calls it), so the view of Christian
existence is shifted away from what the believer becomes in the
eschaton to what he is in the moment of his belief. But chapter 17
of the gospel does introduce another kind of future hope for the
believer, namely the expectation of heavenly perfection. The
heavenly unity of all believers is the johannine spiritualization
of the older apocalyptic hope which has been detemporalized and
put into a metaphysical context.[14]

Blank and Ricca both understand the johannine eschatology out
of the context of a salvation history scheme. Blank finds the
evangelist stressing most heavily the concept of Jesus as the
"turning point of the ages." The concept of the "world" in the
fourth evangelist's thought is similarly to be understood, proposes
Blank, as a salvation history category.[15] Ricca is more thorough
in his interpretation of johannine eschatology as an element of
salvation history. He makes a rather careful case for the prevalence
of the salvation history motif in the gospel. He then explains that
it is because the evangelist sees the saving work of God in three
distinct periods that he does not dissolve the whole of the future
hope of the Christian into the present. But the present and future
dimensions of this eschatological view are united. (That is, the

---

[13]Schnackenburg, *Gospel*, vol. I, 159-160, quote, 160;
Johannesevangelium, Bd. II, 532-540.
[14]Käsemann, *Testament*, 13-21, 70-73.
[15]Blank, 345, 282, 196.

present and future are consistent with one another in a manner
corresponding to the distinctiveness but unity of the saving
epoch.)[16]

Riedl avows the persistence of temporal categories in the
johannine view of Christ's work and the future, but he does not in
so many words declare that those categories mean that the eschatology
of the gospel functions out of a salvation history model.[17] In
contrast, Schnackenburg stresses that the evangelist has abandoned
temporal categories altogether in his articulation of the Christian
eschatology and employs ontological ones instead.[18] This seems to
resemble the judgment of Käsemann that the eschatology of the gospel
is a spiritualization and detemporalization of early Christian
apocalyptic thought.[19]

Some tantalizing contrasts and comparisons are evident. Most
intriguing, perhaps, is the effort of some to understand the
relationship of the fulfilled and the unfulfilled dimensions of
johannine eschatology in terms of the relationship between the present and the future in the consciousness of the believer. Ricca
and Riedl find this to be the key to the johannine present-future
tension; while Blank is satisfied to leave the tension unexplained.
This use of the human experience of the aspects of time to understand biblical eschatology is a promising one, to be sure, although
it is far from new. The danger faced by Riedl and Ricca and others
who attempt to have the evangelist think in terms of a new experience of temporality thanks to the advent of Christ is that they
may be imposing contemporary concerns upon the author. From that
perspective Blank's admission to the unexplainable relationship
of present to future in johannine thought looks appealing. To come
to Riedl and Ricca's defense, however, it may be said that what
they are attempting to say is that such an unprecedented temporal
experience as the advent of Christ is the phenomenon which the
evangelist may have been articulating, and not that he would offer
it as a general model for understanding human temporality.

A similar issue is involved in the difference between those
who would understand johannine eschatology in salvation history
terms (Blank, Ricca, and Riedl) and hence in terms of some appre-
hension of time, and those who would claim that the evangelist has
left temporality behind and is thinking in nontemporal, metaphysical

---

[16]Ricca, 130-153. Ricca's view compares favorably with Cullmann,
Salvation in History, 289-290.
[17]Riedl, 35.
[18]Schnackenburg, *Johannesevangelium*, Bd. II, 540.
[19]Käsemann, *Testament*, 72.

terms (Käsemann and Schnackenburg). It seems to me that the
positions of the latter two scholars depends too much upon their
insistence that the evangelist is influenced by or embraces a
proto-gnosticism. At the same time, the salvation history scheme
seems unsatisfactory, as I have argued in the section on christology. The truth lies somewhere in between. The evangelist is
perhaps dealing with a sense that history and time are known among
believers in a manner quite different than ever before, and he
stresses the vertical or ontological dimensions of Christian
experience. But he does this not in a philosophical or gnostic
sense but in order to express the radical Christian experience of
the collapse of the epochs of time (past, present, and future) into
one. He is, on the other hand, not imposing a salvation history
scheme upon the events he knows, but is speaking as one who believes
that the final things have happened and continue to happen in the
midst of the Christian community.

Against Käsemann and the Bultmannian school in general, Ricca
and Blank each maintain that the evangelist looks toward a future
resurrection and that resurrection is not to be understood as
demythologized or spiritualized by the evangelist. The advancement
of contemporary scholarship on this point is found in the fact that
there is no appeal to a post-johannine redactor theory in order to
account for the presence of future resurrection texts in the gospel.
But the answer may not lie in the rather strange contentions of
Blank and Ricca that the Christians possess "life" but still "die"
so that they may be "resurrected" at the last day. It more likely
may lie in the suggestion of Schnackenburg and others that the
tension between the present, realized eschatology of the gospel and
the futuristic, resurrection passages is the fruit of the tension
between the evangelist and his tradition. Tradition-source
criticism may enable us to understand better the way in which the
evangelist has preserved traditions and interpreted them in his
gospel, sometimes in a manner which does not produce a smooth,
ideologically consistent text. My suggestion is that just as the
apparent conflicts over the role of the signs may be understood
as the result of the evangelist's use of a source or oral tradition
(see Part One), so the inconsistent eschatology may be similarily
enlightened.[20]

---

[20]Attempts to understand the tension between realized and
futuristic passages in the gospel in the light of the evangelist's
use of tradition include Brown, *Gospel*, vol. I, cxviii, and Kysar,
"The Eschatology of the Fourth Gospel," 26-31.

In conclusion, two other comparisons might be noted with approval: First, Ricca, Blank, and Riedl have all commented on the meaning of the eschatological "now" (*nun*) as rooted in the evangelist's own experience in the church of his day. That perception, it seems, is accurate and adds to our appreciation of the eschatology of the gospel. It is not simply an expression of what was actualized in the coming of Christ and what promises to be actualized later, but the *experience* of the actualization of the eschaton in the evangelist's church.[21] Second, Blank and Schnackenburg are surely correct in stressing, far more than Ricca, the self-activating quality of judgment in the fourth gospel. To the credit of the genius of the evangelist, judgment is the self-imposed consequence of the decision (*krisis*) in response to the revelation.[22]

---

[21]This is the merit of Robert Gundry's suggestion that John 14:2 has a reference to the place of the believer both in the community of faith and in a future heaven. "'In My Father's House Are Many *Monai*' (John 14:2)," *Zeitschrift für die neutestamentliche Wissenschaft*, 58 (1967), 68-72.

[22]L. van Hartingsveld, review of Ricca, *Novum Testamentum*, 9 (1967), 315-318.

CHAPTER III

THE JOHANNINE DUALISM

One does not read far into this gospel before being struck by
its symbolism and especially by the profuse appearance of opposites.
The entirety of the johannine theology seems to be suspended within
a conceptual framework of a magnificent dualism expressed in a wide
variety of language--"from above, from below,""light, darkness,"
"truth, lie," "life, death," etc. The investigation of the origins
of this kind of dualistic language and thought is one sort of
critical enterprise, the contributions of recent scholarship to
which we have already examined in Part Two. But once the critic has
argued for a certain intellectual milieu for the dualistic thought
of the gospel, it is necessary then to attempt to articulate the
evangelist's view itself, given the likely influence from this or
that intellectual predecessor. This is to say that the critical
task occasioned by the dualism of the gospel is not completed by the
investigation of the intellectual milieu out of which that dualism
stemmed; at the very least, the scholar must show how the evangelist
has *used* the dualism which is borrowed from another environment.
But what of the evangelist's own contribution to the dualism, his
adaptation of the concepts, his tailoring other ideas to the dualistic
framework, and generally how he understood that dualism whatever its
roots? This kind of treatment of the dualistic thought of the gospel
falls within the purview of this chapter.
        Contemporary scholarship has produced two major examinations of
the general nature of the dualism of the gospel: The work of Luise
Schottroff, which we have already mentioned several times now, and
a monograph by Günter Stemberger. The reader should be able to

anticipate the sort of general construction of johannine dualism
proposed by Schottroff. For her, the basic antithesis of the gospel
is the pole of salvation and its opposite, the absence of salvation,
or total deprivation. These two poles are the basic realities from
which the individual emerges and is defined. The evangelist can
speak of each with a variety of interchangeable terms (e.g., "from
truth"--18:37--means the same as "from God"--8:47); this inter-
changeability of the dualistic terms alerts the reader to the fact
that the meaning of the dualism lies not in the peculiar content of
each word but in its negative or positive quality in the context
of the dualism.

This dualism is determinative for the whole of the evangelist's
argument; everything is defined by the distance from one or the
other of the poles. Salvation, for instance, is defined negatively
as the distance from the fiendish world, and that distance is
expressed in terms such as "life" and "love." All the dualistic
concepts are related to revelation--its acceptance or rejection
(e.g., 15:22, 24; 9:41). This prevalent dualistic framework is not
temporal in its conception, Schottroff maintains. The prologue is
without a time scheme, for instance, and its mythology is without
reference to the temporal plane. The primary thing for the evangelist is the existentially conceived dualism of acceptance and
rejection of the revelation, and all mythology is mustered for the
elucidation of this polarity. He takes the mythology at face value;
he does not demythologize it, as Bultmann argues. There really is,
then, no ethical dualism, as such, just as there is no cosmic,
apocalyptic or anthropological dualism (e.g., 8:23 and 3:6). What
appears as the ethical dualism of the gospel is really only a form
of the dualistic possibilities of responding to the revelation of
God in Christ.[1] Schottroff's view is but the framework of her
understanding of the johannine use of the signs (see Part One) and
of christology (see Chapter I of this Part).

Stemberger's treatment of johannine dualism is in sharp contrast
to Schottroff's. Stemberger seems to conceive of the dualism in
the gospel as basically a moral discernment. He believes that it
provides the evangelist with the conceptual outline of a moral theology. The symbols, then, taken as a whole constitute the gospel's
moral teachings. "The moral decision consists for John of the sole
acceptance by man of the light, the life, the freedom and, as a

---

[1]Schottroff, *Der Glaubende*, 228-234, 237-238, 293-294. See
also, "Johannes 4:5-15 und die Konsequenzen des johanneischen
Dualismus."

consequence, the acceptance of Christ...." So moral decisions are a question of faith in the gospel. Being and action are one for the evangelist; faith is not just dogma, but morality as well, Stemberger argues. It is understandable then that Stemberger should stress that the dualism of the gospel is ultimately a monism, that the only *reality* is the force of good and that the force of evil is "purely and simply *non-being*."

The opposition of God and Satan provides the evangelist with the roots of his dualism, thinks Stemberger, but he does not imagine two static worlds but thinks in terms of the human choice between these two forces. The evangelist has radicalized the symbolism of the dualistic concept because of the situation in which he wrote, namely, the situation of the church amidst crisis and opposition. The symbolism should not, however, be taken as a diminishing of history. The symbols of the dualism make discernible in the gospel the concept of salvation history and without that concept the dualism would have no meaning. Christ, of course, is the full symbolization of the good; all the symbols used for the good are transferred to him. The result is that the ethical in the fourth gospel is personal, that is, it is christocentric. "Christ is the ideal image of the moral Christian...."[2]

The contrast could hardly be more drastic and more obvious! We need mention only the two fundamental views which separate Schottroff and Stemberger from one another. The first is their respective conceptions of the basic polarity implicit in the johannine dualism--is it a matter of salvation as Schottroff claims or morality as Stemberger argues? Schottroff would seem to conceive of johannine salvation as beyond morality; but Stemberger understands the moral distinction between the forces of good and evil to be the core of johannine thought. Second, they differ fundamentally in their conceptions of the relationship of this dualism to history--does the evangelist set his dualism within a scheme of salvation history, as Stemberger contends, or does he essentially collapse temporality into mythology, as Schottroff would have us believe? The difference is vital not only for the subsequent understandings of christology and other theological concepts, but directly for the interpretation of johannine dualistic terminology itself.

If one were forced to a choice, Schottroff or Stemberger, surely the third choice--"none of the above"--would be preferable. The best understanding of johannine dualism must certainly lies somewhere

[2]Günter Stemberger, *La Symbolique*, 239-244, quotes 241, 239, and 244, respectively.

between the mythological, gnostic conception proposed by Schottroff
and the salvation history, moral theology proposed by Stemberger.
Schottroff is, however, far closer to what seems a viable interpretation of the gospel at this point. It is hardly contestable
that the salvation motif with the question of the relationship to
(or distance from) salvation is closer to johannine conceptuality
than the question of the forces of good and evil. In the gospel
which seems to be least concerned with moral theology, it is risky,
even foolhardy, to propose that the whole of johannine dualism
be taken as a moral polarity.[3] Moreover, the persistent effort
to find the salvation history scheme in the gospel must again be
rejected. Generally, it seems to me that the work of Stemberger
has a propensity to find the interpreter's interests in the gospel
rather than allowing the gospel to speak for itself.[4]

Schottroff's reading of johannine dualism is in itself vulnerable only in its radicality. That is, it seems that Schottroff is
correct in her reading of the polarity, but the question that must
be asked is whether the evangelist really intended it to be taken
in the extreme fashion Schottroff offers. Does the employment of
timeless mythology necessitate that the evangelist nowhere has an
interest in history? Is it not conceivable that mythology and
history have been wedded--perhaps not without pain--in the gospel?
Schottroff has radicalized the essentially johannine dualism and
has over-emphasized its consequences.[5]

There are a number of points at which Stemberger and Schottroff
are in agreement, and these may be taken as some evidence for the
direction of contemporary scholarship on the johannine dualism.
They both agree that the opposites of the gospel invite, and in

---

[3]This does not mean that the effort to speak of moral values
implicit in the fourth gospel is entirely fruitless. Noël Lazure,
Les Valeurs morales de la théologie johannique (Paris: Gabalda,
1965) is a provocative and somewhat successful study. Lazure
surveys topics such as the "economy of salvation," truth and spirit,
law, faith, agape, hope, and sin. His conclusions are hardly
startling: (1) Johannine moral values are founded in the kerygma
and the relationship of the individual to God and Christ, and (2)
have to do with the "interior condition" of the human (329-332).
Such an enterprise as Lazure's, however, seems inevitably fated to
ask questions of the johannine text which it was never intended to
answer. "Moral values" can hardly be claimed to be an intentional
johannine motif, and the effort to construct a moral theology from
the fourth gospel is a bit like nailing water to the wall!

[4]For a less unfavorable view see C.K. Barrett, review of
Stemberger, *Biblica*, 53 (1972), 586-587.

[5]Siegfried Schulz's view of the dualism, although only briefly
described, seems comparable to Schottroff's without suffering the
latter's excesses. *Das Evangelium*, 67-71.

some cases describe, the results of human decision. Bultmann's
proposal that the dualism of the gospel is a dualism of decision
is for the most part sustained by these two investigators.[6]
Stemberger more by implication than direct statement agrees with
Schottroff when she claims that the individual terms of the
polarities are interchangeable and are to be read in reference to
the dualism rather than so much in terms of their individual content.
This agreement leads us on to the second kind of research in johannine dualism--the investigation of the individual poles of the
dualism and the terms employed to describe them.

Here our survey must be more representative than exhaustive,
and the attempts to describe the negative pole of the dualism are
best represented in the studies of the johannine concept of "the
world" (*kosmos*). These studies are in turn best represented by two
efforts to articulate what the evangelist means by the use of "the
world" as a symbol of the negative pole.[7] Heinrich Schlier understands the negative meaning of "the world" within the context of
the symbol of darkness. The world, as a negative phenomenon,
obscures the purpose and direction of human existence. The world's
"lie" is its pretense that it is independent of its Creator (8:30-
47). "Men desire to be independent and self-centered and so shut
themselves off from the true being of an unobscured life bestowed
by the Word." The world is man in revolt for autonomy.[8] Thomas
Olbricht puts the same point only slightly differently when he
stresses that the negative sense of the term, "the world," characterizes human existence in rebellion against God, and "the world
is therefore man who fails to maintain the proper relationship with
God."[9] This kind of interpretation of the negative pole of the
johannine dualism seems typical of contemporary scholarship. The
evangelist was characterizing human existence in its prideful,
rebellious effort to live entirely out of its own resources as "the
world."[10]

_____

[6]Bultmann, *Theology*, vol. II, 15-21. "The cosmological dualism
of Gnosticism has become in John a *dualism of decision*," 21. See
also Schulz, *Die Stunde*, 346.

[7]Of course its use in the gospel is sometimes more positive or
even neutral. See, for example, Kümmel, *Theology*, 288.

[8]Heinrich Schlier, "The World and Man According to St. John's
Gospel," *The Relevance of the New Testament* (New York: Herder and
Herder, 1968), 161-164, quote, 164.

[9]Thomas H. Olbricht, "Its Works Are Evil (John 7:7),"
Restoration Quarterly, 7 (1963), 242-244, quote, 244.

[10]This view seems also to sustain Bultmann's interpretation,
Theology, vol. II, 26-32. Other recent discussions of the johannine
concept of the "world" include the following: N.H. Cassem, "A
Grammatical and Contextual Inventory of the Use of *Kosmos* in the

The positive pole of the johannine dualism is perhaps symbolized most frequently in the gospel with the expression "the truth" or "true." Among the studies of the concept of truth there seem to be two slightly different kinds of interpretations. On the one hand are those who would understand the term primarily as a christological expression. Ibuki's monograph on truth in the Gospel of John concludes that the johannine concept is first of all to be understood as *event*. Truth in the fourth gospel is an event, supremely the event of the Word (word-event), but consequently as the event of love. But this does not mean, Ibuki stresses, that the concept of truth is overwhelmingly a functional concept. For the being of Christ itself is the truth. "The nature of the truth is the nature of Jesus Christ." Hence it refers especially to the unity of the Father and the Son--a unity of being and love. "The truth is this revealed nature of the Son." While Ibuki's conclusions do not diminish the salvific nature of the truth in John, it is clear from what he says that the critic understands the fundamental meaning of truth to reside in the nature of the person of Christ and his appearance in history.[11]

Such a christological reading of the truth concept in the fourth gospel finds support elsewhere: Josef Blank argues, too, that the concept of truth in the gospel is revelation, but the revelation is concerned with nothing other than the person of Christ (14:6). "The truth in John is not be understood without this personal basis..." and is defined christologically.[12]

While to push the distinction too far would distort the truth, it is necessary to observe a differentiating nuance between Ibuki and Blank and another group of critics. The latter seems more inclined to stress the redemptive quality rather than the christological root of the concept of truth in the fourth gospel. S. Aalen, for instance, writes, "The truth is that which saves, through the life-giving power of the Son (John 5, 21)...what is untrue is

Johannine Corpus with some Implications for a Johannine Cosmic Theology," *New Testament Studies*, 19 (1972-73), 81-91; Leon Morris, *Gospel*, 126-128; Donald Heinz, "Kosmos-Men or Men for the Kosmos," *Concordia Theological Monthly*, 41 (1970), 360-365.

[11]Yu Ibuki, *Die Wahrheit im Johannesevangelium* (Bonn: Peter Hanstein, 1972), 355-357, quote, 355.

[12]Josef Blank, "Der johanneische Wahrheits-Begriff," *Biblische Zeitschrift*, 7 (1963), 167, 170, quote, 167. See also Ignace de la Potterie, "La verità in San Giovanni," *Revista Biblica*, 11 (1963), 3-24. Also in *San Giovanni. Atti Della XVII Settiman Biblica. Associazione Biblica Italiana* (Brescia: Paideia, 1964), 123-144. Heinrich Schlier, "Meditationen über den Johanneischen Begriff der Wahrheit," *Besinnung*, 272-278.

what has no power to overcome death." Aalen arrives at this understanding of the salvific quality of truth in the gospel on two
bases: The proposed Old Testament background of the concept, and
the polemic intent of the gospel against false claims to salvation.
The basic question lurking within the johannine use of the term is,
"which of the various claims of the way to salvation is the authentic one?" So, truth has nothing to do with the "heavenly realities,"
but with the life-giving gift of God in Christ.[13] Lester Kuyper
likewise reads the johannine concept in Old Testament terms and
arrives at a similar understanding: Truth has to do with the
redemptive faithfulness of God.[14]

Thus a case may be made for the solidly Old Testament-early
Jewish character of the johannine concept of "the world" and "the
truth." These explorations seem to be harmonious with the general
tendency to see the gospel against a backdrop of Old Testament and
Jewish thought, and make Blank and Ibuki's effort to read the
johannine concept of truth as a christological notion (that is,
referring to the nature of Christ's person predominantly and not
the redemption he effects) seem too dogmatic an emphasis. It is
true that a dogmatic character to the gospel has been detected in
its treatment of the Christ figure, but are we able to say that that
christological dogmatism extends to the very definition of truth in
the gospel?

Another and related question pertains to the implications of
the general understanding of the johannine dualism for these
individual terms. If Schottroff is correct in her interpretation
of the dualism in general, then the individual concepts such as
truth should be read as exclusively as possible in terms of their
salvific function. It is, therefore, to be judged more likely for
a number of reasons that the redemptive content of the symbolism
of the positive pole and the corrupting content of the symbolism
of the negative pole should be emphasized.

---

[13]S. Aalen, "'Truth,' a Key Word in St. John's Gospel,"
Studia Evangelica, vol. II, pt. 1, 3-24, 20. Aalen opposes the
arguments of C.H. Dodd, *The Interpretation of the Fourth Gospel*,
170-178.
[14]Lester J. Kuyper, "Grace and Truth. An Old Testament
Description of God and Its Use in the Johannine Gospel," *Interpretation*, 18 (1964), 3-19. See also Schnackenburg, *Johannesevangelium*,
Bd. II, 279-280; Leon Morris, *Gospel*, 293-296.

CHAPTER IV

WITNESS, SIGNS, AND FAITH

One of the many theological problems of the fourth gospel
arises out of the meaning of belief in that gospel. What occasions
faith? What forestalls it? What is the function of the witness
of Jesus and others in arousing faith, and similarly, what is the
function of the signs in connection with faith? The problem of
faith is further complicated by the manner in which other terms,
such as "to see," "to hear," "to know," etc. are used, sometimes
as synonyms for faith and sometimes to describe conditions independent of faith itself. We cannot attempt here an introduction to
the whole problem of faith in the fourth gospel and would refer
the reader instead to the numerous analyses of the terms in the
gospel.[1] A number of studies, however, have attempted more creative
investigations of this topic in the gospel, and it is upon them
that we will focus our attention in this section. The logic of our
ordering of the survey is something like this: First, we will
survey a number of studies having to do with the theme of witness,
and second, the attempts to articulate the nature and function of
the signs in the gospel. These two topics presumably have to do
with that which arouses faith in some way. The third section of
this portion of the chapter will then examine studies related to
faith itself and associated concepts, such as "seeing" and "knowing."

---

[1]For example, Schnackenburg, *Gospel*, vol. I, 558-575; Kümmel,
Theology, 299-306; Bultmann, *Theology*, vol. II, 70-78.

A.   *Witness*

One major book and one significant article on the subject of
witness beckon for our attention. The book-length study of witness
by James Montgomery Boice becomes a rather thorough theology of
the fourth gospel by the time it reaches its conclusion. (This
often happens in the case of many would-be monographs on a single
theme in the fourth gospel. Because the concepts of the gospel
are so interwoven, one cannot be treated in isolation from the
others.) The article by J.C. Hindley is a rather philosophically
oriented inquiry into the notion of witness and evidence in the
johannine writing. His conclusion rejects the thesis that faith in
the fourth gospel stands independent of evidence, but equally that
it is the simple result of inference from evidence.[2]

Boice's study attempts to show that the johannine use of the
terms "witness" or "testimony" (*martyrein* and *martyria*) expresses
a whole concept of revelation. "For John the witness of Jesus is
revelation, and the witnesses which cluster about it are expressions
by the evangelist of those aspects of revelation which concern the
subjective appropriation and objective verification of religious
truth." Jesus' witness to himself and the Father is, according to
Boice, the direct expression of johannine christology; since Jesus'
knowledge of the Father is direct and absolute, he is able to
witness to himself and the Father. Christ's witness is then self-
authenticating, because it arises out of his consciousness of his
own being, his origin, and his mission. That makes Christ's witness
to the Father a revelation, for it is out of his unity with the
Father that Christ bears witness. He is the content of his own
witness; this is so by necessity of who he is. By virtue of the
fact that word and act are inseparably bound together in the ministry
of Jesus, however, one may not conclude that the revelation is without content or without proposition. True, it is Christ himself who
is the content of the revelation, but that content involves the
spoken words of Christ and the propositions arising from those words.
That revelation, furthermore, is a self-authenticating one and a
saving one.[3]

Hindley's analysis of the self-witness of Jesus, considerably
adumbrated from that of Boice's, is similar and distinct at once.

---

[2]J.C. Hindley, "Witness in the Fourth Gospel," *Scottish Journal
of Theology*, 18 (1965), 319-337.
[3]James Montgomery Boice, *Witness and Revelation in the Gospel
of John* (Grand Rapids, Michigan: Zondervan, 1970), 14-74, quote
31.

Hindley insists that the self-authenticating quality of revelation in the gospel is not apparent; rather, the witness of Jesus to himself violates the rules of evidence and proves nothing. Moreover, against Boice, he contends that the revelation is contentless, or more precisely, it has no content except the bare assertion of the Jesus-God unity. Jesus' self-witness "challenges the very distinction we are accustomed to draw between making a statement and giving evidence for its truth," Hindley argues.[4]

Boice pushes his treatment of witness and revelation in the fourth gospel another significant step further when he argues that the witness to Jesus attested by the gospel is authenticating and is itself revelation. The witness to revelation in the gospel (e.g., by the Baptist, scripture, etc.) is revelation itself. These witnesses are forms of a divine testimony to Jesus, Boice believes. He understands that they are of three different kinds: The prophetic word (the Baptist), the acted word (the signs), and the written word (the appeals to Old Testament scripture.) But in addition to the divine witness to Jesus, Boice finds the gospel affirming a human witness to Jesus in the form of the testimony of the apostles. The words of the apostles themselves are revelation, too, thinks Boice, by virtue of the gift of the Spirit.[5] The result of Boice's analysis is a careful argument for an organic concept of revelation in the gospel centered about the notion of witness.[6]

Hindley argues in a much different way regarding the witness of the Father to Jesus in the gospel. While he acknowledges the importance in the johannine scheme of the "divine witness" to Jesus, he contends that it suggests the evangelist's willingness to admit that the witness of Jesus to himself and the Father is not sufficient of itself. The so-called determinism passages in the gospel (e.g., 3:27; 6:37, 44; 18:37) seem to have to do with the Father's "internal witness" to the heart of man regarding the revelation. Jesus' self-witness and the Father's internal witness to Jesus supplement one another.[7]

---

[4]Hindley, 321.
[5]A somewhat different view of the evangelist's understanding of the witness of the apostles is offered by Rolf Walker who argues that 4:39-42 suggests the evangelist differentiates faith grounded on the witness of the apostles (a second-hand faith) from faith arising out of first-hand, personal encounters with Christ. "Jüngerwort und Herren Wort. Zur Auslegung von Joh 4:39-42," *Zeitschrift für die neutestamentliche Wissenschaft*, 57 (1966), 49-54.
[6]Boice, 75-130.
[7]Hindley, 325-328.

The contributions of both Boice and Hindley must be considered further under our treatment of scholarship on the johannine signs, but the reader will pardon a critical interlude at this point to evaluate the work of these two on the question of witness alone. Boice's study is an immensely valuable treatment of this subject and is argued about as carefully as one would ever want. His book is in some ways a surprisingly worthwhile study, in the light of the fact that it is seldom referred to in critical works. It offers, I believe, a viable view of fourth gospel theology from a rather conservative Christian perspective.

The weakness of the study is that in spite of its careful logic and systematic discussion, the writer's own theological presuppositions seem to control his reading of the gospel. His own conservative Christian theology precludes a careful investigation of the question of the relationship between evidence and faith in the gospel. He is too prone to utilize the category of "self-authenticating witness" without examination of the texts to discover if this was indeed the evangelist's conviction. Moreover, Hindley's article is correct (against Boice) in concluding that the revelation of the gospel is nearly without content--the one content is the unity of the Father and Son. Only Boice's insistent marriage to a propositional Christian faith would seem to prevent his admission of this interpretation. Hindley furthermore is surely correct when he writes that the fourth evangelist "is concerned with the logical structure of the revelation in Jesus and its acceptance, rather than with its content."[8] On the other hand, Hindley's concerns are not those of the evangelist. That is, Hindley raises philosophical questions of evidence, rules of inference, etc., which are not the interest of the evangelist.

B. *The Nature and Function of Signs*

In Part One the studies of the proposed *sēmeia* source and the evangelist's redaction of it were surveyed, and attention is given there to the relationship between the view of faith in the proposed source and the view of the evangelist. A number of studies have been done of the concept of sign in the fourth gospel without, necessarily, asking the question of the pre-johannine history of the signs materials. These studies are concerned with the three

---

[8]*Ibid.*, 324. This is a reaffirmation of Bultmann's famous declaration, "Thus it turns out in the end that Jesus as the Revealer of God reveals nothing but that he is the Revealer." *Theology*, vol. II, 66.

essential questions: First, what is a sign in johannine parlance
and what is its character? Second, what is the relationship of the
signs to the person and work of Christ? And third, what is the
relationship between the sign and faith? (The discussion in Part
One should be referred to as a supplement to what follows.)

Boice conceives of the signs as one of the forms of the divine
testimony to Christ which point decisively to his divinity. Boice
summarizes the nature of the signs in the gospel by suggesting that
they are at once symbols pointing toward the reality they symbolize,
bearers of that reality itself, and trials, occasions for belief or
unbelief.[9] Sebald Hofbeck finds to his satisfaction that the signs
function as a sort of johannine theory of cognition. Whereas the
synoptic gospels have Jesus distinguishing between himself and
the kingdom of God toward which his miracles point, in the gospel
of John that distinction is overcome and Jesus is identical with
the kingdom. The result is that the "entire message of salvation
is Jesus." The signs concept is introduced by the evangelist to
further this insistence that the kingdom and Jesus are synonymous.[10]

Rudolf Schnackenburg's view of the signs is comparable, for he
understands the signs primarily as a means of asserting the full
presence of the eschatological salvation in Christ.[11] The authenticating function of the signs seems to Peter Riga to be the essence
of that phenomenon in the gospel. They authenticate the son of man
and create a decision-making situation in which the participant is
forced to decide for or against the one to whom the sign points.
Riga adds an analysis which shows the sense in which the signs have
a certain parabolic quality and function. Primarily the literary
similarity of parables and signs is found in the fact that both
call for decision.[12]

About the christological character of the signs, there seems
to be no debate. Hofbeck stresses that the signs are intended to
demonstrate that Jesus is the expected messiah of the last days, so
that they are both messianic and eschatological in their meaning.
But the person of Christ is their basis and the messianic, eschatological, and soteriological features of the signs are all encompassed in their christological character.[13] Schnackenburg agrees

[9]Boice, 88-94.
[10]Sebald Hofbeck, *Semeion*. *Der Begriff des "Zeichen" im
Johannesevangelium unter Berücksichtigung seiner Vorgeschichte*
(Münsterschwarzbach: Vier-Türme, 1966), 158-160.
[11]Schnackenburg, *Gospel*, vol. I, 522.
[12]Peter Riga, "Signs of Glory: The Use of 'Semeion' in St. John's
Gospel," *Interpretation*, 17 (1963), 402-410.
[13]Hofbeck, 161-166.

that they have messianic and eschatological significance. They
declare that "the Son of Man on earth is the place of God's
presence and action; God's eschatological action is realized in
him." But Christ is himself the true sign. "Thus the christological
significance proves to be the most important element of the Johannine
'signs', the most characteristic of their properties and the heart
of their theology."[14] Riga maintains that the evangelist intends
to proclaim that the glory of God which was manifested in the mighty
acts of the exodus is now present in Jesus; but the signs are not
simply expressions of extraordinary power but are introductions to
Christ. Moreover, they are presented in their deepest sense in the
fourth gospel as works of the Father performed by Jesus. The unity
of Christ and God in action is the motif of the signs, and they
invite men to ascertain that unity, if they will.[15]

C. Faith and Related Concepts

In Part One we encountered the question as to whether or not
the signs are intended by the evangelist to produce faith, a
genuine belief in Christ and not just a superficial belief in this
wonder worker, Jesus of Nazareth. Hofbeck gives the fullest
theological treatment of this question in his study of the signs.
The signs have a double character, he points out--to reveal and
to veil at the same time. For belief, the signs are a revelation;
they unveil the divine glory of Christ (2:11; 11:4, 40). For
unbelief, on the other hand, they only veil the true identity of
Christ, and they result in confusion and misunderstanding. They
are related to the witness theme of the gospel. All faith is born
of witness of some sort, according to the gospel, and likewise the
signs are witness which yields faith. There are, however, different
kinds of faith--different levels of faith--and the faith provoked
by the signs is a faith that has yet to grow. But pure "signs-
faith" (2:23 and 4:48) is not the genuine faith which the signs can
produce. A purely wonder response to the signs is a basic misunderstanding of the signs. So, in effect, Hofbeck discerns two possible
responses to the signs: A simple interest in the wonders of Jesus,

---

[14]Schnackenburg, *Gospel*, vol. I, 521-525, quotes 521 and 525
respectively. Comparable is John Wilkinson's conclusion regarding
the meaning of the healings in the gospel: "They reveal Jesus as
the Christ, as the Son of God already invading the kingdom of evil
and defeating Satan on his own ground." "A Study of Healing in the
Gospel of John," *Scottish Journal of Theology*, 20 (1967), 442-461,
quote, 458.
[15]Riga, 410-424.

which is not faith at all, and an initial, immature faith which can
lead to a personal encounter with Jesus.[16]

Boice and Hofbeck are in essential agreement, then, that the
signs have a witness character and are part of the total witness
scheme of the gospel. But Boice pushes this observation further to
conclude that the signs have evidential value, and they provide a
kind of independent verification of the teachings of Christ.[17]
Morris Inch defends the apologetic use of the signs in the fourth
gospel and hence argues that they are evidence for faith. He
qualifies this, however, by asserting that the signs are witness
and not purely miraculous event. Therefore, he suggests they are
"faith giving evidence [rather] than...evidence demanding faith."[18]
Inch would soften the evidential quality of the signs so strongly
affirmed by Boice.

The treatment of signs by Hindley is, however, still more
distinctive. Hindley distinguishes two values in the signs--
evidence-value and sign-value. The first refers to the extent to
which the signs yield grounds for inference, while sign-value is
"the quality of event and response by which the spiritual significance of an event is perceived." The evidence value of the signs
is simply that *some* divine power is at work; but the signs value
is the faith perception of God's presence in Christ. The evidence
value is not denied, as 10:38 seems to imply, but leads toward the
perceiving of the sign. Miracle as such, however, does not provide
the grounds for true faith in the gospel of John; one must perceive
the glory expressed in the sign.[19]

Schnackenburg, interestingly enough, dissents from this approach
to the relationship of signs and faith. The signs are not combined
with the notion of witness, he argues. The signs show the individual
Christ but do not have the force of testimony. They are restricted
to the earthly ministry of Jesus.[20] Witness in John does not prove
or authenticate. It "enlightens" the reason of the searcher, but
it does not persuade. Witness leaves the responsibility of faith
with the individual.[21] Schnackenburg would seem to suggest that the

---

[16]Hofbeck, 177-186.
[17]Boice, 99.
[18]Morris Inch, "Apologetic Use of 'Sign' in the Fourth Gospel,"
The Evangelical Quarterly, 42 (1970), 35-38, quote 37.
[19]Hindley, 330-331.
[20]Schnackenburg, *Gospel*, vol. I, 519-520.
[21]Schnackenburg, "Revelation and Faith in the Gospel of John,"
Present and Future. Modern Aspects of New Testament Theology
(Notre Dame, Indiana: University of Notre Dame Press, 1966),
135-136.

signs have no evidential value but are a sort of neutral presentation of Christ for the eyes of faith.

Two critical responses are evoked at this point. The first
may be taken as a warning: It is dangerous to read too much of
the contemporary theory of symbolism into the johannine use of signs.
Boice and others tend to do just that, namely, to make the evangelist sound like a post-Tillichian theologian. Hofbeck is closer to
the sense of the evangelist, as I read him, when he sees a special
johannine identification of kingdom and Jesus which is developed
into a sort of theory of cognition in the signs notions. This
means that the evangelist or his tradition has wedded the kingdom
of God proclamation and the person of Jesus himself. Similarly,
Riga's comparison of the signs and the parables is helpful, for as
different literary types they have remarkably similar functions.
The explanation for this lies in the history of the pre-johannine
tradition and its adaption by the evangelist.

The second general critical remark is this: The key to the
evangelist's understanding of the relation of sign and faith lies
in the discovery of that relationship in the signs source, and
its adaption (or correction) in the work of the evangelist. In
other words, the way to understand the relationship of faith and
sign in the fourth gospel is to do source-tradition and redaction
criticism, not theological analysis alone. The former would, it
seems to me, produce more helpful insights into the questions of
authentication and evidence as they relate to the signs. It is
most likely that the *evidence value* of the signs--their authenticating value--is found in the signs source materials, and the
sign value in the redactional work of the evangelist. Without this
kind of analysis, the enigma of the signs will not be solved, namely,
how can they provoke faith, if faith is the condition for their
perception? As valuable and interesting as these studies we have
just reviewed are, they are impotent before the task of understanding
the total johannine view of the signs until they are teamed with
the source-tradition and redaction critical studies of recent years.

The nature of faith itself in the fourth gospel is widely
discussed, but the creative contributions to the question are fewer.
For instance, there is almost unanimous consent that faith in the
gospel involves a personal relationship with Christ.[22] Little that
has been written lately on that subject merits our attention here.

---

[22]For example, Pierre Grelot, "Le Problème de la foi dans le
quatrième évangile," *Bible et Vie Chretienne,* 52 (1963), 61; Morris,
Gospel, 335-337; Josef Heer, "Glauben--aber wie?" *Geist und Leben,*
46 (1973), 165-181, especially 175-178.

There are, however, two other questions which seem to have evoked
more serious and creative work: First, the question of what we
might term the "conditions" for faith in the fourth gospel, and
second the relationship of faith to two other terms, "seeing" and
"knowing."

To the question of why persons either believe or do not believe,
the gospel seems to give three different kinds of answers, according
to James Gaffney. Moral predisposition seems to determine the
capacity for faith in some passages (e.g., 3:20-21), but in others
it is clearly a divine influence or its absence which accounts for
faith or its want (5:44). Finally, some passages seem to credit
the testimony of either words or works with the birth of faith
(e.g., 5:36).[23] A. Vanhoye has argued, however, that it is not
the evangelist's view that predisposition accounts for the capacity
to believe. Rather, the gospel is to be understood as saying that
belief arises out of a combination of the exterior witness of Jesus
and the interior witness of the Father--6:36-37, 43-45, 64-65.
This latter divine intervention does not overpower freedom; it is
"an interior invitation" as 6:45 must be interpreted. Vanhoye's
view is nearly identical with Boice's (see above) but also reminds
one of the position of Hindley on the effectiveness of witness:
"It is [God's] speaking in the heart which enables a man to accept
Christ."[24] Vanhoye extends his position, however, by insisting
that the roots of unbelief lie in disinterest, in the sense of the
sufficiency of the materialistic, the exterior, the worldly.[25]

Herbert Schneider finds this question of the roots of unbelief
in the teachings of the fourth gospel much more complicated than
Vanhoye would admit. The gospel gives two reasons for the human
failure to believe the revelation of God in Christ. The first
roots squarely upon human failure. The ambiguity of the flesh is
no excuse for human unbelief according to the evangelist. The
inability of the human to penetrate the ambiguity of the flesh to
perceive the divine *doxa* in Jesus is clearly the result of human
sin. But the other explanation of the phenonemon of unbelief
according to the fourth gospel is the hiddenness or the incomplete-
ness of Jesus' messiahship until its manifestation or fulfillment
in the cross. John suggests by the persistent reality of unbelief
that Jesus is fully the Son only at the moment of his crucifixion

[23]James Gaffney, "Believing and Knowing in the Fourth Gospel,"
Theological Studies, 26 (1965), 233-236.
[24]Hindley, 328.
[25]A. Vanhoye, "Notre Foi, oeuvre divine, d'apres le quatrieme
évangile," *Nouvelle Revue Théologique*, 86 (1964), 339-348.

and exaltation; it is only then that Jesus is the perfect Son and
his revelation, as it were, is obvious. So the gospel offers an
explanation of the rejection of Jesus in terms of human sin, on
the one hand, and in terms of Jesus' identity, on the other.
Schneider confesses in conclusion that another kind of johannine
resolution to the problem is found in the assertions that faith is
a gift from God (6:37, 29).[26]

These studies seem to present us with the problem without
really solving it. That is, these analyses demonstrate that there
is a sense in which the divine is involved in the birth of faith,
according to the fourth gospel--call it "the interior witness of the
Father," the gift of faith, or whatever. But they do not lead us
to a very clear understanding of the johannine view of the relationship of that divine initiative and human freedom. The full force
of the passages which seem to declare the responsibility of God for
human faith (e.g., 6:39, 44, 65; 17:2, 6, 12, 24) is not taken
seriously in any of the studies of faith in recent years. Nor has
their relationship with the implicit appeal to human freedom been
adequately explained. Two observations may be made: First, perhaps
it is a latent dogmatic resistance to the concept of determinism
which prevents the interpreters from taking the role of God in
creating the disallowing faith seriously. Second, perhaps it is
again necessary to ask if this johannine contradiction (between
determinism and freedom) is solvable by means of the analysis of
the source materials and the evangelist's use of them as opposed to
a strictly theological analysis.

On the relationship of faith to "seeing," there has been one
major study worthy of our notice. C. Traets has examined the use
of the verbs meaning "to see" or "behold" (*horan, theorein, theasthai,*
and *blepein*) and their use with Jesus and the Father as their
objects. He begins by noting that the visual perception of the man
Jesus is affirmed by the fourth gospel as the starting point for
faith. The deeper insight of faith perception, however, sees the
mystery of Jesus' being, his unity with the Father. At this latter
level the Father is the object of what is seen in Jesus. "To see,"
then, in the gospel has reference to both the events of Jesus' life
and the mystery of his person. To see Jesus determines the distinction between those open to the mystery of his being and those
blind to it.

---

[26]Herbert Schneider, "'The Word Was Made Flesh,' An Analysis
of the Theology of Revelation in the Fourth Gospel," *Catholic
Biblical Quarterly*, 31 (1969), 344-356.

"To see God" expresses a particular accessibility to God
which permits the reception of his revelation. "To see
glory" designates the experience of the intervention of
divine salvation within the consciousness of the communion
with the life and love of Jesus and the Father. Neverthe-
less, "to see God" and "to see glory" implies also a visual
perception.

Likewise, seeing Jesus has a double temporal dimension, namely,
the historical events of Jesus' life and the retrospective view of
those events from the vantage point of the church. The same verb,
"to see," is used then to comprehend the historical Jesus and the
presence of Christ as Lord in the church. Traets concludes that
the evangelist has fashioned a concept with the verbs for perception
which involves a dynamic relationship between visual seeing and the
vision of faith by which one attains the mystery of the person of
Christ. This involves among other things an essential historical-
temporal dimension and an organic connection between the grasp of
history and the vision of the church. At the same time, Traets
notes in passing, this vision of the unity of the Father and Son
in Christ remains in tight relationship with the hearing of the
word.[27]

The relationship between believing and knowing has received
less thorough attention than Traets gives to the matter of vision
and faith, but there are three shorter studies which might be
briefly mentioned. James Gaffney compares the subjects, objects,
conditions, and consequences of believing and knowing, and then
he comes to some interesting conclusions: First, believing and
knowing are not, he suggests, quite synonyms. Believing in the
fourth gospel is "the idea...of accepting testimonies, of freely
submitting to the moral force of a certain kind of religious
evidence." Knowing, on the other hand, is "a kind of discernment
of signs, a quality of insight into the transcendental reference
of various symbolisms, ambiguities, and veiled allusions...believing
has a more volitional, and knowing a more intellectual, flavor."
This distinction, Gaffney maintains, is important even though his
second conclusion stresses that both believing and knowing are
concerned with one matter and that alone: Christ and revelation.[28]

Schnackenburg concurs, it would appear, when he writes that
revelation cannot be grasped rationally, according to the fourth
evangelist, but involves a personal, total submission along with
an understanding (19:37ff). Schnackenburg recognizes that the

---

[27]C. Traets, *Voir Jesus et le Pere en lui selon l'Évangile de
Saint Jean*, 51-52, 120-121, 197, 244. Traets' position shares
much with the broader study done by Mussner and cited earlier.
See especially Mussner, 18-23 and 82-88.

[28]Gaffney, 215-240, quote 240.

evangelist sometimes uses the verb "to know" seemingly to describe
a state of affairs in advance of faith (6:69; 10:38; 14:20), but
it is more characteristic of knowledge in relationship with faith.
Faith opens deeper understanding.[29] Heinrich Schlier is content to
say merely that faith and knowledge, along with love, are at their
roots in the fourth gospel (and 1 John) bound inseparably together.
Faith is bound up with seeing and hearing. Knowing and believing
can be used interchangeably and stand in a reciprocal relationship
with each other.[30]

These studies of the relationship of faith and seeing, on the
one hand, and knowing, on the other, are valuable contributions.
Traets has very nicely caught one of the subtleties of johannine
language with his analysis of the matter of perception. What he
says about the double focus of seeing in the gospel and the double
temporal dimension adds considerably to the understanding of the
evangelist both as a theologian and as a historian. The studies of
Gaffney, Schnackenburg, and Schlier are similarly useful, if somewhat less conclusive. The nagging suspicion one has as attempts
are made to split so nicely the distinctions between knowing and
believing, as say Gaffney attempts to do, is that the evangelist
was not really that deliberate and precise in the use of his
language. Without demeaning his stature as a theologian, one can,
I believe, suggest with some evidence that the evangelist may not
have possessed all of the philosophical sophistication that some
interpreters would attribute to him. His use of the verbs to
see, know, believe, hear, obey, etc. may well have been simple
variations in expressing the single act of acceptance which he had
in mind. Let the interpreter beware lest he or she find in the
evangelist more theological sophistication than was ever intended!

---

[29]Schnackenburg, "Revelation and Faith in the Gospel of John,"
131, 136-138.
[30]Schlier, "Glauben, Erkennen, Lieben nach dem Johannesevangelium," *Besinnung*, 279-293.

CHAPTER V

THE SPIRIT-PARACLETE

Another of the fourth evangelist's innovative concepts is
that of the Paraclete and its identification with Spirit. Scholarly
enterprises related to this complex of ideas are generally of three
kinds: There are those efforts to determine the intellectual milieu
which contributed to the evangelist's language and conceptuality at
this point. Second, there are efforts to itemize the data about
the Spirit-Paraclete given in the johannine text itself. And,
third, there are endeavors to articulate the meaning of the evangelist's thought on the basis of the proposed milieu and the gospel
data. The concern of this section is with the third of these
projects, in so far as it is separable from the other two. The
reader is referred to Part Two for a survey of those studies having
to do with the background of the evangelist's thought as it bears
on this subject, and to the several excellent summaries of the
evidence of the gospel on the theme of the Paraclete and Spirit.[1]
Our attention here will focus on the studies which propose interpretations of four related questions: What is the concept of
Spirit in general in the fourth gospel? What is the Paraclete and
what is his relationship to Christ? What specifically is meant
by the "Spirit of Truth"? And finally, what are the functions of
the Spirit-Paraclete in the gospel?

_____

[1]Without doubt the best of these in the current literature
is Raymond Brown, *Gospel*, vol. II, 1135-1136. The same material
is stated in much the same way in an earlier article, "The Paraclete in the Fourth Gospel," *New Testament Studies*, 13 (1966-67),
113-114; also in *Studia Evangelica*, vol. IV. 158ff.

A. *The Concept of the Spirit*

The question regarding the general nature of the Spirit in the
fourth gospel is dealt with by the biblical theologians primarily
in terms of seeing the johannine pneumatology in relationship with
other major themes in the fourth gospel. For instance, James
Montgomery Boice understands the concept of Spirit in the gospel
within the framework of the evangelist's view of witness. The
Spirit provides the understanding which makes possible the witness
of the apostles, according to Boice's interpretation of the gospel,
and provides an "internal witness" which in turn enables the personal comprehension of the meaning of the Christ event. It is the
internal witness of the Spirit, says Boice, which allows for the
conviction that the kerygma is truth and leads the individual to
the consequent salvation available in the kerygma. Hence, the
concept of the Spirit in the fourth gospel is part of the evangelist's scheme of the problem of belief--how the kerygma is received
and affirmed. Hence, Boice contends that it is intimately related
to the questions of the meaning of "seeing and believing" in the
gospel.[2]

Since Boice understands that witness to revelation is in every
case in the fourth gospel understood as revelation itself, his
view of the johannine pneumatology is akin to that of Heinrich
Schlier. Schlier's contention is that the concept of Spirit in the
fourth gospel fits the peculiar understanding of revelation embraced
and articulated by the evangelist. Schlier understands that the
evangelist views the world as "self-veiled" and confused by the
revelation of God in Christ; the concept of the Spirit, then, serves
as the means by which the truth of revelation can be interpreted
to the world of darkness.[3] De la Potterie holds a comparable
position which leads him to say that the Spirit is necessary in the
general scheme of johannine salvation, since it is the Spirit which
gives "the interpretation of a previous revelation which remains
obscure and mysterious."[4]

Others view the johannine concept of the Spirit primarily from
the vantage point of the evangelist's eschatology. In that light
the Spirit is called the eschatological fulfillment of the resurrection. "The *pneuma* is the unpassing presence of the past and the

---

[2]Boice, 120-122, 143-145.
[3]Heinrich Schlier, "Der Heilige Geist als Interpret nach dem
Johannesevangelium," *Internationale Katholische Zeitschrift
"Communio",* 2 (1973), 97-103.
[4]Ignace de la Potterie, "Le Paraclet," *La Vie selon l'Esprito
Condition du Chrétien* (Paris: Cerf, 1965), 96.

advancing presence of the future," writes Gottfried Locher.[5]
Similarly Josef Blank goes so far as to declare, "The Paraclete is
the basis, the cause, the principle of the johannine realized
theology."[6]

Our way of presenting the approach to johannine pneumatology
is not to suggest that the two modes of understanding that theme
are exclusive of one another, but that the scholar tends to understand the Spirit in the gospel either in the light of a broader
concept of revelation (Boice, Schlier, and de la Potterie) or of
the johannine eschatology (Locher and Blank). For myself, it
would seem that the latter view is excessively dominated by the
research concerns of the scholars and that the approach to johannine
pneumatology in the context of the evangelist's concept of revelation seems more consonant with the gospel itself. At the same time,
of course, the eschatological importance of the Spirit is not denied
by the insistence that it be understood within the concept of
revelation.

B. The Paraclete and Christ

The identification of the Spirit with the johannine title,
Paraclete, is primarily a problem of the history of religions
approach to the gospel; but one may also ask, what is the meaning
of the evangelist's use of this title, whatever its source in other
religious literature may be? Johnston is clear in his response to
this question. There are really two meanings to the evangelist's
employment of this term. The first is that it had a polemic purpose to repress what he regarded as undesirable claims for an
angel-intercessor in the life of the church. With his identification
of the work of the Paraclete as the Spirit of Truth, he effectively
protected the primacy of Jesus against the intrusions of the angel,
Michael. The angelic being cannot be understood as a Paraclete
somehow rivaling Jesus' revelatory work, for the Paraclete is totally
dependent upon Jesus. The second meaning found in the evangelist's
indentification of the Spirit with the Paraclete is that the
evangelist thereby identified the active power embodied in certain
leaders of the church with the Spirit of God. The evangelist was
thus able to explain certain evidence in the church by reference
to the continuing presence of Christ in the Paraclete in the midst
of the church. "For John the unseen Spirit of Christ is the reality

---

[5]Gottfried W. Locher, "Der Geist als Paraklet," *Evangelische
Theologie*, 26 (1966), 578.
  [6]Blank, *Krisis*, 215.

behind the appearance of inspired teachers in the congregations of Christians."[7]

De la Potterie, however, believes that the intention of the evangelist in identifying the Spirit with the Paraclete is more strictly theological. By this identification, claims de la Potterie, the evangelist sought to distinguish the two stages of the economy of God's salvation--the work of Christ and the work of the Spirit-- and to subordinate the latter to the former. "It is clear that with the general economy of the revelation the role of the Spirit remains essentially subordinate to that of Christ, the unique revealer."[8] In a related interpretation, Brown proposes that the Paraclete is the title John gives to a special role taken by the Spirit, in particular, the presence of Christ with the Christian in the post-resurrection era. Therefore, it is consistent that the evangelist should deliberately stress the resemblance of the Paraclete to Jesus by the fact that almost everything that is said of the Paraclete has been said elsewhere in the gospel of Jesus (e.g., the Father gives the Paraclete, 14:16, and the Father gives the Son, 3:16).[9] It is widely held that the peculiar title "Paraclete" is the evangelist's way of relating the Spirit to Christ, and thus making the work of the Spirit dependent upon Christ and the completion of Christ's work.[10]

C. The Spirit of Truth

On the question of the meaning of the expression, "Spirit of Truth," there is less to be said. It is Boice's contention that the expression is intended to have a two-fold meaning: First, it identifies the Spirit and consequently the Paraclete with God and with Christ, since the essential nature of each is "truth." Second, it denotes the truth-giving function of the Paraclete; it is he who delivers the truth.[11] Locher's word on this issue supplements Boice's: The Paraclete is called the Spirit of Truth in order to

---

[7]Johnston, *The Spirit-Paraclete*, 119-146, quote, 128.

[8]De la Potterie, "Le Paraclet," 90-96, quote, 96.

[9]Brown, *Gospel*, vol. II. 1139-1141. See also Morris, *Gospel*, 662. Brown's view is similar to Kuhl's who understands the title "Paraclete" to have been used in an effort to personalize the meaning of the work of the spirit. *Die Sendung*, 135.

[10]Locher, 578; Schulz, *Stunde*, 359; Blank, *Krisis*, 329; Ernst Bammel, "Jesus und der Paraklet in Johannes 16," *Christ and Spirit in the New Testament*, 199-217; A.R.C. Leaney, "The Historical Background and Theological Meaning of the Paraclete," 158.

[11]Boice, 152.

affirm the conviction that it is by the work of the Spirit that
persons are brought out of ignorance and placed within the truth.[12]

D.   The Functions of the Spirit-Paraclete

More discussion of the evangelist's concept of the Spirit-
Paraclete is devoted to the question of the functions assigned to
this agent.   It is commonly held that the function of the Paraclete
is different for two different realms--the disciples and the world.[13]
To the first group the Paraclete has a positive function which may
be expressed in two ways: First, the Paraclete interprets the
revelation of Christ to the disciple. Second, the Paraclete
provides for the personal appropriation of the revelation of Christ.
Boice speaks of these two functions as if they were separable, but
de la Potterie seems to suggest that the interpretative function
of the Paraclete is precisely the "interiorization and spiritualization" of the witness of Christ, so that the two functions are really
one.[14] Schlier, on the other hand, does not speak of the internal
appropriation made possible by the Paraclete, but of the continuation of the divine self-revelation of God begun in Christ.[15] To
the world, the Paraclete has what is essentially understood to be
a negative role, at least by Brown and de la Potterie. The witness
of the Paraclete is an indictment of those who oppose Jesus. This
function acts at the same time secretly to reassure the disciples
faced with the hostility of the world, and it demonstrates the
wrong of the world to the conscience of the disciples.[16] Schlier
prefers to put this function in a more positive way. The Paraclete's
witness has the result of enlightening the situation of the world,
and revealing its alienation from its creator.[17]

Scholars have seen the relationship of the function of the
Paraclete with that of Jesus but also with the function of the
disciples in the gospel. Schlier understands that the interpretative work of the Paraclete appears in the words of the disciples

---

[12]Locher, 577.

[13]E.g., Blank, *Krisis*, 330-331; Brown, "The Paraclete in the
Fourth Gospel," 114.

[14]Boice, 153; de la Potterie, "Le Paraclet," 92, 99; see also
H.F. Woodhouse, "The Paraclete as Interpreter," *Biblical Theology*,
18 (1968), 51-53.

[15]Schlier, "Der Heilige Geist," 101-103.

[16]De la Potterie, "Le Paraclet," 97-103; Brown, *Gospel*, vol.
II, 1136.

[17]Schlier, "Der Heilige Geist," 104-105. Locher can say then
that the functions of the Paraclete continue the process begun in
the incarnation (577).

and that the Spirit in the fourth gospel is linked with tradition.[18]
There are obvious parallels between the sending of the Spirit and
the sending of the disciples, so that these two are supportive of
one another and are intended by the evangelist to suggest the two
constituents of the church. The functions assigned to the Paraclete
are precisely the functions assigned by the gospel to the disciples.[19]

Finally, Brown suggests two cogent reasons for the importance
of the Paraclete concept in the evangelist's thought. First, it
was important because it supplied the evangelist with a way of
understanding the continuation of the tradition between the church
and the historical Jesus in spite of the death of an increasing
number of apostolic eyewitnesses. Second, Brown proposes that
the Paraclete is the johannine response to the problem caused in
the early church by the delay of the second coming of Christ.[20]

These studies provide a remarkably consistent and accurate
interpretation of the Spirit-Paraclete in the fourth gospel.
Johnston's thesis that the evangelist had in mind a polemic against
the dominant role played by the angel Michael among some Christians
is, however, an unnecessary and unfounded proposal. The purpose
of the Spirit-Paraclete concept seems much better expressed in the
two suggestions advanced by Brown, namely, to fill the gap left by
the death of eyewitnesses and to respond to the delay of the second
coming of Christ. There is no hint of a polemic quality in the
language of the gospel in the Paraclete passages. But Johnston may
be correct in his contention that the Paraclete concept explained
and supported certain leaders of the johannine community. My own
resolution of the meaning of the Paraclete title would simply be
that the johannine tradition had adopted this expression (under the
indirect influence of Qumranian thought) as a means of Christianizing
the notion of Spirit. At the hand of the evangelist, the Paraclete
became a christocentric understanding of the Spirit by which John
hoped to provide an intellectual link between the historical
revelation believed to have occurred in Jesus of Nazareth and the
contemporary experience of the vitality of that revelation in the

----

[18]Schlier, "Der Heilige Geist," 106-107.

[19]Kuhl, 130; Locher, 575-576. Johnstone G. Patrick claims,
quite without johannine basis, it seems to me, that the Paraclete
in the gospel assures the church against error. "The Promise of
the Paraclete," *Bibliotheca Sacra*, 127 (1970), 337-339.

[20]Brown, *Gospel*, vol. II, 1142-1143. Schlier, too, has
suggested that the coming of the Paraclete in the fourth gospel
is identical with the second coming (the Parousia) of Christ. "Zum
Begriff des Geistes nach dem Johanesevangelium,"*Besinnung*, 268.

johannine community.

To this extent, then, de la Potterie is quite correct in discerning the implication of two stages of the divine economy in the johannine concept. He is also correct in stressing the interiorization and spiritualization accomplished by the Paraclete, according to johannine thought. But the point is not so much that the evangelist thought of the Paraclete as making the external internal as he did of the Paraclete making the past revelation present to the believer. De la Potterie seems most relevant too when he speaks of the so-called negative function of the Paraclete-- the indictment of the world--as a function performed within the consciences of the believer. The johannine concept does not so much propose that the Paraclete actually judges the world but that the Paraclete is the divine support of the believer in his or her struggle with unbelief. The evangelist is quite deliberate in his identification of the functions of the Spirit-Paraclete and the disciples; the point being that the community is the locale in which the work of God begun in Christ is continued.

CHAPTER VI

THE CHURCH

Bultmann boldly declares, "No specifically ecclesiological
interest can be detected [in the fourth gospel]."[1] Needless to
say his judgment has not been widely accepted on this matter. On
the contrary, a large number of critics have argued that the
ecclesiological themes of the fourth gospel are prominent and
important in the total picture of the evangelist's thought, and
it has been urged that a proper understanding of his view of the
church would greatly enhance our grasp of his Christian perspective.[2]
The literature of the recent criticism suggests that interest in
the johannine view of the community of faith is very much alive and
vigorous. Discussions of johannine ecclesiology most often have
concerned themselves with five themes: The dualistic view of the
church and the world, the unity and the mission of the church, the
polemic nature of the church, and church order.

A. *The Church and the World*

The issue of the relationship of the community of believers to
the world has grown out of investigations of chapter 17 for the
most part.[3] That chapter is the primary expression of the dualistic
concept of the church and the world which seems to hold sway in the
fourth gospel. Pierre Le Fort's study of the church in the johannine

[1]Bultmann, *Theology*, vol. II, 91.
[2]Nils Dahl, "The Johannine Church and History," *Current Issues
in New Testament Interpretation*, William Klassen and Graydon F.
Snyder, eds. (New York: Harper, 1962), 124-142.
[3]For a literary analysis of the chapter, see Rudolf Schnackenburg, "Strukturanalyse von Joh 17," *Biblische Zeitschrift*, 17
(1973), 67-78.

literature stresses that the sanctification of the believer (17:19) presupposes and furthers the opposition of the world (*kosmos*) and the believer. The johannine ecclesiology is then basically a dualistic one with the world and the church defined and constituted in opposition to one another.[4]

Käsemann agrees: Johannine dualism is basically a result of the Word which splits humanity into two spheres. This means the community of believers is representative of the heavenly realm over against the world, and there is no sense of solidarity between the church and the world. The believer is concerned only to take the elect from the world and not to transform the world itself. Hence, the community of believers has little affinity with the world; it is heavenly. "The accepted Word of God produces an extension of heavenly reality on earth."[5] Consequently, the believers in a unique sense belong to God and to Christ; they are those "given to me" (17:6).[6]

The only weakness evident in these arguments regards the ambiguous use of the word "world" (*kosmos*) in the fourth gospel. It does seem that the world and the community are posed as opposites in John 17, but does that occasionally positive or even neutral use of "world" elsewhere in the gospel (e.g., 3:16) in any way necessitate a revision of the radical opposition of world and church expressed in chapter 17? Käsemann and Le Fort are probably correct; however, the world, to which the church is so opposed, elsewhere in the gospel is the realm of the divine creation and the object of divine love. Therefore, the ultimate dualistic split of church and world cannot be made, and the evangelist is not unmindful of the fact that the world, while it is the fortress of unbelief, is also the realm in which the potential believer still resides. This is only to say that to speak as Käsemann and Le Fort do of the dualistic opposition of the world and the community may be exaggerating the johannine separation of the two. It is symptomatic of both the works of Käsemann and Le Fort that they pay minimal attention to the johannine data outside of the particular passages with which they deal. (For Käsemann it is only chapter 17; for Le Fort it is that chapter plus several others.) It is that

---

[4]Pierre Le Fort, *Les Structures de l'Église militante selon Saint Jean* (Genève: Labor et Fides, 1970), 102, 180.

[5]Käsemann, *Testament*, 63-69, quote, 69.

[6]Le Fort, 101; Beda Rigaux, "Die Jünger Jesu in Johannes 17," *Theologische Quartalschrift*, 150 (1970), 202-204. See also Anne Jauberg, "L'image de la vigne (Jean 15)," 93-99, and Jürgen Heise, *Bleiben. Menein in der Johanneischen Schriften* (Tübingen: J.C.B. Mohr, 1967).

oversight in their methods which may cause their exaggeration of this johannine theme.

B. *The Unity of the Church*

Interest has also been expressed in the theme of the unity of the community in the gospel of John. Käsemann and Le Fort agree that the unity of the believers is to be understood as arising out of the unity of the Father and Son. In the words of Le Fort,

> The communion of knowledge, of obedience, and of love which unites the Father and the Son constitutes the model and more than the model, the root of the ecclesial unity...[7]

Kuhl and Käsemann call the Father-Son relationship the prototype of the solidarity of believers.[8] For Käsemann this means that the unity of the believers has a christological basis. The relationship of the Father and the Son is transferred to the community by the activity of the Son. Christology is both the point of origin and the general orientation of johannine ecclesiology.

That unity which has its basis in the unity of the Father and Son is, in turn, the basis of the love which characterizes the community, Käsemann continues. Love is the concrete expression of Christian unity. It is not surprising then to find that Käsemann understands the unity of which the evangelist speaks to have a heavenly quality, for unity is entirely a heavenly reality which finds its earthly projection in the Christian community. Le Fort expresses the same points with only slightly different language. The unity of the community is a communion of love and the unity experienced in love is the realization of divine life. Le Fort and Käsemann even seem comparable in their insistence that the unity of the community is a consequence of the essential eschato-logical character of that community. The community represents the presence of the eschatological realities. Käsemann similarly sees that unity as an expression of the heavenly unity, and believes that the evangelist articulates a future hope for the perfection of that unity in a heavenly existence.[9]

---

[7]Le Fort, 108. See also John F. Randall, "The Theme of Unity in John 17:20-23," *Ephemerides Theologicae Lovanienses*, 41 (1965), 373-394 and Severino Pancaro, "'People of God' in St. John's Gospel," *New Testament Studies*, 16 (1970), 114-129.

[8]Käsemann, *Testament*, 69; Kuhl, 198.

[9]Käsemann, *Testament*, 57-73; Le Fort, 106-113. F.-M. Braun has found the unity of the church expressed in four other passages --6:12-13; 11:47-52; 19:23-24; 21:1-11. His exegesis, however, seems strained and overly influenced by dogmatic considerations. "Quartre 'signes' johanniques de l'unité chrétienne," *New Testament Studies*, 9 (1963), 147-155.

Although their general approaches to johannine thought are quite distinctive, Le Fort and Käsemann are in impressive agreement on the issue of the unity of the Christian community in the fourth gospel. Their otherwise differing approaches add validity to their agreement on this subject, for one senses that their expositions have not been shaped by their peculiar perspectives. I find their interpretations sound and accurate.

C. *The Mission of the Church*

The third theme in johannine ecclesiology which has been subjected to investigation in the recent past is that of the mission of the church. Josef Kuhl's impressive study of the mission of Jesus and the mission of the church in the fourth gospel is the most extensive work done on the subject. The greatest contribution of Kuhl's study is that he clearly establishes the correlation of the sending of the Son, the sending of the Spirit, and the sending of the disciples. Each continues the mission of the former and depends upon the former.

James McPolin makes the same point with the exception that he understands the mission of John the Baptist to be portrayed in a parallel manner; all four missions have the same features (e.g., they all are originated by the Father).[10] Radermakers and Käsemann, like Kuhl, find the mission of the disciples conceived on the model of the mission of the Son, and the two constitute one mission.[11] Kuhl proposes that the mission of the disciples is structurally conceived to parallel the mission of Jesus. The church is conceived as embodying both the disciples and their mission and the Spirit which empowers the disciples' mission. These two--disciples and Spirit--are coordinated in the total mission of the community. That mission, according to Kuhl, has as its object the world, even though the ones sent in mission to the world are distant from it by virtue of their faith in Christ.[12] The disciples are sent to the world to transmit life and to witness for the truth.[13]

---

[10]James McPolin, "Mission in the Fourth Gospel," *Irish Theological Quarterly*, 36 (1969), 113-122.

[11]J. Radermakers, "Mission et apostlat dans l'Évangile johannique," *Studia Evangelica*, vol. II, pt. 1, 100-121; Käsemann, 65.

[12]Günter Baumbach similarly stresses the mission of the disciples to the world--that constitutes the essence of the relationship of the community to the world. At the same time, the community of faith owns an origin out of the "above." "Gemeinde und Welt im Johannes-Evangelium," *Kairos. Zeitschrift für Religionswissenschaft und Theologie*, 14 (1972), 121-136.

[13]Kuhl, *Die Sendung*, 141-174.

It is precisely this undeniably accurate representation of the johannine conception of mission which is needed to correct the so-called dualistic interpretation of the church and world in the fourth gospel. As real as the distinction is between the community and the world, its mission is to that very realm from which it is distinct. Again the prototype is Christ, who was not of this world but who nonetheless was sent in mission to the world. Kuhl and others make clear that the community of faith in the fourth gospel is a community in mission, and there can be no doubt that just as the internal unity of the church is christologically founded and modeled, so too its external mission has christological roots.[14]

D. *The Polemic Nature of the Church*

Le Fort has made a case that the fourth evangelist's conception of the church is polemically conceived. The church is thought by the evangelist to be a defense against gnostic distortions of the faith. Two ecclesiastical texts in the gospel, chapters 10 and 15, portray the community of faith resisting the influence of heresy. The theme of chapter 10 is the divine protection of the church against false intruders. The believers are assured in this passage that they will be able to recognize the true revealer and resist the false leaders. Chapter 15 expresses a similar assurance, namely, the promise that the purity of the community will be preserved by the exclusion of the false members. Moreover, the faithfulness of the church is assured by the intercession of Christ and the permanent presence of the Spirit. The evangelist is confident, then, that the purity of the church can be maintained. Le Fort thinks that purity is the maintenance of the apostolic kerygma and its doctrines.[15]

Le Fort's study is an important one and many of his points well made. However, on his major thesis, that the evangelist presents a concept of the church significantly shaped by polemic interests and more specifically by a defense against the onslaught of heresy, he has misread the evidence. He is led into this error by two major deficiencies in his method: First, he assumes a common authorship of the epistles and the gospel.[16] Second, he disregards the findings of source and tradition criticism. In both cases, the result is that

---

[14]Other literature which understands the community of faith in the gospel as missionary includes Ferdinand Hahn, *Mission in the New Testament* (Naperville, Illinois: Allenson, 1965).

[15]Le Fort, 77-78, 83-88, 90-94, 97-100, 180-181.

[16]Raymond Brown, review of Le Fort, *Biblica*, 52 (1971), 454-456. See also review by E. Cothenet, *Esprit et Vie*, 81 (1971), 612-614.

he reads a later concern in the johannine community back onto the
gospel itself without perceiving that gnosticism posed no threat
to the community until the gospel reached, at least, its final and
minor redaction.

Le Fort's error is not that he perceives a defensive ecclesiology in the gospel; his error concerns from what it was the evangelist supposes the church must be defended. The passages Le Fort
exegetes do indeed suggest that the evangelist's image of the church
was one which highlighted protection, but the threat is not false
doctrine, not the contamination of the pure kerygma. It is rather
the church's necessarily defensive stance toward the synagogue,
and those who would admonish the believer to surrender Christian
identity in order to perserve Jewish identity. These are the thieves;
these are the branches which wither; it is for this situation that
Christ intercedes on behalf of the community. In other words, it
is the concrete situation of the dialogue with the synagogue that
occasions John's ecclesiology.

Le Fort's study must also be emended by that of Kuhl. Le Fort
is correct when he understands johannine ecclesiology as defensive,
but the community of faith in the gospel is also described as sent
into the world. The defensive-polemic stance described by Le Fort
is not the whole picture, but neither is the offensive-missionary
one Kuhl would have us perceive. The church is thought of by the
evangelist as defending itself against the attacks of the synagogue,
but at the same time witnessing to the world. (It may be that the
missionary motif represents an older stratum in the gospel than
the defensive motif.)

E. *Church Order*

Finally, the question of church order in the fourth gospel has
come under some discussion recently. Le Fort recognizes that there
is no reference to the orders of ministry in the gospel except for
chapter 21; still, he argues that Peter is presented in the gospel
as a prototype of ministry. The absence in the gospel of attention
to the institution of the church is not due to a johannine mistrust
of or polemic against church order. It is only that the evangelist
wanted to stress faith and love as the essentials of community life
and thereby emphasize the responsibilities of ecclesial existence.[17]

Käsemann reads the evidence differently, to be sure, but he
also accumulates other evidence. Käsemann understands that the

_____
[17]Le Fort, 81-83, 161-162, 182.

evangelist de-emphasizes the place of Peter and his authority. 20:21 gives the office of ministry to a wider circle than just the twelve. The prominence not only of Peter but the circle of the twelve is diminished in preference for the significance of all believers. "Unmistakably, John represents a Christianity in which ministerial functions are not yet connected with privilege." The community is led by Spirit-filled persons with a variety of gifts, as 3:34 demonstrates. "Disciples" is a term used of all Christians; "friends" and "brothers" are titles which imply the "democratization" of leadership in the community. This view of church order results, Käsemann says, from an emphasis upon the activity of the Word in the community and the role of the Spirit as the mediator of that Word. (Käsemann entitles his chapter on the church in John 17, "The Community Under the Word.") Such a pneumatic conception of church order does not fit the pattern of developing institution-alization in first century Christianity, Käsemann admits, and can only mean that the johannine community was a conventicle outside the main stream of the Christian movement.[18]

The evidence of a dissenting form of church order in the fourth gospel is more substantial than Le Fort is willing to admit. Cer-tainly it is persuasive enough to withstand the simple suggestion of a de-emphasis of institutional structure. Käsemann is closer to the truth. Something quite different is in process in the johannine community than in the synoptic communities. The emerging pattern of church structure perceivable in the synoptics and other New Testament literature is not evident in the fourth gosepl. Käsemann is correct that ministry is not structured, according to the fourth evangelist, but still charismatic. But Le Fort is not wrong when he objects to finding a polemic against church order in the gospel. It is more likely that the johannine community was excluded from the "normal" development of institutionalization in the church. It is less likely that the evangelist intended to depreciate Peter than to honor the beloved disciple.

It would appear that Bultmann's negative appraisal of the fourth gospel as a source of ecclesiological thought is amply refuted by the studies we have so briefly examined. There is an ecclesiological interest in the fourth gospel; however, Bultmann is correct if what he means is that that interest does not stand apart from other concepts. For surely it is demonstrated by these studies of recent years that the evangelist's view of the community of faith is indivisibly bound to his view of Christ, the eschaton, and the Spirit-

---

[18]Käsemann, *Testament*, 27-32, 45-46, quote, 29.

Paraclete. Most especially have a number of these works (Kuhl,
Le Fort, and Käsemann) shown that christology provides the foundation for and structure of the johannine view of the church. One
might correctly infer that the evangelist's view of the church is
but the logical extension of his affirmations regarding the person
and work of Christ. Thereby a fundamental feature of johannine
religious thought is vividly illustrated, namely, the indissouble
interrelatedness of that thought and its thoroughly christocentric
orientation. One final observation is this: The evangelist's
view of the church reflects the concrete situation out of which
he wrote. His ecclesiology is not an abstract theory of the church,
but a picture of a community in a concrete, living circumstance.

CHAPTER VII

THE SACRAMENTS

The question of the sacraments is one of the most vigorously
debated matters in the area of the religious thought of the evangelist. Herbert Klos's valuable survey of the critical options in
the interpretation of the sacraments in John isolates no less than
five distinctive categories of opinions; they range from those
who maintain that the evangelist was consciously and polemically
antisacramental to those who insist that he emphasized the sacraments. Klos's book presents us with an excellent survey of mid-
twentieth century scholarship on this question.[1] But our survey
must be necessarily brief and selective. Six johannine passages
are most often occasions of debate on this question. For each of
these passages we will present examples of the evidence employed
to argue either for or against sacramental meaning. Second, we
will try to characterize the interpretations of the evangelist's
general view of the sacraments.

A. *The Major Passages and Their Interpretation*

John 2:1-11 This passage is occasionally taken to have clear
sacramental meaning. Mathias Rissi argues that the wine at the Cana
wedding feast is intended to evoke eucharistic allusions. The wine
is connected with the messianic joy (Isaiah 25:6f), and John intends
the miracle to declare the presence of the new covenant in Jesus.

---

[1]Herbert Klos, *Die Sakramente im Johannesevangelium* (Stuttgart:
Katholisches Bibelwerk, 1970). But see James Swetnam's review of
Klos, *Biblica*, 53 (1972), 590-593.

The wine points to the character of the third period of God's saving activity among his people in which the eucharist is celebrated.[2] Brown has more cautiously concluded that "if there is eucharistic symbolism, it is incidental and should not be exaggerated." The association of the miracle with the Passover (2:13), thus linking it with the multiplication of the loaves (6:4) and the last supper, may be a poetic allusion to the sacrament.[3] Schnackenburg, on the other hand, explicitly denies the sacramental interpretation. He argues that the meaning of the new wine is a christological one: The wine symbolizes wisdom now present in the person of Christ. Eucharistic interpretations only inhibit this christological reading of the passage.[4]

The only basis for finding a sacramental insinuation in this passage is the role of the wine, and it seems quite unnecessary to assign it that referent. The metaphorical use of wine is, as Schnackenburg points out, far richer and diverse than its Christian allusions to the cup. Moreover, the dating of the event on the Passover is hardly sufficient evidence for even an "incidental" reference to the eucharist. I must conclude that this passage is not sacramental, in spite of proponents to the contrary.

John 3:5 This verse is often taken to be a reference to baptism, and one finds a number of scholars recently defending that point of view. Klos's argument for the baptismal sense of the passage is perhaps representative of the proponents of a sacramental reading. He argues that the evangelist intends to say that the rebirth is bound to the son of man, that faith in Christ is demanded for rebirth, and that faith in Christ is concretized in the act of baptism. 3:5 therefore presents the requirement that one's faith find concrete expression in the sacramental act.[5] De la Potterie's discussion of this passage recognizes the tenuous status of the words, "water and" (*hydatos kai*), and argues that 3:5 existed in the evangelist's tradition without a reference to water. The evangelist added the reference to water in order to make it speak of baptism. The result is that the passage is made to say that both faith

---

[2]Mathias Rissi, "Die Hochzeit in Kana (Joh 2, 1-11)," *Oikonomia. Heilsgeschichte als Thema der Theologie*, 80-81, 91. See also André Feuillet, *Johannine Studies*, chapter 1.
[3]Brown, *Gospel*, vol. I, 109-110.
[4]Schnackenburg, *Gospel*, vol. I, 338-339. See also Lindars, *Gospel*, 125.
[5]Klos, 69-73. See also, Schnackenburg, *Gospel*, vol. I, 369-371; Lindars, *Gospel*, 152; and Rudolf Pesch, "'Ihr müsst von oben geboren werden'--Eine Auslegung von Joh 3, 1-12," *Bibel und Leben*, 7 (1966), 208-219.

and baptism are required.[6] De la Potterie's suggestion that the
reference to water may be detachable from the rest of the text is
also the conclusion of F.-M. Braun. He argues, however, that the
words, "water and," were added not by the evangelist to a piece of
tradition but by a later redactor to the text of the evangelist.
Thus, for Braun the baptismal meaning is a later one, and the
evangelist himself did not intend such a meaning.[7]

Brown argues for a secondary or incidental reference to the
sacrament in this verse. He confesses that originally the specific
baptismal reference may not have been intended or may not have
existed in the text; but in time the obvious reference became
clearer. Perhaps the baptismal phrase was added to bring out the
sacramental theme.[8] D.W.B. Robinson asks the question, is it possible to interpret 3:5 without recourse to baptism. He finds that
it is. "Born of water and spirit" denotes successive rebirths one
might go through; water represents the old religion (as it does in
the Cana miracle), and spirit the Christian religion. The sense of
the verse is then much the same as that in 2:1-11, namely, the
passage from the old to the new--a common theme in the gospels.[9]

Robinson's argument lacks cogency because it necessitates that
one conceive of the old religion (Judaism) as a rebirth from some
other state and Christianity as the second rebirth. There is little
basis in the gospel for claiming that Judaism is represented as a
reborn existence. His interpretation is a contortive one, it seems
to me. The likelihood is that 3:5 as it stands does stipulate
baptism as the means of rebirth through faith. The question becomes
whether the evangelist included the words, "water and," or whether
they represent a later addition. With Brown I see little reason
for attributing them to a later redactor; however, de la Potterie's
thesis is intriguing, namely, that somewhere in the total process of
the johannine tradition the rebirth by the spirit became associated
with the act of baptism. So, while the text as it stands represents
an allusion to baptism, I would want to reserve the possibility of
that allusion emerging later in the composition of the gospel.

----

[6]Ignace de la Potterie, "Naître de l'eau et naître de l'Esprit
--Le texte baptismal de Jean 3:5," *La Vie selon l'Esprit. Condition
du Chrétien*, 56-61.

[7]F.-M. Braun, "Le Don de Dieu et l'Initiation Chrétienne,"
Nouvelle Revue Theologique, 86 (1964), 1025-1048.

[8]Brown, *Gospel*, vol. I, 143.

[9]D.W.B. Robinson, "Born of Water and Spirit: Does John 3:5
Refer to Baptism?" *Reformed Theological Review*, 23 (1966),
15-22.

John 6:1-13 and 51c-59   These are doubtless the most debated
passages in the gospel when the issue of the sacraments is raised.
A substantial majority of contemporary interpreters have opted for
the sacramental reading of these passages and for attributing them
to the evangelist himself.[10]   Two scholars will have to suffice as
examples of the kinds of arguments posed in favor of the eucharistic
reading of the passages.   G.H.C. MacGregor holds that the sacramental meaning of the whole of chapter 6 is clear from a number of
characteristics: The Passover reference (v. 4), the fact that
Jesus himself distributes the food, the technical expression "give
thanks" (*eucharistēsas*, v. 11) is explicitly used, the sacredness
of the bread is stressed (v. 12), Jesus claims to be the bread of
life, the use of "flesh" (v. 51), and the reference to eating and
drinking (v. 53).

> In view of the fact that we have echoes in the chapter
> of almost the whole terminology of the sacramental ritual,
> it can hardly be denied that the identification of the
> life-giving bread with Christ's flesh, and in particular
> the use of the double symbolism in v. 53, is intended to
> place the Eucharistic seal on the whole discourse.[11]

MacGregor's contention for the eucharistic meaning of verses
51c-59 builds upon the eucharistic tone of the feeding narrative
earlier in the chapter.   Herbert Klos's argument takes a different
direction.   He does not argue for the eucharistic tone of the
feeding miracle but interprets 51c-59 as a sacramental restatement
of the speech in verses 48-51b.   The passage, verses 51c-59, moves
the assertions of the bread analogy in the previous section from a
christological and soteriological level to a eucharistic one.   The
later verses are a parenthesis in the argument which binds the
sacrament to the redemptive event of the incarnation expounded in
verses 48-51b.   Moreover, the relationship of these two sections again
suggests that the evangelist understand the sacrament as a concre-
tization of faith.   Verses 48-51b demand faith in Christ as the living
bread; verses 51c-59 declare that that faith may be expressed concretely

---

[10]E.g., in addition to those below, Josef Blank, "Die
johanneische Brotrede," *Bibel und Leben*, 7 (1966), 193-207; John
Bligh, "Jesus in Galilee," *The Heythrop Journal*, 5 (1964), 3-26;
Oscar S. Brooks, "The Johannine Eucharist--Another Interpretation,"
Journal of Biblical Literature, 83 (1963), 293-300; André Feuillet,
Johannine Studies, 118-127; Kümmel, *Theology*, 310-312; Heinrich
Schlier, "Johannes 6 und das johanneische Verständnis der Eucharistie,"
Das Ende der Zeit, 102-123; T. Worden, "The Holy Eucharist in
St. John," *Scripture*, 15 (1963), 97-103 and 16 (1964), 5-16; Théo
Preiss, "Étude sur le chapitre 6 de l'Évangile Jean," 144-167; Borgen,
Bread, 188-192; Brown, *Gospel*, vol. I, 287-291.   See a critique of
Brown;s eucharistic interpretation of chapter 6, M.M. Bourke, review
of Brown, vol. I, *Catholic Biblical Quarterly*, 28 (1966), 342-345.
   [11]G.H.C. MacGregor, "The Eucharist in the Fourth Gospel," *New
Testament Studies*, 9 (1963), 114-116, quote, 116.

in the act of the eucharist.[12]

A concern of critics is the use of the word "flesh" (*sarx*) in verses 51, 53, etc., instead of the traditional word "body" (*sōma*) which is found in the institution of the eucharist in the synpotics and Paul (Matthew 26:26ff; Mark 14:22ff; Luke 22:14ff; and 1 Corinthians 11:23ff). If the speech in verses 51c-59 is an explication of the meaning and the necessity of the eucharist, why is the more traditionally eucharistic word not used? Marie-Francois Berrouard supplies a number of reasons for this change, and those reasons are representative of the argument of the scholars who favor a eucharistic interpretation of the passage under consideration. First the original Aramaic of Jesus' own words might have been translated into Greek in two different ways--"body" and "flesh"-- in different traditions, and the evangelist is simply using that translation common to his tradition. Second, the evangelist may select "flesh" for its obvious anti-docetic implications. Third, it may also be that "flesh" was the Greek rendering in a liturgical pattern known to the evangelist (see, for instance, Ignatius of Antioch, Epistle to the Romans 7:3).[13]

James D.G. Dunn uses the appearance of the word "flesh" as one clue to the essentially secondary nature of the eucharistic meaning of this passage. If the entire chapter has a eucharistic tone to it, why is there no mention of the breaking of the bread which is so central to the sacramental celebration? Can we be sure that "gave thanks" has such a narrow, technical, and hence eucharistic meaning at the time of the evangelist? Moreover, the manna and the bread of the miracle are the themes that are con- trasted and are used to symbolize Jesus, not the eucharistic bread. Verses 62-63 seem to intimate that the section 51c-59 is not eucharistic. Dunn concludes that the evangelist in chapter 6 is addressing a situation in which docetic christology has made a marked impact upon the Christian community; some Christians have responded with a literalistic interpretation of the eucharist. The evangelist is trying to combat both the docetic christology and the literalistic sacramentalism used to combat docetism.   "In other words, the 'eucharistic overtones' of the passage are secondary and negative in import...the eucharistic element 'does no good whatever, it is the Spirit who gives life through the words of Jesus."[14]

---

[12]Klos, 66-69, 73.

[13]Marie-Francois Berrouard, "La multiplication des pains et le discours du pain de vie (Jean, 6)," *Lumière et Vie*, 18 (1966), 70.

[14]James D.G. Dunn, "John VI--A Eucharistic Discourse?", 328-338.

Dunn's thesis that an anti-docetic motif lies embedded in the passage is the contention of other scholars who use that fact to argue for a much different thesis. Bornkamm maintains that 6:51c-59 is a later redactional insertion into the gospel. The similarity between this passage and that found in Ignatius of Antioch (Epistle to the Romans 7:3) should alert us to the fact that its origin is late. It has been inserted into the text for anti-docetic purposes and has been carefully shaped to give the impression of a johannine address.[15]

Again we have a three-fold variety of critical opinions: Sacramental, secondarily sacramental, and, in this case, redactional. I am persuaded that the feeding miracle has no intentional eucharistic overtones, and that verses 51c-59 are more than likely a later addition.[16] The latter persuasion grows out of the mounting evidence that the gospel underwent a number of additions in the final stages of its composition in order to include an anti-docetic theme. It seems to me that the revision was within the johannine community by a friendly redactor who believed that he was giving fuller expression to the mind of the evangelist; perhaps he was also the author of the first epistle of John. Hence, Bornkamm is correct, I believe, in regarding the passage as redactional.

The feeding miracle is not eucharistic in any deliberate way. The eucharistic "overtones" that MacGregor and others find in the passage are to be understood in two ways. First, some of the words used in the passage which are later closely linked with the eucharist should not be read as signals of eucharistic meanings. Is it not possible that the evangelist might have Jesus give thanks without necessarily wanting images of the eucharistic celebration to flash into mind? Are we ro assume that certain words out of the sacramental services could be used in no other way? Of course not!

---

[15]Günther Bornkamm, "Vorjohanneische Tradition oder nach-johanneische Bearbeitung in der Eucharistischen Rede Johannes 6?", 51-64. See also Bornkamm,"Die Eucharistische Rede im Johannes-Evangelium," *Geschichte und Glaube. Erster Teil* (München: Kaiser, 1968(, 60-67; and Georg Richter, "Zur Formgeschichte und literarischen Einheit von Joh. vi. 31-58," *Zeitschrift für die neutestamentliche Wissenschaft*, 60 (1969), 21-55.

[16]Among those who view 51c-59 as an interpolation are Bultmann, *Gospel, ad. loc.*; Bornkamm, "Vorjohanneische Tradition," and "Die Eucharistische Rede,"; Eduard Lohse, "Wort und Sakrament in Johannesevangelium," *New Testament Studies*, 7 (1960-61), 117ff. Those who maintain the integrity of the chapter include Ruckstuhl, *Die literarische Einheit*; Peder Borgen, "The Unity of the Discourse in John 5," *Zeitschrift für die neutestamentliche Wissenschaft*, 50 (1959), 277-278. H. Schürman, "Joh. 6, 51c, ein Schlüssel zur grossen johanneischen Brotrede," *Biblische Zeitschrift*, 2 (1958), 244-262; and Feine, Behm, Kümmel, *Introduction*, 150.

So it is not that these words are deliberately meant to denote the eucharist. The second explanation of the so-called eucharistic overtones is that the feeding narrative was later given more and more eucharistic associations, since there are obvious points of contact between that narrative and the sacrament. But those associations must not be read back upon our evangelist. The evangelist in this narrative is shaping the feeding in such a way that others later in his tradition may have associated it with the eucharist; but he himself, I am convinced, had no such meaning in mind.

   John 13:1-17 This passage is sometimes understood sacramentally and sometimes not.[17] Some stress heavily that at the very point one would expect to find the institution of the eucharist in the johannine gospel one finds instead the footwashing. The point is that the washing of the feet of the disciples is the symbolic act by which the evangelist signals his understanding of the eucharist, namely, its identification with the incarnation.[18] On the basis of the word, "to wash" (*niptō*), some have cautiously proposed a baptismal reading of the footwashing. Lindars, for instance, writes that, "what John is saying is certainly close to the theology of baptism."[19] Others argue for the thesis that the sacramental quality of the narrative is due to later additions to the text. Boismard maintains the original form of passage had a simple moral meaning-- the imitation of the servant act of Jesus. This form was unsatisfactory to some readers of the gospel who went about adding words, phrases, and sentences until a baptismal sense had been incorporated. The result is that verses 6-10 appear as a rite of purification necessary for those who would enter the kingdom (i.e., baptism) and verses 12-15 an example of humility and love for other people.[20]
   The refutation of the baptismal sense of the narrative in chapter 13 involves a number of arguments. The first is that the whole point of verses 9 and 10 is that the physical washing itself is not important; therefore, the spiritual cleansing would not seem

---

   [17]For a survey of scholarship on the footwashing narrative see Richter, *Die Fusswaschung im Johannes-Evangelium* (Regensburg: Friedrich Pustet, 1967). See also J. Swetnam, review of Richter, *Biblica*, 49 (1968), 439-444 and Brown, review of Richter, *Theological Studies*, 30 (1969), 120-122.
   [18]Brooks, 298-299.
   [19]Lindars, *Gospel*, 451. See also Brown, *Gospel*, vol. II, 566-568.
   [20]M.-E. Boismard, "Le Lavement des Pieds," *Revue Biblique*, 71 (1964), 5-24.

compatible with the baptismal message.[21] The second argument is
that the meaning of the narrative is obviously soteriological and
christological: Hence, the sacramental interpretation violates
the major sense of the passage.[22] These refutations are surely
successful and leave little ground for a baptismal (and even less
for a eucharistic) interpretation. The mere appearance of the word
"to bathe" does not properly signal baptismal meaning.

It is a misfortunate error of the sacramental interpreters
that they assume the widespread popularity of the sacraments in
the early church. Only such a popularity could possibly justify
the claim that almost any use of one of the standard terms associated with the celebration of the sacraments indicates sacramental
meaning. Such omnipresent sacramental meaning is hardly evidenced
in the johannine gospel. The evangelist can use the word "to bathe"
without necessarily meaning a reference to baptism as surely as he
can have Jesus "give thanks" without wanting the reader to immediately think of the eucharist.

John 19:34 The sixth and final johannine passage is often
subjected to sacramental interpretation. Brown believes that the
reference to water provides a sufficient basis for a secondary
baptismal meaning in this verse. By this he means that the evangelist's intent was to communicate another meaning; but he was not
unmindful of the possible association of his words with the sacrament, and allowed that possibility to stand in his text. Less
certain is the eucharistic meaning arising from the appearance of
the word "blood" in the text. "Thus, at most we can give a probability to the double sacramental reference of xix 34b (on a
secondary level), with better proof for the baptismal than for the
Eucharistic reference."[23]

Opposing such an interpretation is Klos, who understands that
the primary meaning of the passage--the redemptive significance of
the death of Jesus--is all that may be read from the passage.
Moreover, Klos is convinced that the evangelist understood the
sacraments as concrete expressions of religious faith; and Klos
is not able to discern in this passage a relationship between faith
and its concrete expression. Therefore, he thinks it is unlikely

---

[21]James D.G. Dunn, "The Washing of the Disciples' Feet in John
13:1-20," *Zeitschrift für die neutestamentliche Wissenschaft*, 61
(1970), 247-252.
    [22]Klos, 85-93; Richter, "Die Fusswaschung Joh 13, 1-20,"
Münchener Theologische Zeitschrift, 16 (1965), 13-26.
    [23]Brown, *Gospel*, vol. II, 952.

the evangelist intended a sacramental meaning.[24] Richter has not
only argued against the sacramental meaning of this passage, but
ventures the opinion that it is not from the hand of the evangelist
at all. It is another bit of evidence of the work of the anti-
docetic redactor. The meaning of the blood and water for the
redactor is christological; the humanity of Jesus is real.[25]

Again, it seems that the interpreters who find sacramental
meaning here are stretching the reference of the words. In a passage designed only to demonstrate the reality of the death of Jesus,
it is unnecessary to load the words "blood and water" with sacramental freight. The evangelist must be permitted to use these
words without sacramental meaning, even though they are later closely
associated with the sacraments. Richter's efforts to see the hand
of the anti-docetic editor here are perhaps right on target. It
might be, however, that the anti-docetic purpose of the words is not
to be set at odds with the sacramental reference, if Dunn is correct.
It could be that our anti-docetic editor has in mind both the affirmation of the reality of Christ's death and the allusion to the
two sacraments. But I would hold that he is working in a later
environment than the evangelist.[26]

B. *The Evangelist's General View of the Sacraments*

The interpretations of the key passages demonstrate that the
critical appraisals of the evangelist's general view of the sacraments are varied. The problem is, of course, more complex than
finding or not finding sacramental meaning in the several passages
we have examined. It also involves a justification for the glaring
omission of an account of the institution of the lord's supper and
(less seriously) the ambiguity of a sanction of baptism. My
perception is that there are three positions among scholars in
recent years with regard to the evangelist's view of the sacraments.

The first of these views is that he was a profound and vigorous
sacramentalist. Raymond Brown may be taken as one of the leading
proponents of this view. He is critical of those who find sacramental references too easily in the gospel, but is at the same time
convinced that the evangelist himself has a strong commitment to the

---

[24]Klos, 74-80. See also Lindars, *Gospel*, 586-587.
[25]Richter, "Blut und Wasser aus der durchbohrten Seite Jesu
(Joh 19, 34b)," *Münchener Theologische Zeitschrift*, 21 (1970),
1-21.
[26]Excluded from consideration here is a weak argument for the
eucharistic meaning of the vine allegory in chapter 15. Björn
Sandvik, "Joh. 15 als Abendmahlstext," *Theologische Zeitschrift*,
23 (1967), 323-328.

sacraments and that the final redactor of the gospel has only
strengthened that commitment. It is Brown's contention that the
institution of the eucharist has been omitted in favor of the
explication of the sacrament in 6:51c-59. By doing this the evangelist elevates the eucharist from an act commencing near the end
of Jesus' life to a motif on his lips throughout his ministry.[27]

The second view holds that the evangelist believes the sacraments to be very important but that he subjects them to his own
peculiar interpretation. MacGregor is of the opinion that the
evangelist wanted to offer a "spiritual interpretation" of the
sacraments. One of the reasons for the substitution of the narrative of the footwashing for the institution of the lord's supper
was to check what the evangelist considered a materialistic conception of that sacrament. The footwashing narrative is an
exemplification of the spirit of one who participates in the eucharist. "We conclude then that for John the spiritual interpretation
of sacramental efficacy is primary and normative."[28]

Herbert Klos concludes his study with a sketch of the johannine view of the sacraments. He affirms that the sacraments are
viewed as the continuation of the historical work of Christ in
which they are rooted. But it is in the area of the relation of
the sacraments and faith where the unique interpretation of the
evangelist is most evident. Klos believes that the evangelist
did not want the sacraments to be understood in a mechanical way;
he wanted to show that they depended totally upon faith. Consequently, "The sacrament is understood correctly in the sense of the
Gospel of John only when it is seen as a concrete expression of
faith in Jesus Christ, as the confirmation and execution of faith."[29]
Still a third form of this view is offered by C.L.J. Proudman who
argues that the evangelist is trying to disassociate the sacraments
from the primitive Christian eschatology. His omission of the
institution of eucharist is due simply to the desire to strip it
of its apocalyptic colorations. All of the early traditions about
the lord's supper are centered in the hope of the imminent consumma-
tion, and the evangelist wants to "rehabilitate" the sacrament
independent of those implications.[30]

The third view we can only infer from those who find no sacramental meaning in the passages from the hand of the evangelist him-

---

[27]Brown, *Gospel*, vol. I, cxiii-cxiv. See also Schlier,
"Johannes 6," 123.
[28]MacGregor, 118.
[29]Klos, 97-99, quote, 99.
[30]C.L.J. Proudman, "The Eucharist in the Fourth Gospel,"
Canadian Journal of Theology, 12 (1966), 212-216.

self. None of them has developed his understanding of the evangelist's general view of the sacraments, but it would appear that they hold the evangelist to have been either anti-sacramental or asacramental. My opinion is that the latter is closer to the truth. I believe that the early form of the gospel (the redaction of the source-traditions into a gospel) had no sacramental reference because the johannine community at that time was essentially non-sacramental. Could it be that the absence of the institution of the lord's supper from the fourth gospel is due to the fact that that narrative was not part of the johannine tradition and that the johannine community did not know the institution narratives in any form? While this thesis cannot be pursued in this context it is proposed that primitive Christianity was not totally sacramental.

The fourth gospel represents a maverick form of Christianity, to be sure, in which the sacraments, at first at least, were not known or practiced. We need not infer from this an anti-sacramental position, for there is no evidence of that save an argument from silence. To the contrary, it might be maintained that johannine theology is the most sacramental of all the New Testament theologies in the sense that it stresses that the love of God is communicated to humans through concrete, historical persons and acts. At the same time, that theology shows no clear evidence of having included the rites of baptism and eucharist as continuing acts in the Christian community.

CONCLUSION OF PART THREE

To structure some general conclusions out of the bulk of the literature and issues we have just surveyed is no mean task. It seems, however, possible to propose three kinds of conclusions for consideration: First, there are a few affirmations one could make concerning the fourth evangelist as a religious thinker (or if you prefer, theologian). It is necessary to say at the outset that he and his community were either extremely astute or else very naive! That is, the evidence of the gospel dictates that one of two things is the case: It is the product of sophisticated theological minds capable of posing fine subtleties and imaginative paradoxes and discerning relationships. If that is the case, then the ponderous efforts of critics to disentangle those subtleties and analyze those relationships are not only necessary but rewarding.

The other possibility is that the gospel is the product of
theologically unsophisticated and naive minds who have clumsily
put together unrelated thoughts and narratives and who have perpetuated numerous contradictions out of sheer ignorance. If this
situation obtains, then it makes a farce of the enterprise we have
just reviewed. The precise investigations and profound explications are for naught! That the latter is the origin of the religious
thought of the gospel is not seriously held, of course, by anyone
within the critical quest to understand the document. Still, the
mandate of critical scholarship requires that the question be posed
and the possibility considered. Perhaps there is heuristic value,
too, in raising the question. There is this much truth in the
unkosher proposition that the evangelist and his community were
theologically unsophisticated: It may help us resist the tempta-
tion to suppose that the originators of the fourth gospel are
contemporary theologians. The serious critic of the thought of
the gospel may tend to find more in the ideas of the gospel than
are there. He or she must be tempered with the sober possibility
that the document is the result of very primitive and immature
reflection, that it is the cautious quest of Christian novices.

Putting aside the proposition that our document is not worthy
of careful investigation of its religious thought, one evident
conclusion of the studies we have surveyed is the interrelatedness
of the evangelist's ideas. Recent investigations have decisively
demonstrated that each religious theme in the gospel is tied with
many, if not all, of the other themes. The result is that the
critics find the thought of the gospel to be a complex of interrelated affirmations and explications--eschatology cannot be
articulated without reference to christology, pneumatology is bound
up with christology and ecclesiology, etc. The consequence of this
observation is surely to deny that the document is entirely the
work of intellectual inferiors. This interrelatedness of thought,
however, leads to another observation regarding the evangelist as
a theologian, namely, the unqualifiedly christocentric character
of his thought. All of the intellectual roads of the gospel seem
to lead to Christ, some more circuitously than others, but all
eventually terminating in the affirmation of the nature and person
of Christ. It might be an exaggeration to say that there are no
theologies of the fourth gospel, only christologies, but the element
of truth contained in that statement has been borne out by the
scholarly work we have examined.

Two other general observations about the religious thought of

the evangelist: First, he and his community seem to be representative of an independent and distinctive Christian community of the
first century. My own orientation doubtless contributes to the
construction of this conclusion, for many of the critics would
argue adamantly for the commonality of johannine, pauline, and synoptic Christianity. Still, there is overwhelming evidence that the
fourth gospel and its thought are expressions of another branch
of the primitive Christian movement which held a number of highly
peculiar conceptions. The dualism of the gospel exemplifies this
sort of independence and uniqueness characteristic of the gospel.

Finally, the religious thought of the evangelist seems to have
been significantly influenced by the concrete occasion of the
production of the gospel. The theology of the minds responsible
for the gospel is a "community theology" in the sense that it roots
in the real life situation of the community and attempts to deal
with the unique problems of that community. This point is verified
by the fact that the gospel seems to have grown up in a community
in accord with the concerns of that community. A case in point
is the anti-docetic motif which seems to have entered the composition
of the gospel late in that process because of a threat to the
community's faith. Those nurtured in the redaction criticism of
the synoptic gospels are not surprised by this observation, for
the same feature pervades the theologies of the first three gospels.
(Furthermore, it might be said that all religious thought, all good
theology, is intimately tied up in the life of its community, and
always reflects that life and is designed to influence that life.)

These observations are made as general characterizations of
the religious thought of the evangelist; but other observations must
pose what seem to be the most problematic areas in the understanding
of that thought for contemporary scholarship. There are three such
areas, as has been evidenced by our survey.

First, there is the area of the resolution of the relationship
of faith and history in the thought of the evangelist. His perception of the meaning of the past and its relationship to his and
his community's present experience is a vital key to the whole of
his thought. How did he understand the distance between himself
and the historical fact of Jesus of Nazareth? How did he conceive
his involvement in that past? What was his view of the relationship
of the historical Jesus and the so-called Christ of faith? These
are questions which seem to bring the inquirer directly into the
subject of the hermeneutic of the fourth evangelist—his interpretation of the past and his way of understanding both that past and

the data of his own experience. Franz Mussner's monograph on this
subject opens up a vastly important discussion which holds the
vital force of johannine christology, eschatology, and pneumatology,
if not the whole of the religious thought and perception of the
gospel.

This hints at the second area of need in the further study of
johannine thought, namely, christology. For if the evangelist's
thought is christocentric as we have observed and if one of the
crucial areas of his thought is his hermeneutical perception, surely
the understanding of his view of Christ is pivotal. What we must
conclude from the surveys of contemporary scholarship is that the
matter of johannine christology has not been adequately settled,
although foci have emerged, as I have already stated. What is
needed now is a concentrated effort to bring together all of the
best johannine research--literary and historical, as well as theo-
logical--to bear upon the question of the gospel's portrayal of
the Christ figure. As one makes that declaration, however, the
realization surfaces that this thorny problem of old still pricks
us, and doubtless will for some time to come.

The third and final problematic area goes to the heart of the
difficulty in johannine christology and is not irrelevant to the
issue of faith and history. It is what we might call the quest
for adequate categories. The old struggle between salvation-
history and existentialist interpretation goes right on. This
struggle signals for us the need for adequate categories by which
the interpreter might comprehend the thought of the evangelist
without distorting it in the image of contemporary thought. Another
symptom of the malaise of inadequate categories in fourth gospel
criticism is the tension between those who would employ cosmic
models and those who would evoke temporal-historical ones for
articulating the evangelist's thought.

What is needed is the rare combination of solid historical
inquiry into the intellectual milieu of the fourth evangelist, on
the one hand, and free imagination, on the other. Only that
combination would liberate the scholar from his or her imprisonment
in modern thought and from preconceived notions of how the evangelist thought. That combination, moreover, would allow the critic
to move into the mind of the johannine community and expound its
thought from within. That utopian situation is not likely to be
achieved in the near future, but advances toward it will result
when we take seriously the need for more adequate categories and
when historical inquiry and creative imagination are wed to fill

that need. It is this quest for new categories which will
eventually, I believe, yield up a more adequate proposal for the
hermeneutic of the evangelist and for his christology.

Finally, one observation must be tendered regarding the method
of research on the religious thought of the fourth evangelist.
The survey of the works produced in the recent past has confirmed
two notions expressed in the introduction of Part Three. The
problem of the critic's presuppositions shaping the results of his
or her inquiry is much in evidence in the works we have examined.
Second, the interrelatedness of literary and historical criticism
with theological analysis has been amply corroborated. The method
of theological analysis must attend more consciously to these two
problems before the results of its work will merit hardy endorsement. But I am confident that with a disciplined method and a
diligent quest for new categories the enigma of the religious thought
of the fourth evangelist can be transformed into clarity.

PART FOUR:

RESULTS OF

THE INVESTIGATION

Our map of the terrain of recent johannine scholarship is completed despite the ommission of some important details here and there. What is necessary now is some general assessment of this critical work. What can be said in the way of general achievements and failures? Where have we been led by all of the investigations and theses? Certainly it is only history which finally assesses the work of scholarship; for it is only as the efforts of future scholars are able to test and reformulate the work of the recent past that its importance in the entire quest to understand the fourth gospel will become known. A glance into the annals of eighteenth century scholarship shows, for instance, how mighty hypotheses are eventually brought low and humbler pro-posals gradually given a status of honor. The pursuit of histori-cal truth is a long and arduous one that never finally ends as long as humanity is curious about the past. How contemporary johannine scholarship will fair in the longer trial of the on-going history of scholarship, no mortal dare predict.

Still, given that awesome condition, we must venture some evaluations from the vantage point of the mid-nineteen seventies. It is a foregone conclusion that many of these judgments will not prove accurate, but they must nonetheless be tentatively ventured. They, of course, reflect my peculiar perspective with my own presuppositions, commitments, and interests. There is, first, the task of trying to issue some verdicts on the advances gained by recent scholarship. Then, there is the matter of the vital questions which emerge from this scholarship to be dealt with by future generations of scholars.

CHAPTER I

RECENT ACCOMPLISHMENTS

What recent scholarship has accomplished may not in every case
be novel. Each advancement in scholarship is not an innovation,
at least on a major scale. Since the progress of scholarship (when
it manages to progress at all) is tediously slow, what merits
status as "advancements" may be little more than the clarification
of questions to be asked, refinements of more innovative hypotheses,
and further substantiation of tentative conclusions from a previous
era. The advancement of johannine scholarship has been in the
literary, the historical, and the theological areas of study of
the gospel, and each has had significance for the total range of
the critical enterprise. I propose the following as the major
accomplishments of recent years.

*A. The efforts of critical study have shown quite decisively
that the fourth gospel incorporates a body of traditional material
and was composed over a period of years in what might have been a
rather complex process.*

That traditional material may have come to the evangelist in
written or oral form or a combination of both. It may have come
to him exclusively through the community with which he was identified
or from outside of that community. It may have already been in
some sense or another a gospel, or it may still have been fragmentary
and specialized. Whatever its previous history, its form, and its
specific contents, that tradition had some association with one or
more of the synoptic traditions but was essentially independent of

the synoptic gospels. It may have had its roots in an apostolic
personage, but its origin is beyond recovery by our historical
methods. It is that tradition which forms the first base of material
for what we today call the Gospel of John. It was revised, expanded,
corrected, commented on, and joined with other materials to produce
the first form of the gospel. The fourth evangelist, an anonymous
figure working about 80-90, is responsible for the redaction of
the traditional materials into the earliest form of the gospel.

Associated with the recognition of the traditional materials
embodied in the fourth gospel is the agreement that the gospel as
a whole is the result of a complex process spread over a period of
years. At the very least the gospel represents the result of the
merging of a number of sources and traditions with the creative
work of the evangelist, and very likely there were still further
stages before the document reached the form in which it comes to
us. This is surely not a new hypothesis, but the advancement of
current criticism is that so many scholars agree that some such
process of composition must be assumed in the critical work done
on the gospel. The gospel, then, represents a collection of
narratives and discourses which have been brought together through
a number of stages or periods. The process may have been as long
as the developmental theories of composition propose. On the
other hand, the process may have involved only the evangelist's
one-time redaction of his tradition material and minor additions
by later members of the community. Either way, the composition of
the gospel was a process involving a number of persons and historical
situations, and that insight is of monumental importance.

The implications of these accomplishments in source-tradition
and composition criticism of the gospel are far reaching for
johannine studies. They mean that we may not credit the gospel as
it stands now to the genius of one individual, no matter how
important and creative we may regard the redactional work of the
evangelist. Whatever the gifts of the evangelist himself, his
work stands on the shoulders of a body of material which he inherited
and for which he may not be credited. Moreover, we must acknowledge the strong possibility that his work has undergone revision
and expansion at the hands of later figures in his community. The
traditional materials in the gospel have their roots in the life
of the people of the community of faith; it is in the true sense,
folk literature, belonging to, arising out of, and preserved by the
people themselves. These materials may be very old--as old or
older than synoptic materials. The quest of the historical Jesus

in and through the johannine materials is an authentic enterprise, if that quest has any virtue at all.

The traditional basis of the gospel means that historical and theological analysis must be done with the basic methods of redaction criticism. This involves viewing the evangelist as an editor who did his work on a body of older material in a given situation for certain reasons. The critic must seek to ask how it is that the evangelist used that material, if the historical situation of the emergence of the gospel is to be discerned. Likewise, the study of the religious thought of the evangelist must be done by means of that redactional method. The thought of the evangelist may be found superimposed upon the religious thought of his source-tradition materials, and his particular contributions must be detected and articulated in relationship with those of this tradition. In a word, we have seen in recent years the birth (but not the conception) of the redaction critical study of the fourth gospel.

Similarly the compositional process has impact upon the historical and theological study of the gospel. The historical setting of the gospel as it is deduced from the data of the document may really be three or fourfold: In addition to the historical settings of the traditional materials of the gospel and the evangelist's redaction of those materials, there may be indications of the historical circumstances surrounding the work of later revisers of the gospel. In the quest of an understanding of the thought of the gospel, the critic must be sensitive to the possibility that shades of differences in an idea are due to the differences among the source-tradition materials, the evangelist, and his revisers. The final result is a far more complex view of the gospel, perhaps, but it is one that will prove to be richly rewarding as its consequences are worked out. The firm footing recently achieved by source-tradition and composition criticism may very well prove to be its most significant contribution to the johannine criticism.

B. *Contemporary johannine criticism has confirmed that the gospel is a community's document.*

In this case, the advance of this period of scholarship has not been to innovate but to confirm in a substantial manner inclinations long found in the scholarly literature. The works associated with source-tradition and composition criticism, the quest of the concrete situation of the evangelist, and theological

analysis have all merged upon a common tenet: The contents of the
gospel are the result in large part of the conditions of a community
of persons. We have asserted that the traditional materials of the
gospel should be regarded as folk literature. Redaction criticism
stresses that the work of the evangelist in editing the first form
of the gospel was motivated by the needs he perceived in the
Christian community with which he was related. Composition criticism
holds that the later revisions of the gospel were not mere whims
of individuals but were responses to significant changes in the
conditions of the community. The theology of every stratum of the
gospel relates to the community of faith; it addresses the needs
of that community at that moment. At every turn of our study, the
involvement of the document with its parent community has been
stressed.

The implications of this achievement are obvious. We have
long been accustomed to speaking of the New Testament as the book
of the community of faith, but the demonstration of the reality of
that fact for the fourth gospel is now accomplished. The gospel
cannot be read meaningfully apart from some understanding of the
community out of which and to which it was written. Certainly no
significant level of understanding of the text can be achieved
without a prerequisite historical knowledge. Moreover, as I have
asserted several times, the fourth gospel must then be viewed as
an occasional writing. It was produced (and reproduced) for a
specific occasion, and its thought is sustained in the atmosphere
of that occasion and nowhere else. It is incumbent upon the reader
to know as much about that occasion as possible. This may indeed
be the primal ingredient for a grasp of the religious thought of
the gospel of John, so long eluding us. The concrete situation of
an evangelist is the seam down the garment of his thought.

*C. It is the accomplishment of current johannine scholarship
that the evidence for the syncretistic, heterodox Jewish milieu of
the gospel has become irresistible.*

The studies of the intellectual milieu of the gospel are still
widely varied, but they have increasingly zeroed in on some form of
Jewish environment for the gospel. That environment must have been
exceedingly syncretistic and must have sustained a kind of Judaism
quite different from what we for a time were accustomed to call
"normative Judaism." But basically Jewish it was, founded upon Old
Testament scripture and subsequent interpretations of it. That

those subsequent interpretations contained notions which were later to become separated and regrouped around a Christian center and called gnosticism seems most likely. It is also likely that the multiformed Judaism influencing the fourth evangelist was not dissimilar to the sectarian form of Judaism known to us through the Qumran literature. It is to the credit of present-day johannine scholarship that the Qumran evidence has been put in perspective and carefully assessed. Qumran alone does not offer any easy solution to the intellectual background of the gospel, just as a proposed pre-Christian gnosticism does not. But criticism has lately strongly sustained the proposition that a very complex form of Jewish thought does offer an enlightening milieu for the gospel.

The implications of this achievement are no less important than those of the above-mentioned achievements. The gospel must be read within that scope of meaning which can be established by imaginative reconstruction of this proposed environment. The ideas of the gospel must be placed against a broadly Jewish background, if they are to be rightly comprehended. If this hypothesis is sustained by future generations of scholars, it may be the case that the gospel of John will provide some sort of source for the understanding of heterodox Judaism of the first century; for as Jewish parallels more and more enlighten the gospel, the gospel in turn may begin to cast a reflection of one form of Judaism whose existence is elsewhere insinuated but not clearly proven.

It is my conviction that current scholarship portends the demise of the gnostic hypothesis as a viable background of the gospel. Further, this advance may allow us to understand better the contributions of Judaism to the emergence of Christian gnosticism. Finally, the result of this kind of conclusion is that our quests for parallels to johannine thought in all of the extant literature of the period must go on. It is not as if we were to halt our investigations in all non-Jewish literature because the thesis is that John originated in a Jewish atmosphere. The proposed Judaism which influenced the evangelist seems to have been so syncretistic that investigations in all literature may result in our better understanding that form of Judaism. The reward of the vast amount of work done in the intellectual milieu of the fourth gospel during the past few years may be that we will be enabled to put behind us once and for all the false choice of Jewish *or* hellenistic when it comes to the background of the fourth gospel.

*D. That the dialogue between the church and the synagogue
comprises the major element in the concrete situation of the fourth
evangelist appears to be the emerging consensus of critics.*

Criticism has lately produced an impressive array of studies
which unanimously point toward a similar understanding of the purpose and immediate setting for the gospel. That setting consists
of a strained and hostile relationship between the Jewish and
Christian communities; the former was more and more aggressive in
resisting the inclusion of the latter within its circles. Amid
this crisis setting, which may have erupted in violence from time
to time, the fourth evangelist set about to rework his tradition
in order to speak to the Christians. It may well be that the
actual expulsion of the Christians from the local synagogue was
the occasion for the evangelist's specific motivation to write.
The result is that the first form of the gospel was produced around
two focuses: The venerable past, the history of Jesus of Nazareth,
and the decisive present, the life of the evangelist's own community.
The work of the evangelist moves between these two focuses freely
and frequently, and often the two are mingled inseparably together
in his work. It is a worthy achievement that this understanding
of the concrete setting and purpose of the evangelist has been
more sharply focused and demonstrated with increasing detail.

What this proposed setting for the gospel implies is of great
substance. The gospel was written primarily for intra-church
consumption, if this concrete setting is accurately discerned. The
evidence for the missionary purpose of the gospel may reside
exclusively in one of the earlier traditions embodied in the document, and the evangelist may still have held out hope for the
conversion of some Jews. However, the major task of the writing
was not evangelism but Christian nurture. This setting gives
support to those theses which would relegate evidence for other
purposes of the gospel to later strata of the document (e.g., the
anti-docetic theme). It would mean, too, that the gospel of John
as a whole must be read within the framework of this Jewish-Christian
struggle, and its peculiar treatment of "the Jews" understood as
an occasional and emotional attack. This would defuse once and for
all the efforts to utilize the fourth gospel as justification for
any kind of Christian anti-semitism.

The fourth gospel, if this proposed concrete setting is correct,
reflects the final stages of the process of the separation of
Christianity from its Jewish roots. That this separation was still in

progress when the fourth evangelist produced the first form of his
gospel necessitates that the dating of that document not be as late
as some would propose. Still, the growing evidence for the separation of the johannine community from other Christian communities
allows for the likelihood that this separation does not antedate
the stage of the struggle described in the pauline literature.
Most important, perhaps, among the implications of this achievement is the fact that the johannine community is pictured as
conceiving itself to be the true descendant of the old covenant
heritage. Johannine Christianity, whatever else it is, is not a
radically hellenistic form of the gospel, but a thoroughly Jewish-
based expression of the Christian faith.

   *E. Research on the religious thought of the gospel demonstrates
that it is an innovative and sophisticated mode of Christian thought
radically christocentric in all its expressions.*

   Such an assertion can hardly claim to be new; its origin is
far back in the history of criticism. Still, the achievement of
recent scholarship must not be eclipsed by such a fact. Through
vastly different approaches to the thought of the gospel, recent
critics have shown the same point, namely, the creativity, expertise,
and consummately Christian orientation of the evangelist. Taking
up different studies of the thought of the gospel, critics have
consistently unearthed the christological foundation of the evangelist's work. They have shown that even with the use of a wide
assortment of syncretistic Jewish materials, the evangelist is
thoughtful and imaginative in his own articulations. They have
found the thought of the gospel is impregnated with subtleties and
insinuations which continually seem to be deliberately planted in
the text. Fourth gospel research on religious thought has perhaps
not been as creative as that done in the literary and historical
fields, but still the contemporary scene has witnessed an impressive
production of material. That material tends to prove over and over
again that the work of the evangelist is no sophomoric enterprise.
Perhaps most telling in this matter are the number of monographs
which profess to focus upon a single theological theme in the
gospel, but which, in the process of elucidating that theme, are
led into the discussion of almost all of the other major religious
motifs of the gospel. All monographs on johannine religious thought
seem to end up as surveys of the whole gospel!
   What does this achievement in the theological analysis of the

gospel suggest? It certainly points toward the fact that as an
evangelist the author of the substance of the gospel was no mere
copyist. It is true that he employed a body of traditional
material, but in his employment of that material he gave expression
to a wide number of religious motifs which were distinctive to
him and/or his community. If some of the other achievements of
recent criticism have stressed that we may not credit the evangelist as an innovative genius and thereby overlook the contribution
of the traditional material to his document, this point must qualify
the others. He was indeed a creative and wholistic thinker and that
is evidenced in his use of other materials.

Second, this advance of critical scholarship indicates that
the fourth evangelist was one of the first formative Christian
thinkers. It is he who must be made responsible for a number of
significant steps in Christian thought, for instance, the emergence
of an early form of dogmatic faith. Finally we may argue that
the implication of the findings of recent scholarship on the thought
of gospel is that the evangelist was the first really "systematic"
thinker of the Christian community. That is, it is he who first
dealt with such a wide range of themes in such a way as to inter-
relate them and root them all in a christology. By "systematic,"
of course, we mean to imply that he saw interrelationships in an
encompassing manner. His "system" is surely not a modern one and
his relationships are not "logical" in every case, in the modern
sense of that word. Still, he holds together a multitude of motifs
in a well-conceived framework. What is amazing is that he does
this in a literary genre such as the gospel and that it is done out
of the stimulation of and as a response to a concrete historical
occasion.

One of the achievements of recent theological analysis has
certainly been to show how the evangelist dealt with the historical
past and related it to the community's present. His skillful
handling of history and faith has been shown again and again in the
studies we looked at in Part Three. What this implies is that
the fourth gospel employs the literary genre of gospel in the most
creative and theologically rich manner. He understood, apparently,
that the gospel genre was the enabling means by which the past
could be grasped in a meaningful way in the light of the present.
It is the implication of this point that the fourth evangelist
may be the most perfect artist of his genre known to history. While
the research on the thought of the gospel has not been as rich in
its achievements as have the other two areas, the critics are to

be especially commended for having advanced our appreciation for
the evangelist's conception of faith and history.

    *F. Finally, the recent criticism of the gospel attests fully
to the fact that the johannine community is a distinctive form of
early Christian life and thought.*

    All three fields of the work done on the gospel have shown in
their own way how the johannine community stood in a separate and
distinct relationship with other forms of early Christianity.
The studies of the traditional material in the gospel and the
relationship of the gospel to the synoptic traditions have shown
the independence of the johannine tradition and the distinctiveness
of its material. The quests for the historical milieu and the
concrete setting of the gospel point decisively toward the uniqueness of the gospel. Its milieu was, so far as our knowledge at
this point has taken us, peculiar as compared with the other early
Christian literature; and its concrete setting is paralleled only
by the gospel of Matthew, perhaps, and in that case the occasion
seems to have been different. Theologically, there can be little
question about the independence and uniqueness of the gospel. The
consensus seems to be that johannine Christianity cannot be regarded
as a simple variation on the other forms of Christianity known
to us through the other New Testament literature, but it is
something quite different in many ways. While not all critics would
endorse this sort of emphasis, it is my opinion that scholarship
has moved us more and more in this direction.
    Therefore, we must recognize (again) the variety of forms of
Christianity existent in the first century, and remove once and
for all any remnant of the concept of a single, harmonious Christian
church in this era. This is, of course, not a novel suggestion--far
from it. But the evidence for this thesis coming out of johannine
studies is fresh and newly compelling. This advancement must also
shape our conceptions of the so-called "development" of Christian
theology in the first two centuries. The independence of the
johannine form of Christian life and thought may mean that the so-
called "high christology" of the gospel is not so much an indication
of the lateness of the gospel as it is of its peculiarity. It would
appear that johannine Christianity articulated a "high christology"
early and in isolation from other developing forms of views of Christ.
In other words, the old evolutionary schemes of Christian thought
are undermined in an absolute way. In a similar fashion, dates

for the gospel must be reassessed. This achievement has obvious
implications for the canonical process in the early church which
cannot be explored here. It is certain that the canonical process
had the unfortunate result of attempting to level the valuable
uniqueness of the fourth gospel.

Finally, a question is to be inferred from all this: What
might have accounted for the independence and the uniqueness of
this form of early Christian thought? Was it spatial separation
from other Christian communities, or a form of self-isolation
preferred by the johannine community? The distinctiveness of the
gospel has import for a whole range of matters pertaining to the
interrelatedness of early Christian communities.

These six observations, then, are the achievements I find
growing out of the mass of recent johannine research. How accurate
these perceptions are you will want to judge for yourself, but it
does seem that each of these six has some clear roots in current
critical work, That these achievements will be borne out by future
scholarship is uncertain. Probably future scholarship will over-
turn some of them, confirm others. Some may be followed up with
more intense and better research; others may go unattended and
hence unverified. Whatever the future, the present time must be
judged as one of the most vigorous periods of johannine scholarship,
even if some questions of its accomplishments remain. The thesis
of the last few pages has been, of course, that the vigor of the
research has not been wasted, that solid and worthy advancements
of knowledge have been made.

CHAPTER II

THE VITAL QUESTIONS REMAINING

Whatever the appraisal of the accomplishments of recent
johannine scholarship may be, the fact that a number of important
questions have risen to the surface is undeniable. The accomplishments may be far less significant than the questions posed and the
enigmas uncovered. Indeed, one could observe that for every
proposed advance in johannine scholarship, a half-dozen new problems
have been born. I would not attempt to enumerate all the new
problems but only what I think are the four issues which must be
dealt with if the current achievements are to be as fully exploited
as possible. These are the knotty issues--the ones on which progress
will hinge.

A. *What are the contours of the traditional materials employed
by the evangelist?*

Current scholarship has, I believe, established the fact that
such a body of traditional material does underlie the gospel; furthermore, the critics have already taken some steps toward defining
what those materials are. Still, the contours of that traditional
material remain too vague. The disagreements among the major
source theories are so sharp as to leave too much difference among
their assessments of traditional materials. The task now before
scholarship is to reach some greater degree of consensus between
what is traditional and what is redactional in the gospel. That
may be done by the persuasive demonstration of one or more of the
hypotheses from current scholarly work or by the advancement of new

ones which surpass their predecessors in their evidential basis.
However it is accomplished, the outline of that material must
become clearer to a great many more critics than is now the case.

Should this question be resolved with any sort of decisiveness,
the results would be significant. With such contours of the
traditional material established, the task of redaction criticism
could proceed with much greater precision and accuracy. The
religious thought of the evangelist could then be sharply distinguished from that of his tradition, and theological analysis would
be greatly improved. Redaction research could flood the situation
of the evangelist with light and make invaluable contributions to
our knowledge of first century life and thought. One segment
of the history of Christianity in the first century could be
enriched beyond measure if johannine redaction were able to proceed
without such a precarious basis. Finally, the traditional material
could be subjected to examination with form critical methods and
the pre-johannine tradition probed. Such a possibility might reveal
the missing link between the johannine and synoptic traditions so
long eluding the critics. The definition of the contents of the
evangelist's tradition must be a number one priority in future
scholarship.

*B. What was the character of the amorphous Judaism claimed
by some to have been the intellectual milieu of the evangelist?*

The Judaism which influenced the evangelist seems, on the basis
of the critical studies done thus far, to be so expansive and
encompassing as to be formless. How is it that a mode of first
century Jewish thought could include Old Testament motifs, apocalyptic
schemes, Essene (Qumranian) conceptuality, mystical beliefs,
rabbinical exegesis, and pre-gnostic mythology? Is this possible
at all? The proposal seems so sweeping as to be self-defeating, and
unless further definitions can be attained the proposal appears to
be a monster whose destiny is to destroy itself by virtue of its
own expansiveness. The mode of further definition may be to delimit
the hypothesis we have constructed out of the research on the
intellectual milieu of the gospel. Perhaps it is not the case that
the so-called pre-gnostic mythologies are actually assumed in certain
fourth gospel passages, and we may eliminate those from our model
of the Judaism relevant to the fourth gospel. Or it may be that
further research will be able to show how it might have been that
a form of Jewish thought could have encompassed such divergent ideas

and language. Perhaps the clue will lie in the more intense
investigations of the literature we now have at our disposal, perhaps in the discovery of new documents, perhaps in the reassessment of the traditional rabbinic literature. Whatever the means
of dealing with this question, it seems inescapable that it be
brought into the center of our attention.

Should the matter be more precisely dealt with, our reading
of the gospel could, of course, be much enlightened. The importance of having a convincing and workable milieu for the gospel
need not be rehearsed again. But the results of such achievements
would also contribute to the history of Judaism in the first
century. That in turn might put the whole body of Qumran literature
into a perspective which would clarify it. What significance such
a clarification might have for other early Christian literature
cannot be anticipated. Surely, students of the history of johannine
scholarship have declared many, many times that it is necessary to
define the milieu of the gospel more precisely. My admonition is
different only in so far as it may be that the results of scholarship have lately brought us to a new understanding of that background which must now be further defined and demonstrated.

*C. What are the categories which best enable us to apprehend
the thought of the evangelist?*

I have pointed out several times in Part Three what seems to
me the crying need for new categories by which to comprehend the
ideas of the evangelist and in particular the relationships among
some of the major motifs of his gospel. The categories recently
employed are burdened with modern connotations which get in the
way of their elucidation of the evangelist; or they are so narrow
as to be inadequate. Often when the effort is made to articulate
the thought of the gospel in terms of one of the gospel's own
categories (e.g., witness or glory), that category is not fully
understood or is simply not the operative fundamental of the evangelist's thought that it is claimed to be. It is my contention that
the evangelist's own basic categories have not yet been discovered.
That is, that lying perhaps unexpressed beneath the thought of the
gospel are a number of basic presuppositions which, if they were
to be manifested, would put handles on the ideas and language of
the evangelist. The discovery of those categories is obviously
bound up with the further refinement of our understanding of the
evangelist's intellectual milieu. Therefore, as that work continues

the critics of the religious thought of the evangelist must probe
the possibility of articulating the basic foundations of his
thought.

If this could be done, the theological analysis of the gospel
could advance far beyond its present status. Such a real comprehension of the way the mind of the evangelist works would release
us from the sometimes fruitless discussions of johannine ideas
which seem to mirror the minds of the exegetes more than the evangelist. Such an advancement would further help us understand the
distinctiveness of the gospel. For while it is true that that
distinctiveness roots in the johannine community and not alone in
the evangelist, to understand the way the mind of the evangelist
works would surely tell us something about the community that
nurtured his thought. Hence the distinctive quality of the gospel
could be discerned at its most fundamental level. The quest for
new categories must be the pressing item on the agenda of any who
would profess to work at the task of penetrating the mystery of
the evangelist's thought.

D. *What are the results of doing theological analysis of the
gospel on the basis of the findings of the most recent literary
and historical criticism?*

I have already anticipated my contention that the most exciting
and important task of the study of the thought of the evangelist
lies in doing theological analysis in close dependence upon literary
and historical criticism. What results would come from carefully
distinguishing the thought of the evangelist from the thought of
his traditional materials and from his later revisers? What would
the results be if the theological analyst kept always before him
or her the image of both the intellectual milieu of the evangelist
and the concrete situation of the evangelist? The results, of
course, would be an excitingly new perspective on the thought of
the gospel. The very failure of some contemporary scholarship has
been in this area. Critics of the thought of the gospel do not
avail themselves of a well-defined view of source-tradition and
composition criticism of the gospel. The failure of much of current
johannine research presents us with a vital, remaining question.

What is proposed, of course, assumes that the theological
analysis of the gospel cannot be done simply on the gospel as it
stands before us. That assumption will be debated by some, but it
seems that attempting to discuss the thought of the gospel without

fully comprehending the evangelist's use of tradition, or his
intellectual or concrete situation is paramount to a dogmatic,
pre-critical method. The theological critics have asserted the
principle that their work stands on the shoulders of the best in
literary and historical criticism, but the evidence of that is
sometimes wanting. The task, then, is for that principle to be
taken with the utmost seriousness. The result would be, it seems
to me, approaching the thought of the evangelist with the hermeneutic question foremost in mind. That is, what was the evangelist's method of interpreting his tradition, on the one hand, and
his own situation, on the other? What were the presuppositions of
that method (which is to ask the same question as the one posed
in number three above)? Thus, the question facing the theological
analyst of the gospel is the explication of the hermeneutical
thought and method of the fourth evangelist.

These four questions present a formidable agenda for future
johannine criticism, and I have no illusions that the agenda can
be completed with any decisiveness in the near future. But if
the critical method is to advance, if it is to make any measurable
progress, it must take as obligatory the burdens of the questions
from the past work and make them the subject of future work. Otherwise the critical enterprise will become an endless circle and the
scholarly community will dissolve into pointless individualism.
These four questions(and surely there are many others left unmen-
tioned) provide the direction for our work on the gospel. What
the prospects of success are only the future will reveal.

Certainly, the future for johannine studies, along with biblical
studies in general, is promising and exciting. Given the momentum
of the present, the future will produce a great deal of good work
in an ever widening range of approaches. The enigma of the fourth
evangelist and his gospel will not disappear into splendid certainty, to be sure; but the future promises to yield up some of
the secrets of the fourth gospel still buried beneath its puzzles
and our ignorance.

INDEXES

AUTHORS